ALTERNATIVE B(

CW00927475

From Robin Hood to Jack Sparrow from *Pirates of the Caribbean*, outlaws have been a central part of 800 years of culture. These are characters who criticize the power of those in the castle or the skyscraper, and earn their keep by breaking the law. Outlaws break categories, too. They are fact and fiction, opposition and product, culture and economy, natural justice and organized crime.

Beginning with Robin Hood stealing from the rich, and covering along the way pirates, smugglers, highwaymen, the Wild West, the Mafia and many others, Martin Parker offers a fresh and exciting insight into the counter culture of the outlaw – one that rebels against the more dominant and traditional forms of economy and organization and celebrates a life free from wage slavery.

Alternative Business is a highly readable, entertaining book that will prove a helpful study tool for all students and lecturers working on organizations, cultural studies and criminology.

Martin Parker is Professor of Organization Studies at the University of Warwick, UK. He has authored and edited several volumes on many topics, including anti-management thought, conspiracy theory and utopianism. He co-wrote *For Business Ethics* and co-edited *Science Fiction and Organization* – both of which are also available from Routledge.

ALTERNATIVE BUSINESS

Outlaws, crime and culture

Martin Parker

Routledge
Taylor & Francis Group

LONDON AND NEW YORK

First published 2012
by Routledge
2 Park Square, Milton Park, Abingdon, Oxon OX14 4RN

Simultaneously published in the USA and Canada
by Routledge
711 Third Avenue, New York, NY 10017

Routledge is an imprint of the Taylor & Francis Group, an informa business

British Library Cataloguing in Publication Data
A catalogue record for this book is available from the British Library

Library of Congress Cataloging in Publication Data
Parker, Martin, 1962-
Alternative business : outlaws, crime and culture / Martin Parker.
    p. cm.
Includes bibliographical references and index.
1. Outlaws in popular culture. 2. Crime in popular culture. 3. Brigands and
robbers. 4. Economics – Sociological aspects. I. Title.
HV6441.P48 2011
364.1–dc22   2011016988

ISBN: 978-0-415-58647-4 (hbk)
ISBN: 978-0-415-58648-1 (pbk)
ISBN: 978-0-203-55329-9 (ebk)

Typeset in Bembo
by Taylor & Francis Books

Printed and bound in Great Britain by the MPG Books Group

My Daddy was a bankrobber
But he never hurt nobody ...
A lifetime serving one machine
Is ten times worse than prison

The Clash, 'Bankrobber' (1980)

CONTENTS

Acknowledgements   *vii*

1   Knowing the outlaw   1

2   The many myths of Robin Hood   16

3   Pirate utopianism   32

4   Robbers and romantics   52

5   Outlaws and the frontier   70

6   The Mafia   91

7   Modern bandits   111

8   The counter culture and organization   129

9   Popular political economy   142

Notes   *160*
Bibliography   *166*
Index   *175*

ACKNOWLEDGEMENTS

Thanks to a whole variety of people for helping me think through the ideas in this book over a period of several years, and at conferences and seminars at quite a lot of different universities since 2005 where I have done talks about my 'imaginary book'. There are too many of you to name, but thanks to all, because this book is a collage of all the things that you have said. More specific forms of help and inspiration, and comments on early drafts of bits of what follows, came from Peter Armstrong, Simon Bainbridge, René ten Bos, Jo Brewis, Phil Hancock, Stefano Harney, Gavin Jack, Mark Jancovich, Ruud Kaulingfreks, Tom Keenoy, Simon Lilley, Alf Rehn, Carl Rhodes and Jeroen Veldman. Rob Cluley, Valerie Hamilton and Jeroen Veldman were all kind enough to comment on an earlier draft of the book. So was Terry Clague from Routledge, who was also imaginative enough to see a book where about 30 other publishers couldn't. Thanks also to Carolyn, who took me to Whitby to meet Jack Sparrow, and love to Jude.

Earlier versions of some of these chapters have been published elsewhere, but they have all been substantially revised to bring them together as the argument in this book. Chapter three is based on 'Pirates, Merchants and Anarchists: Representations of International Business,' *Management and Organizational History* 4/2 (2009), 167–85. Chapter five on 'The Wild West, the Industrial East and the Outlaw,' in *Culture and Organization* (2011, 17/4). Chapter six on 'Eating with the Mafia: Belonging and Violence,' in *Human Relations* 61/7 (2008), 989–1106 and 'Tony Soprano on Management: Culture and Economy in Fact and Fiction,' in *Journal of Cultural Economy* 2/3 (2009), 379–92. Chapter eight is based on 'The Counter Culture of Organization: Towards a Cultural Studies of Representations of Work,' in *Consumption, Markets and Culture* 9/1 (2006), 1–15, and 'The Little Book of Management Bollocks and the Culture of Organization,' in R. Westwood and C. Rhodes (eds), *Humour, Organization and Work* (London: Routledge, 2007), 77–91. Finally, an early review of the whole argument, parts of which appear in chapter nine, was published as 'Heroic Villains: The Badlands of Economy and Organization,' in M. Kostera (ed.), *Organizational Epics and Sagas: Tales of Organizations* (London: Palgrave, 2008), 105–17.

1

KNOWING THE OUTLAW

In February 1632, an English writer of ballads called Martin Parker entered his 'A True Tale of Robin Hood' into the London 'Stationers' Register', an official list of publications established as a means of enforcing copyright. Parker had already written ballads about the misty tales of King Arthur and St George, and here produced a poem about another legendary English figure. He subtitles this work:

> A brief touch of the life and death of that Renowned Outlaw, Robert Earle of Huntingdon vulgarly called Robbin Hood, who lived and dyed in A.D. 1198, being the 9 yere of the reigne of King Richard the first, commonly called Richard Cuer de Lyon. Carefully collected out of the truest Writers of our English Chronicles. And published for the satisfaction of those who desire too see Truth purged from falsehood.
>
> *(Knight and Ohlgren 1997)*

There was a popular proverb at the time that 'tales of Robin Hood are good for fools', but Parker's Robin Hood claims both historical accuracy and nobility. In the poem, Robin was outlawed as the result of the plotting of a rich abbot, and takes to the woods with a hundred men. He robbed from the rich, castrated any clerics he didn't like, and was kind to the poor:

> But Robbin Hood so gentle was,
> And bore so brave a minde,
> If any in distresse did passe,
> To them he was so kinde
> That he would give and lend to them,

To helpe them at their neede:
This made all poore men pray for him,
And wish he well might speede.

(op. cit., lines 73–80)

This other Martin Parker's wasn't the first account of Robin Hood, but it certainly contains most of the key elements of the narrative that we would recognize nowadays (Holt 1960). An outsider, a criminal, a hero who cared about the poor and showed us what freedom might mean.

The story has, in the globalizing culture of the global North, been something of a touchstone for ideas about the noble robber. A cowed local population, a company of bold men hiding somewhere, and a cruel authority figure. Perhaps most importantly, some idea of stealing from the rich to give to the poor. It is a heroic story of resistance to oppression, and of the justifiable use of violence. An inspiring tale, and one that has been retold in many ways over the centuries through ballads, songs, poems, novels, films, TV series and children's plastic play sets made in the third world. The names for the goodies and the baddies will alter, but what is consistent is the distribution of power and justice. The people in charge might have the castle, the army and the money, but the sparking-eyed rogues in the shadows have right on their side.

This book begins with Robin Hood because I think that it isn't merely a children's fantasy, or an interesting bit of social history or literature, but an enduring story about power, organization and economics. Built into the narrative is the idea that what one person assumes to be the necessary order of things, another might think of as injustice. Or that crime is what the powerful call any economic activity that damages their interests. Or that a gang can be as organized as an army. The seventeenth-century Martin Parker does his best not to question the authority of King Charles the First's power in his poem, preferring to suggest that this is a history, and such events couldn't happen in these days of 'plenty, truth and peace' (line 462). Not a very good prediction, given that Charles was beheaded by revolutionaries 17 years later. This twenty-first-century Martin Parker has the opposite problem. I want to untame the outlaw, and show that even a blockbuster Hollywood film like the 2010 *Robin Hood* starring Russell Crowe can be understood as a radical text. I think that these are deeply subversive stories, and that we can find the politics of Robin Hood in many different guises – as pirate, smuggler, highwayman, train robber, bandit, outlaw, Mafiosi, bank robber, jewel thief, revolutionary icon and so on. We can also find the Sheriff of Nottingham, of course – as king, captain, detective, policeman, businessman, mayor, banker, general, president, manager and so on. I am interested in these ideas, in these stories, because it seems to me that their ubiquity and endurance tell us something rather important about popular culture, and about political economy. To put it simply, I think that a great deal of popular culture is and has long been hostile to the forms of organization and economy that are contemporary with it. Stories about outlaws, whether in medieval ballad or blockbusting film, appear to fit into this interpretation pretty neatly. Blackbeard, Jesse James, Dick Turpin, Ned Kelly and many, many others reflect a deep suspicion of those in power, and also sometimes present ways of living, and forms of character, which present radical alternatives to the present.

More widely, I want to argue that a whole variety of questions about the political economic order are expressed through popular culture. Whether (for example) Hollywood musical, horror film, *The Godfather* or episode of *The Office*, there is a reading of all these materials which presents them as engaged in a critical commentary on contemporary culture. Hidden in plain sight, the legitimacy of markets and power are actively contested, either by offering a 'utopian' alternative in 'entertainment' (Dyer 1993), by metaphorizing the bloody contradictions of capitalist relations (Newitz 2006), or laughing at the pomposities of power (as we will see in the rest of this book). Of course, against my general positive reading of the 'popular', there are also those who would dismiss 'mass' culture as merely one part of an assembly line of product which makes money for some Hollywood mega-corporation, or distracts consumers into stupefaction (Horkheimer and Adorno 2002). In this book I will argue that there's an odd sort of denial going on here, as if we have to explain away all these representations by insisting that they don't mean anything very much. Perhaps one of the most powerful things that ideology does is to allow us to see something, and then encourage us to ignore it and assume that it isn't what it is, but is actually something else instead.

The outlaws that this book tracks down are part of a broader 'counter culture' which continually problematizes power and authority, and hence to some extent de-naturalizes the dominant forms of economy and organization. In that sense, Captain Jack Sparrow from *Pirates of the Caribbean* plays a similar function to David Brent from the TV show *The Office*. They both show the stupidities of the powerful, and celebrate the limits of control. But this isn't the end of the story, because a detailed consideration of representations of the outlaw shows us quite a lot else, too. To be more specific, I think that this is a figure which both makes and blurs a series of structural oppositions which we often keep separated. The outlaw certainly problematizes the relation between natural justice and the laws of the state, but so too does their endless re-presentation for money raise questions about the boundary between accommodation and resistance. Captain Jack is both a product manufactured by Disney and a fantasy of freedom, and the two seem inseparable. So a *Pirates of the Caribbean* school lunchbox is both a clear example of global capitalist economics, as well as an enduring cultural image of dissent which goes back at least four centuries. Finally, the noble robber questions the divide between fact and fiction, history and myth. As we shall see in most of this book, stories about outlaws shaped what outlaws did, and discovering the 'truth' of the outlaw is always difficult, and sometimes impossible.

I think that it is very difficult to understand Robin Hood, Captain Jack and the rest unless we see them as straddling these supposed contradictions. The point is that each side of the opposition makes the other, so they are really both/and, rather than either/or. It is easy enough to think that the structures of the world give us certain sorts of categories – facts, the market, the law, power – and that we can then compare and contrast them to their opposites – fictions, culture, crime, resistance. The outlaw both makes and confuses these distinctions, being an impossible object that marks a boundary and restlessly erases it. The story of Robin is both fact and fiction; he is loyal to the King and at the same time a rebel against authority; his stories are part of 700 years of European culture and are also products being sold by ballad writers and global entertainment corporations for money. Finally, Robin asks us to question the boundary between crime and law, between the bandit and the King. The outlaw both organizes and disorganizes our common sense (Cooper 1990). Understanding the economic outlaw means not deciding to choose which box to put Robin into, but noting that his endurance comes from an ability to trouble simple classifications. Out there, in the woods, he asks us questions about who we are, and why we are so sure about what we are doing.

Social bandits

> The traditional 'noble robber' represents an extremely primitive form of social protest, perhaps the most primitive there is. He is an individual who refuses to bend his back, that is all.
>
> *(Hobsbawm 1972a: 56)*

I am certainly not the first or the only person to have thought about the political implications of the economic outlaw. Eric Hobsbawm, in *Primitive Rebels* (1965) and *Bandits* (1972), writes about the idea of the 'social bandit', suggesting that 'in one sense banditry is a rather primitive form of organized social protest' (1965: 13). Hobsbawm, a radical historian, is searching for the ways in which 'official' histories hide resistance as deviance or criminality. In his first book, originally published in 1959 as *Social Bandits and Primitive Rebels*, Hobsbawm collects a series of essays on what he calls 'primitive' or 'archaic' forms of social agitation. His distinction here is largely between peasant protest and working-class organization, and he often implies that the former is politically confused, ineffectual and so on, when compared to self-conscious revolutionary movements. There is something interesting here about the assumption that social bandits are somehow 'pre-political', situated within a realm of imagination and desire, but incapable of the formulation of coherent political demands and co-ordinated action. The division of politics into categories of reality and fantasy is an important one, and I will come back to that repeatedly in this book.

Hobsbawm begins with Robin Hood, and notes that many of the secret societies, mobs, gangs, sects and bandits that he is concerned with exist in societies in which there is some sort of tension between tradition and modernization, or forced social change. For those who resist, change 'comes to them from outside, insidiously by the operation of economic forces they do not understand and over which they have no control' (op. cit., 3). So though Hobsbawm sees the social bandit as a historically interesting figure, he is continually concerned to stress its limitations.

> *Social banditry*, a universal and virtually unchanging phenomenon, is little more than endemic peasant protest against oppression and poverty: a cry for vengeance on the rich and the oppressors, a vague dream of some curb upon them, a righting of individual wrongs. ... Social banditry has next to no organization or ideology, and is totally inadaptable to modern social movements. Its most highly developed forms, which skirt national guerrilla warfare, are rare and, by themselves, ineffective.
>
> (op. cit., emphasis in original)

He goes on to catalogue some characteristics of the social bandit, that they are young, male, have the support of the people and so on. I'll go into these 'structural' descriptions in more detail in the next chapter, but when I first read the book I found it remarkable just how many figures Hobsbawm manages to unearth – Oleksa Dovbush and Juro Janosik in eighteenth-century Carpathia, Angelo Duca or 'Angiolillio' from Naples in the same period, Schinderhannes in 1790s Rhineland, Diego Corrientes from eighteenth-century Andalusia, Nikola Shuhaj, a Czech robber from the early twentieth century. Of course these names might be well known in particular localities, but they certainly suggest that the better-known figures covered in this book – Dick Turpin, Black Bart, Billy the Kid and others – are really just the English-speaking tip of a very big iceberg.

Importantly, Hobsbawm also includes mafias as a developed and systematic example of social banditry. Here he is focussing primarily on nineteenth-century examples and not the twentieth-century US versions we will meet in chapter seven and which were popularized in so many films from the 1970s onwards.[1] He is at pains to stress the political ambiguity of mafia arrangements, because they often repress the peasantry themselves, but suggests that secret societies like this are common, though often undocumented, and that they represent a partially organized form of social protest. Interestingly, he doesn't suggest that they are examples of 'organized crime', which would be the more common label nowadays. He notes their valued character traits, the secrecy, initiation rituals and language that unify this 'network of local gangs' (op. cit., 33) and suggests that they share the same sort of glamour that attaches to the social bandit. However, he claims, the two are not the same. 'One of the commonest misconceptions about *Mafia* ... is the confusion between it and banditry. *Mafia* maintained public order by private means. Bandits were, broadly speaking, what it protected the public from' (Hobsbawm 1965: 40).

Much of the rest of Hobsbawm's book concerns the connections between religious millenarianism and peasant uprisings, with the city mob, religious organizations of working men in Britain and secret societies of various kinds. The direction of his argument is to show how rational forms of working-class organization can grow from irrational roots – from religion, gangs, crowds and

fraternities – but he leaves us in no doubt as to the superiority of properly organized political parties in terms of securing social change. A few years later, in
Bandits, he expands on the nature of social banditry as 'peasant outlaws' who 'are
considered by their people as heroes, as champions, avengers, fighters for justice,
perhaps even leaders of liberation' (1972a: 17). He locates the 'noble robber' as a
rural phenomenon, and explicitly excludes robbers who regard the peasants
as their prey. This latter group would not have popular support, and hence be
regarded as simple criminals. As in the previous book, he is clear that social bandits
are not revolutionaries, and not to be regarded as part of a social movement. They
are instead 'the exception that proves the rule', an example of individual rebellion
which does not turn into collective protest (op. cit., 36).

Bandits contained a lot of new examples, from China, India and the USA, a
more systematic discussion of the vengeance and expropriation that social bandits
engage in, and a description of the necessary economic relations between the
robber and their community. Hobsbawm also discusses examples of social bandits
becoming politically motivated guerrillas, but again dismisses their politics. 'As
bandits they could at best, like Moses, discern the promised land. They could not
reach it' (op. cit., 108). Like the anarchists that he also dismisses, it is as if the
social bandit were a symptom of a form of mass false consciousness. Charming, in
their way, but needing to have the principals of party organization and mass
mobilization explained to them by someone who really understands politics. But
then, in his final chapter, 'The Bandit as Symbol', Hobsbawm shows us why he
does think that the bandit matters:

> What survives from the medieval greenwood to appear on the television
> screen is the fellowship of free and equal men, the invulnerability to
> authority, and the championship of the weak, oppressed and cheated. … In
> a society in which men live by subservience, as ancillaries to machines of
> metal or moving parts of human machinery, the bandit lives and dies with a
> straight back.
>
> *(1972a: 132)*

These ideas stimulated much debate, most of which was concerned with the
extent to which Hobsbawm's presentation of bandits was itself romanticized, and
perhaps even bad history. As Anton Blok argued, 'Rather than actual champions
of the poor and the weak, bandits quite often terrorized those from whose very
ranks they managed to rise, and thus helped to suppress them' (1972: 496). In his
reply, Hobsbawm agrees that not all bandits should be understood as examples
of rebellion, but asserts that some can (1972b). Central to their disagreement, and
to later reviews of the 'social bandits debate' in the 40 years since (Slatta 2007),
is the question of evidence. Is the social bandit a creature who can be measured
against some sort of historical or ethnographic evidence, as Hobsbawm seems to
imply, or are they largely mythical creatures, as Blok wishes to have it? Secondly,
if they are (at least partly) mythical, what does this myth tell us? For Hobsbawm,

and those social historians who have since developed the idea of 'social crime' (Hobsbawm *et al.* 1972, Hay *et al.* 1977, Lea 1999), it seems to be a myth that can express protest at injustice. For Blok on the other hand, it seems to be a form of ideology that usually conceals interests and naturalizes oppression. Again we will return to these issues all the way through this book, particularly when repeatedly discussing the relation between 'real history' and 'cultural representation'. For now though I simply want to note that it seems that bandits sell. Hobsbawm's book has been reprinted many times, and went on to have a second revised edition in 2000. Just like poems about Robin Hood, perhaps the images that Hobsbawm collected somehow had meaning to readers which exceeded his rather definitive political judgements, and Blok's solid dismissals.

The outlaw and the business school

I'll say a lot more about all this later, but also want to note here something rather specific about my approach in this book. Unusually perhaps, for someone writing about popular culture, I am academically located within a business school. Over the last 30 years or so, these parts of universities have grown very quickly and become places in which questions of organization and economy are generally regarded as translatable into charts, spreadsheets and strategies. The business school is presented as a place which is only interested in things if they make money, or stop people from making money. Other questions might be academically intriguing, but they will quickly be dismissed as irrelevant or ivory tower because the measure of the business school is business itself. This is the bottom line and, it is often said, nothing can be built if you don't get the bottom line right. On the other hand, other departments within the university claim to be largely uninterested in such brutal evaluations, and so people studying history, literature, cultural studies, film and so on have traditionally not had to worry about whether their research has 'practical' implications.[2] (And by 'practical' here I mean, of course, making money, or helping the public sector to lose less money.) The arts and humanities largely rest on the assumption that things are worth studying because they are interesting in themselves, perhaps because they tell us something about what it means to be human. As a result, I think that universities are often very divided places, and that their knowledge gets divided up, too. One gang of academics studies economy and organization, the other studies culture, and it is easy enough to come to believe that the two fields are necessarily separate and that they do, and *should* do, different things.

But if we take the case of Robin Hood and assorted outlaws, we can see how problematic this quickly becomes. These are stories about the social organization of a particular time and place, and they act as commentaries on the equity of those economies. They tell of who eats and who starves, who works and who has leisure, who pays taxes and where they go, and of the various actions taken by the powerful to ensure that the money stays in the castle. Simultaneously they suggest that there is an alternative to this arrangement, even if it exists on the margins of the social order – in the forest, the canyons, the alleyways of the city, or on the high seas. Often enough, this is an alternative which stresses collective equity, a broader notion of justice and less hierarchical organizational forms. It seems to me that these are matters which could easily be treated as part of business ethics, corporate social responsibility, management history, strategy, organization theory and so on. Of course they are not normally understood like that, and are instead bracketed as 'cultural' questions. This, in a sense, makes them both more and less important. More important because the arts and humanities have higher symbolic status within the university than the business school, but less important because the business school is an important source for the dominant models for running the university, the corporation, and even the state. As a result, the radicalism of the outlaw can become a mere historical and textual matter, and not a persistent commentary on the ways in which we think about organization, economy and questions of justice.

It is easy to come to believe that there is something called 'the economy' which is somehow different from something called 'culture'. I will show in this book that this is a highly misleading division and it leads to forms of enquiry that are one-sided. So we get people from business schools writing as if there were natural laws concerning the organization of the economy, and referring to 'the market' as if it were a creature that had properties independent of people's beliefs and behaviours. But we also have plenty of people from the arts and humanities writing as if economics was an irritating interference to their true purposes, and hence spending a great deal of time worrying about the meaning of texts without embedding them in the context of the global culture industries and forms of organization – the network of things that people make, and sell, and buy. Both positions seem odd to me, and each presents its own caricature of the other – as cold-eyed utilitarians who wish to reduce everything down to exchange value, or as wishy-washy intellectuals who don't understand where their salaries come from. In practice, questions of economy and of culture *must* be entangled in all sorts of complex ways. The anthropologist Maurice Godelier (1985) reminds us how hard it is to imagine any social practice which is not linked to the satisfaction of wants of some sort, or any economic practice which doesn't gain its meaning from social context. What is odd is that those of us who live in complex societies have been convinced that the 'economy' or 'market' is something different from our everyday lives, perhaps a position which is much harder to sustain in smaller and slower places where economy, culture and politics are much more clearly embedded in the same spaces and times (Polyani 2001).

This in turn relates to the politics of the set-up. There is a tendency for those who research and practice management, business and the market to assume that the present distributions of power and reward reflect, by and large, the distributions of talent and effort within capitalism. The politics of the business school is usually conservative, or market liberal. It tends towards smug affirmations of the status quo, and a robust belief that the system is essentially sound, even if it needs some reform from suited experts. Much contemporary analysis of popular culture has the opposite problem. There is a common assumption that the popular expresses discontent and resistance, and much sympathy for and identification with the radical politics that this implies, but not much interest in what this actually means for alternative forms of organization and exchange. Resistance is often bracketed as cultural, and hence disconnected from practical questions about how people might live different sorts of lives. Indeed, and as we shall see later, cultural resistance is then sometimes reframed as a form of accommodation to power, as a 'safety valve' which prevents change rather than encouraging it. So market managerialism (Parker 2002) usually just collides with culturalist idealism, producing little understanding of the way in which what they don't talk about is necessary to produce what they do talk about. In fact, the set-up just ends up hardening differences on both sides and making it less likely that people from the business school will think about popular culture, and that people from the arts and humanities will think about organization and economy.

For both of these reasons, I think the example of the economic outlaw is particularly interesting both for what it is and what it says. The stories are told through a wide variety of forms – ballads, pamphlets, plastic toys, engravings, dime novels, paintings, operas, films, comic books, TV shows, video games and pop songs. In this book, I will pretty much use every single medium as evidence in some way or other. Yet all of these materials are brought to bear on questions of economy and organization. Robin Hood is, in that sense, one part of a seven-century-long multiple cultural text which encourages us to think about forms of power, the appropriation of labour and the possibility of living free, but which also contains a whole series of other elements depending on where and when the representation comes from. As Graham Seal puts it, the 'outlaw hero' is mytho-logized through 'interaction over time and space of any and all forms of cultural expression' (2009: 86). He (because it is usually a he) represents the inseparability of culture and economy, of telling stories and selling products, and helps to show us that art is always on the other side of the coin.

I also think it is important to think about these sorts of issues because, at the present time, many critically inclined business school academics often pay a great deal of attention to 'serious' management thinking and practice, usually in an attempt to expose its empirical or theoretical incoherence. So critical accounts of work tend to look at what management does, or what management gurus claim, and then try to understand this as reflective of the imperatives of capitalism, power, patriarchy and so on (Alvesson *et al.* 2009). Or they might study workers at work, and try to find examples of the places where they resist doing what they are told, or when they criticize management or join unions, and if they do not, then this might be explained in terms of some version of hegemony or ideology. Whilst not disavowing this sort of strategy in principal, this book rather follows Alf Rehn's suggestion that

> To begin with, we would expand our horizon as to what economy and busi-ness is. The notion that only those things that *seem* serious enough to be taken

seriously are the ones that should be studied has hampered our theorising, and one could argue that the 'science' of business and management cannot be taken seriously as a social science until this fact has been addressed.

(2004: 18)

I want to encourage those people interested in critical accounts of work, organizations and economy to have a look at Robin Hood, Blackbeard, Jesse James, Don Corleone and the like, partly because I believe that much of their critical thinking is already found in the cultural texts that are right there in front of them. Resistance to work, management and organization – as well as alternative ways of thinking about organization and economy – can be found in popular culture already. It simply requires that we take trivial matters seriously.

Economics, culture and cultural economy

The German toy manufacturers Playmobil sell a 'Duo Pack Policeman and Bandit 5878'. The small plastic policeman carries a gun and nightstick, wears a tidy blue uniform and has blonde hair. The bandit wears black with red flashes, has tattoos, red eyes, black hair and a mask.[3] They are handcuffed together. Is this economy or culture? Is it ideology or resistance? Could it be all of those things, at one and the same time?

In the previous section I was concerned to dramatize some intellectual divisions – between the business school utilitarians and the floppy-fringed culturalists – which are not quite as neat as I was suggesting. There are some examples of cross-fertilization, though they themselves are quite tightly demarcated.[4] Sometimes, for example, the business school gets interested in culture as a product that can be sold. This leads to thinking about culture in terms of units shifted – whether they be books, songs, DVDs or whatever. In some sense, the selling of cultural products is no different to the selling of any product, and the same questions of manufacture, marketing and distribution apply. Nonetheless, there are some differences. The vast majority of cultural products lose money, with only a fairly small number making profits for people involved in production and financing. *Robin Hood: Prince of Thieves* (1991) made over $390 million, partly because of its star, Kevin Costner, but also because of its soundtrack. The other Robin Hood film released that year, an English production with Patrick Bergin in the title role, went straight to TV in the USA, despite many critics suggesting it was a better film. Cultural products are not very predictable. It is also difficult to manage creative people, because they need autonomy to do what they do, and can not produce ideas to order. These sorts of problems mean that there is now a growing body of work on the 'creative industries', much of which stresses the difficulty of getting it right, but the huge rewards when you do (Hesmondhalgh 2007). This, then, also becomes a form of knowledge which is relevant for public policy and planning, with creative regions and city quarters being marketed as friendly to cultural businesses.

In this way, culture becomes an object to be scrutinized by business. The interest is primarily profitability, and the content of the cultural form is only of interest insofar as it helps to sell the product. If Robin Hood sells, then let's make another film about Robin Hood. The idea that economy and organization could themselves be seen as part of culture is rarely suggested, let alone that the business school itself might be understood as a cultural form. However, since the turn of the century there have been an increasing number of attempts to do precisely that, and these suggest that the separation of culture and economy is a questionable one (Ray and Sayer 1999, du Gay and Pryke 2002, Amin and Thrift 2004). This work on the sociology of economic life, and cultural economy, tends to occupy the space of the social sciences. Writers and researchers from sociology, geography, social history and so on have now turned their attention to economics and business. What they have shown is that economies and markets are constituted socially, by passions and interests, as well as by relations between people and things that produce an area that can be termed 'a market', or described as 'economic' (Callon 1998, Callon *et al.* 2007). Broadly, this has been by highlighting the economic mechanisms that shape cultural production, or showing that forms of apparently dispassionate rational decision making are actually built on habits, rituals and fetishes. The market, in other words, is not a force of nature, but a wide variety of ways in which human beings make sense of exchange.

This book attempts to develop that stream of thought, using representations of outlaws as the example, but with two important differences. First, it often seems to me odd that writers who wish to argue that economies are constituted through passions often end up with thick but dispassionate descriptions. In part, I think that this is because those who choose the label cultural economy have tended to focus on practices rather than cultural products – on the anthropological rather than humanities sense of 'culture' (Williams 1976: 86, *passim*). Showing that economics is cultural (on a trading floor, for example) or that culture is economy (by studying art galleries) has produced a great deal of fascinating work, but is often not very attentive to the wider ways in which cultural representations *themselves* comment on economic relations. So treating culture as a way of life tends to efface concentration on the potential readings and meanings of cultural texts. The context becomes more visible than the content, and hence the traditional concerns of the arts and humanities become relatively invisible, with the production of the paintbrush becoming more important than the painting itself. These are relative matters, of course, but it does seem to me that the many films and novels about city traders, for example, or the sculpture and paintings in a gallery, can themselves become an element in an enquiry about organization and economy. It is curious that taking cultural representations seriously seems to sit uneasily with doing the same for cultural practices.

The second reason I depart from contemporary cultural economy is because of the persistent tendency in much of this writing to assume that we live in new times, in times in which culture is somehow more important than it used to be (Lash and Urry 1994). This is shared with the business school focus on creative industries, and is often associated with some sort of periodization, too. The global North is characterized as going through some sort of sea change, and developing towards a post-Fordist, post-modern, post-industrial economy. This moves production from the primary and secondary sectors, and grows the service sector. The latter includes information technology, the knowledge economy and so on, but also the cultural and creative industries, which are hence assumed to be growing in importance. Two claims are then made: that the economy is becoming more cultural and that culture is more permeated by economic influences. I don't know whether these claims are true or not, but I'm not certain that they need to be made, and in any case I think there is much evidence against them. Conceptually, it is quite possible to suggest that the separation of culture and economy is problematic, without making any claims about the present being different from the past. An anthropologist or historian can easily show that buying and selling something was often inextricably tied to ideas about kinship, religion and authority, for example. Indeed, a small but growing body of work on the construction of ideas of the economy from the early modern period onwards, which comes from historians and literary critics, often does precisely this (Griswold 1983, Agnew 1986, Zimmerman 2006, Poovey 2008). I suppose we might say that there has been a contemporary recognition of the entanglement of culture and economy, but that this is really saying something about the way in which *academics* have changed the conduct of their enquiries, and doesn't necessarily represent a sea change in business or culture itself.

Perhaps more importantly, though, it seems to me that the case of the outlaw is a very relevant example here. When Martin Parker registered his ballad 'A True Tale of Robin Hood' with the Stationers' Company, he was almost certainly doing so in order to try and ensure that no one else copied it and made money that he felt that he should earn. That is how we know when the text was written, at the point at which it intersects with a regulatory body which was attempting to clamp down on unauthorized printing, on what is today called 'piracy'. As we will see in this book, the selling of representations of the outlaw has been crucial to their dissemination and survival. It is very difficult indeed to separate 'history' from 'representation', and 'representation' from 'economy'. Ballads about highwaymen, plays about pirates, newspaper articles about bank robbers, and TV shows about the Mafia were all contemporary to the events that they describe and were themselves sold and bought for money. There is also a great deal of evidence that, in many cases, the representations actually shaped characters and events, and not just the way that history was written. My point is that if we treat about 700 years of representations of outlaws as a sort of case study, we will find it very difficult to decide where culture ends and economy begins. These are texts which are 'about' alternative forms of organizing, and express a critique of a particular economic order. They are also texts which claim to be based on 'truth', which enter circulation as commodities, and in turn trickle back into popular culture to shape what counts as truth. So perhaps culture and economy have always been intertwined, and perhaps the creative economy is not that new after all. The task of this book is to undo some of these ideas, and to show that folding disciplines and concepts into one another is the best way to understand what Robin (and the Duo Pack Policeman and Bandit 5878) means and does.

This book

I mentioned above that this is a book which uses a lot of different sources. At various points, I will employ ideas derived from my reading of historical documents and history books, Hollywood films and TV cartoon shows, romantic poems and academic texts. This sheer diversity of bits and pieces presents me with several problems, none of which I can (or particularly want to) solve. I simply want to note them, and then get on with it. As you read the book there will be plenty of moments where you might think I have broken all the rules of evidence. This little note on 'methods' is just intended to tell you that I know how bad my scholarship is, and to encourage you to read generously.[5]

First, it is evidently true that different sorts of texts are produced by different sorts of people for different sorts of reasons and for different audiences. A contemporary academic book like this one, written by someone like me, is not the same sort of thing as a dime novel about Jesse James from the 1890s. They might both be books and have English words in them, but there's not much else that they share. This problem is exacerbated when we are comparing Byron's poem 'The Corsair', from 1814, with the film *Pirates of the Caribbean* from 2003. Not only are we comparing apples and pears, but cabbages and kings, too. Now without committing myself to the idea that there are definitive meanings to texts, I agree that it does seem sensible to know a great deal about the conditions under which a text was produced, and intended to be consumed, before using it as evidence in an argument. Was it produced for a particular sort of audience? Did the medium constrain or enable particular forms of expression? How does it relate to similar texts of its kind which were around at the same time? How do the words in the text encourage and discourage certain sorts of meanings? Caution and scholarly rigour seem to be the order of the day, if all credibility is not to be lost.

But think for a moment about what is also lost with such rigour. If we only ever compare apples with apples, we might not notice that they are fruit, like pears. Neither would we be able to make a tasty fruit salad. So, to make the metaphor clear, if we don't compare accounts of pirates, outlaws and the Mafia, we might not notice that they are similar to accounts of highwaymen, smugglers and jewel thieves. My point is that, in order to make sweeping arguments, it is often necessary to make sweeping generalizations, even if this is precisely the weakness that Blok identifies in Hobsbawm. The bigger the net, the more likely it is that exceptions will slip through, but nonetheless, I assume that most readers would rather that books were not always too scholastic; even if that means that literature professors will be asking for detailed textual warrants, and historians reaching for their flintlocks. I think there is something about the nature of the argument that I want to make here that requires the amassing of details, and hence the avoidance of too much specificity. I am claiming that, if we collect all these instances together, they start to look rather similar, and that these family resemblances are important. I want to blur the differences of time and context between Robin Hood, Dick Turpin, Jesse James, Ned Kelly and Tony Soprano in order to make a general argument about the cultural representation of economy and organization. Now it seems to me that blurring requires a certain distance. It means that I will not get particularly caught up in the detailed comparison of smugglers and pirates, or spend a lot of time distinguishing between the Sicilian and the American Mafias, or track the changing image of piracy through eighteenth-century ballads. I am trying to find similarities, and am therefore almost inviting readers to find differences. And of course there will be differences, because of the huge variety of characters I am referring to, over a period of about 700 years, in many different Western European and North American contexts (as well as quite a few others). This is a book which works by collecting things together, and though my lack of interest in the differences might annoy you, it does not damage the overall argument.

However, there are plenty of ways in which my evidence could have been *more* general. I have written about what I know, and about the places and characters that Western popular culture has taught me. It pains me to say that I am an overweight, white middle-aged academic, and my standpoint is probably clear enough. I read certain comics and books when I was a kid, watched particular TV shows, played with toys that were pretty predictable for a boy of my age. In some ways, this is a book about my childish fascinations, growing up in the 1960s and 70s, in the Midlands of England. I've tried to widen it here and there, but I am well aware that there are entire swathes of global popular culture with which I am simply not familiar. There will be more things that I have missed than that I have included.

This still leaves probably the biggest problem of all. Any text does not 'mean' one thing. I make the meanings I can see with the resources that I and the text provide. The meanings do not pre-exist me, and I can not assume that everyone else will understand these stories in the same way. This position has now become axiomatic in cultural studies, and I see no reason to depart from it that much here. If you are a young black lesbian from Johannesburg, I guess that you will not be quite so fascinated by the escapades of my twinkling-eyed white boys. You might, but I shouldn't assume that. You might also be conscious that the majority of the heroic villains in this book are white, as well as male, and the radicalism I am trying to read into them does look rather a lot like North Atlantic patriarchy in tights. There are a variety of places in this book where I say something about people who aren't white, or male, and heterosexual, but they are in there most of the time to acknowledge that the standard model-T outlaw is a pretty predictable character. As with the rest of my 'methods', I just have to note this, and move on. It would be very interesting to do an audience study of outlaw texts, looking at how they are understood and what 'effects' they have (Reiner 2002), but this book simply isn't it. Ultimately, you will make the meaning of this text, and there's not much I can do to stop you. All my positioning and caveats can't force you to understand things in the way that I do.

What now follows is six chapters which take a broadly chronological sweep from Robin Hood to contemporary organized criminals. This means covering pirates, bandits, smugglers, highwaymen, gangs, outlaws and jewel thieves as we find them in just about every form of cultural representation imaginable. The next chapter also reflects on the common structural features of the Robin Hood myth, in terms of the narratives that explain the origins of characters like these, as well as the features which distinguish them from ordinary people. In all the chapters, I show how each outlaw reflects the era that produced them, but also how they have now converged into a generalized stock of recognizable characters that can be routinely identified by different hats, accents and plots. This makes them great material for the profit mills of the entertainment industry, but also intensifies a question. Why does popular culture produce so many criminals expressing a principled opposition to power? In order to place an answer to this question in a contemporary context, the penultimate chapter concerns popular culture and work. Here I position the economic outlaw as one element in a wider counter culture which contests ideas about work, authority and slaving for a wage. I want to ensure that the argument is one that places the elderly Robin Hood in a contemporary context of scepticism about what the sheriffs of the twenty-first century get up to in their corner offices. The book concludes with a chapter in which I reflect on the strengths and weaknesses of my analysis, at the same time as I celebrate an impossible object – a character who seems to exist somewhere between fact and fiction, accommodation and resistance, economy and culture, and legal and natural senses of justice. I think Robin does all of these things, which is what made this Martin Parker as interested in him as the other one was almost 400 years ago.

> Both gentlemen, or yeomen bould,
> Or whatsoever you are,
> To have a stately story tould,
> Attention now prepare.
> It is a tale of Robin Hood,
> That I to you will tell,
> Which being rightly understood,
> I know will please you well
>
> *(Parker, in Knight and Ohlgren 1997, lines 1–8)*

2

THE MANY MYTHS OF ROBIN HOOD

Eustace Folville and his gang were English outlaws who, between 1327 and 1330, were accused of three robberies, four murders and a rape. They, and the Cotterell gang, who also hid out in the Derbyshire Peak District, appear to have had a certain popular support – examples of people who took the law into their own hands, and set themselves against an oppressive and corrupt system of power. When times are hard, and choices are few, it is better to steal than starve, particularly if the theft is from those who can afford it anyway. The Norman invasion three centuries before had introduced Forest Laws which often made criminals of honest people, as well as leaving a long-standing sense that resistance to power was a legitimate response to the yoke of occupation. The legends of Hereward the Wake and Fouke Fitz Waryn, for example, are stories of patriotic freedom fighters, rebels with a cause, even if historians nowadays suggest that their actions speak more of aristocratic self-interest (Spraggs 2001: 25). A little later, the early fifteenth-century uprising against the English led by the Welsh prince Owen Glyndwr was described on one side as the activities of a robber chieftain, on the other as heroic rebellion (Rees 2001: 13, *passim*). But then if the law is commonly regarded to be illegitimate, then breaking the law is clearly a sign of virtue.

In old English law, the declaration of a 'Writ of Outlawry' meant that an individual no longer had the protection of the state. The term comes from the Scandinavian *utlah*, which had been incorporated into English by the ninth century (Rees 2001: 4). The idea of outlawing (from *utlagare*), and also of 'inlawing' pardoned criminals (*inlagare*), was well established by the time of Folville. A Latin declaration, *caput gerat lupinum*, meant that the outlaw's head would be treated as a wolf's head, and that the criminal be considered as no more than a wild animal which anyone could kill without any legal punishment. Though by the mid-fourteenth century only a sheriff could kill an outlaw, being outside the law still relegated the person to a non-human category, forfeiting all property, or the possibility of any claim to ownership.[1] It also meant that if they were robbed or injured they would not be able to claim the law's protection. If someone helped an outlaw, they too would become in danger of similar exclusion. To be outside the law was to be outside society, to be spatially excluded from the places of people and symbolically excluded from the category of the human.[2] Like the word bandit, derived from the Italian *bandire*, to banish, outlaws have moved across a border. Yet such movement is not simple in its meaning, because it both constructs and questions the boundary. An outlaw was an extraordinary person, and the danger of that status also brought with it a considerable degree of fascination and glamour. Outlaws may be outside, but they tell us rather a lot about the fantasies of those inside and the resources that they use to make a counter culture.

Robin Hood may be English, but he is known far beyond England. In this chapter, I will explore the early histories of Robin and try to locate him as a sort of archetype. He is not the only character I could have started with, but he is rather important, largely because of the ways he echoes through northern European, and later North American, popular culture. One of the most common ways for subsequent outlaws of various kinds to claim a recognizably moral or political identity was to claim the name of Robin, and become merry men who steal from the rich to give to the poor, and never kill except in self-defence or to protect others. Fifteenth-century Welsh bards compared local outlaws to Robin Hood (Rees 2001: 91), and seventeenth-century highwaymen were commonly referred to as being 'like Robin Hood and his men' (Spraggs 2001: 146). The corsair John Ward renamed a ship that he captured off Ireland as 'Little John' (Lamborne Wilson 1995: 57). Henry Avery, the London pirate of the early eighteenth century, was described at the time as 'the maritime Robin Hood', whilst some pirates tried in Boston in 1718 were described by their capturer as pretending to be 'Robbin Hoods men' (Rediker 2004: 30, 85). And when Mario Puzo is describing the origins and history of the Mafia in his novel *The Godfather*, he explains that justice was never forthcoming from the authorities and so the people went to the 'Robin Hood Mafia' (1969: 328).

Though we might say that 'Robin Hood' now functions as a label for many outlaw myths, we could also look at him as an example of (what is often called) a 'trickster' figure in myth more generally. The trickster appears to occur in many cultures as a character who is able, through wit, cunning and intelligence, to evade the powerful (Hyde 2008). We find the trickster in many guises – as Coyote for Native Americans in the South West of the USA, as Brer Rabbit in US slave stories, the mouse and deer Sang Kanchil for Malays, Eshu and Anansi in West Africa, Hermes in Greek mythology, Loki in Norse myths, the Siang Miang stories in Thailand, the Monkey King in China, and Till Eulenspiegel and Reynard the fox in Northern Europe. Trickster stories tell us about unusual and underdog characters that might be physically small, like leprechauns, or in some way insignificant, but are clever. Using misdirection, deceit, concealment, they send the agents of power the wrong way, or even manage to inflict pain or death upon them. The powerful might be kings or priests, but are more usually alle-gorized as big animals – bears, lions and so on. The trickster also often pretends stupidity, or simplicity, in order to fool the powerful into a false sense of security. Puns and pranks might seem harmless, but sarcasm and satire are powerful weapons. So Puckish tricksters 'play the fool', disguise themselves, and hide in plain sight, or they disappear into the undergrowth, and wait for the right time to strike.

For James Scott, the trickster is an example of the 'arts of resistance', one of the covert ways in which the oppressed manage to satirize their oppressors (1985: 300; 1990: 162, *passim*). It is clear enough that such a figure plays a subversive role in peasant myth, and that there is some sort of connection between an outlaw like Robin Hood, and the fantasy of the trickster. Tales can be told of people who escape the bonds of the everyday, and live a sort of life that can only be imagined. But like the trickster stories, if challenged, these can be presented as mere fictions, or even cautionary tales concerning what happens if you fall outside the law. They allow for an imaginative exploration of radical alternatives, but without it becoming a direct challenge to the authority of the present day. No wonder that the other Martin Parker, the author of the 1632 'True Tale of Robin Hood', chose an outlaw for his topic. It pretty much guaranteed sales by allowing him to write about violence and freedom, but also to self-righteously insist that his was a moral tale:

> A thing unpossible to us
> This story seems to be;
> None dares be now so venturous
> But times are chang'd, we see
> We that live in these latter dayes
> Of civill government
> If neede be, have a hundred wayws
> Such outlawes to prevent
> In those days men more barbarous were
> And lived lesse in awe;
> Now, God be thanked! People feare
> More to offend the law.

(op. cit., lines 429–40)

History and histories

There were other outlaws around the time of Robin Hood, but from 1228 onwards in England there are state records showing that a person who was out-lawed was sometimes given the surname Robehode, Hobbehod, Rabunhod or Robinhood to indicate their status. Robin's first known appearance in literature in English comes a century and a half later in William Langland's poem, *The Vision of William concerning Piers the Plowman*, in about 1377–9. There he is mentioned in

passing as someone who is the subject of popular rhymes, and without any particular introduction, so we can assume he was already a common figure in English
ballad and oral tradition by that time.[3] The poem also makes approving reference
to Eustace Folville, the outlaw who had only died 30 years previously, as a
treasure of grace against the antichrist. The classification of an outlaw was clearly
a contested one.

Though the details of Robin's story become fleshed out in the poems and plays
that follow, the idea that he 'lived in a forest, with other outlaws, used a longbow
to shoot the King's deer, and robbed people on the highway' was established
by the fourteenth century. However, the robbing from the rich to give to the
poor, and the idea that he was 'a dispossessed nobleman or stout yeoman, seeking
revenge and fair play from an unjust system' appears to come some time later
(Rutherford-Moore 1998: 9; Holt 1960). He was certainly violent though, and
particularly towards churchmen, who he is recounted as castrating, slashing their
faces, and stabbing one so hard that his knife stuck in a tree after it had passed
through the unfortunate cleric's body. In the fifteenth century, to be like Robin
Hood and his Merry Men often referred to drunken young men on a spree,
possibly even during the 'Robin Hood games', which were common during the
fifteenth and sixteenth centuries. Mummers' plays, May festivals and carnivals
often had Robin cast as the 'May King', or even the Lord of Misrule, the agent of
disruption who turns the world upside-down. The trickster Puck was sometimes
referred to as Robin Goodfellow, and it seems that Robin may have been vaguely
related to figures like the Green Man of the woods, or the Jack-in-the-Green of
May Day carnivals. Robin might have been a concatenation of all these figures,
a trickster from the woods who set his face against power.

Though he is mentioned in literature at various points in the fifteenth century,
it is the *Lytell Geste of Robyn Hode* from c. 1420 which establishes various elements
of the myth by collecting them together, and begins to assemble the cast of
characters we are familiar with today. It was reprinted seven times by the middle
of the century, indicating a certain commercial success with its rollicking stories of
wicked sheriffs, rescues from the gallows, cunning disguises and archery contests.
In broad terms, this Robin is an outlaw yeoman who is kind to the poor when it
takes his fancy, but often very violent towards the clergy and representatives
of the state (Spraggs 2001: 52). Whilst he is a robber, and not the representative of
an alternative social order, he is certainly resistant to accepting the privileges and
comforts of the powers that be. For the common people, his name appears to
have been a byword for tweaking the noses of the powerful, and a joyful flouting
of social rules, such as when Robin Hood's men stole or collected money from a
crowd on May Day, ostensibly to give to the local church. The name was often
adopted for various revelries that edged into protests, such as the 1441 group
who blocked the road chanting 'We arn Robynhodesmen, war, war, war!' (Cox
1998: 4). Rogues and thieves were also sometimes described as 'Robert's men'
(Holt 1960: 93). A petition taken into the English Star Chamber in 1492 complains about riotous behaviour being caused by men who come to fairs as

Robin Hood and gang. The problem was so severe in Scotland that the characters of Robin and Little John were banned by the parliament in 1555, and Robin Hood plays banned in 1562, on the grounds that they stirred up trouble.

It is from the close of the sixteenth century that Robin becomes a character who begins to assume a certain nobility. Richard Grafton's 1569 *Chronicle at Large* makes the suggestion that 'an olde auncient Pamphlet' he had found suggested that Robert Hood was descended from noble parentage. There is no evidence that such a pamphlet exisited, but its status as fiction claimed to be fact was solidified in 1598, when Anthony Munday and Henry Chettle wrote their influential plays *The Downfall of Robert, Earl of Huntingdon* and *The Death of Robert, Earl of Huntingdon*, which first made Robin into a dispossessed noble (Richards 1977: 190). Like Martin Parker 30 years later, the idea of Robin as a free born and cultured man, loyal to the King in exile, becomes a powerful frame for at least partially de-radicalizing the myth. Robin is not hostile to natural authority, but only to corrupt and illegitimate authority, and this legacy becomes a potential founding story for the nature of the Englishman. But this new pedigree did not entirely domesticate the idea of Robin, because his name still seemed to be associated with radical behaviour. Guy Fawkes and his associates were called 'the Robin Hoods in your part of the country' by Robert Cecil, Earl of Salisbury, in a letter in 1605. In 1640, Radical candidates called 'Robins' and 'Little Johns' stood in elections to the short parliament before the English revolution, and the contemporary legend that Robin attended the signing of the *Magna Carta* in 1215 perhaps gave further credence to the idea that here was someone who righted wrongs against inherited authority (Cox 1998, Dixon-Kennedy 2006: 177). By implication, then, the radical Robin is continually on the look out for injustice, then and now, and the question of the legitimacy of the present order is not settled.

There is a third version emerging around this time, too. In Shakespeare's *As You Like It* of 1600, there is a slightly different treatment, where Robin is mentioned as someone who was able to 'fleet the time carelessly as they did in the golden world'. This reference was probably based in part on Thomas Lodge's *The Tale of Gamelyn* of 1588, which tells the outlaw as 'an oppressed innocent, and the world beyond the greenwood as inhabited, or at any rate dominated, by tight-fisted clerics, corrupt legal officers, ungenerous hearts, liars and oath-breakers' (Spraggs 2001: 138). This Arcadian idea of the greenwood as a simple time before the present day becomes a much more dominant motif two centuries later, and was significantly developed in historical romanticism when Robin joins a cast of characters – including the highlander, bandit, smuggler, poacher and highwayman who we will meet in chapter four – as more authentic, and closer to nature than the present. This Robin is certainly anti-modern, but perhaps more in a nostalgic than radical manner. Indeed, Robin is used for a wide variety of purposes in the seventeenth and eighteenth centuries, being variously positioned as a dangerous radical, a true Englishman, a good Christian, loyal to the King, an anti-Catholic, an anti-Puritan, a radical hero and so on. Ballads, broadsides and comic operas positioned him in whatever way the stories might work, elaborating and adding where necessary, constructing a set of scripts that would make money for the people who sold Robin Hood by giving the audience what they thought they wanted.

In 1746 Dr William Stukeley gave this Earl of Huntingdon an allegedly factual family tree going back before the Norman Conquest. Like Grafton's pamphlet, there is no evidence of any historical accuracy in Stukeley's claims, but if something is repeated often enough it can become true. The fictions of one era became the facts of another. The Robin Hood leisure industry must have begun too because, in 1786, in Richard Gough's *Sepulchral Monuments of Great Britain*, there is an entry about a gravestone with an inscription at Kirklees in Yorkshire. There is no mention of this grave prior to this, and the language of the inscription does not fit with the claimed period, so it was also almost certainly a fake, probably constructed to be visited by tourists. As with so many of the economic outlaws in this book, they were becoming cultural commodities a long time before Hollywood. By 1795, the density of the myth was such that John Ritson's *Life of Robin Hood* could collect together all the existing historical and literary evidence for his existence. Repeating definitively many of the inventions of the previous 500 years, Ritson breathlessly claims Robin as a romantic outlaw, and the model for one of Hobsbawm's social bandits.

> [A] man, who, in a barbarous age, and under a complicated tyranny, displayed a spirit of freedom and independence which has endeared him to the common people, whose cause he maintained (for all opposition to tyranny is the cause of the people), and, in spite of the malicious endeavours of pitiful monks, by whom history was consecrated to the crimes and follies of titled ruffians and sainted idiots, to suppress all record of his patriotic exertions and virtuous acts, will render his name immortal.
>
> *(cited in Cox 1998: 6)*

Ritson's book was reprinted endless times over the following century, and defined Robin as a character with an inbred sense of natural justice, and just the sort of practical patriotism which would also help to define the 'white man's burden' ideology of an expanding empire. Ritson assumes a set of authentic values which define national identity, and transcend the particularities of power in any given age. History defines the meaning of character and, as in Keats's 1818 poem, 'To J. H. R. in Answer to his Robin Hood Sonnets', a nostalgic medievalism becomes a way to mourn the passing of a more authentic way of life increasingly erased by industrialization.

> Gone, the merry morris din;
> Gone, the song of Gamelyn;
> Gone, the tough-belted outlaw
> Idling in the 'grené shaw';

All are gone away and past!
And if Robin should be cast
Sudden from his turfed grave,
And if Marian should have
Once again her forest days,
She would weep, and he would craze:
He would swear for all his oaks,
Fall'n beneath the dockyard strokes,
Have rotted on the briny seas;
She would weep that her wild bees
Sang not to her – strange! That honey
Can't be got without hard money!

(lines 33–48)

Keats's Robin and Marion are anti-modern; repositories of wisdom about a simpler life before the ancient forests of England had been replaced by smoking factory chimneys and everything had a price. The attractions of this sort of escapism no doubt influence the rise of the historical novel, and the beginnings of a widespread sense that the dark satanic mills of the city were places of corruption and despair (Parker 2005). In what became the most influential historical novel of the century, Walter Scott uses Robin as a Saxon rebel against Norman oppression in his *Ivanhoe* of 1820. The greenwood becomes the location for the freedom fighter to be a true Englishman, and the lowering castles the sites of a dark foreign oppression.

> To these causes of public distress and apprehension, must be added, the multitude of outlaws who, driven to despair by the oppression of the feudal nobility, and the severe exercise of the forest laws, banded together in large gangs, and, keeping possession of the forests and the wastes, set at defiance the justice and magistracy of the country. The nobles themselves, each fortified within his own castle, and playing the petty sovereign over his own dominions, were the leaders of bands scarce less lawless and oppressive than those of the avowed depredators.
>
> *(Scott 1996: 87)*

Though contemporary readers might be driven to despair by Scott's windy declamations, his depiction of the outlaw is one that has become the dominant one up to the present day. Robin of Locksley is modest, but twinkling eyed and clever, and the forest is the site of rough but honest manly companionship. He is 'King of the Outlaws', his authority over the merry men seeming somehow as natural as that of the real King, who he deferentially assists to regain his throne. Robin has no need for organized religion, as 'the nearer the church the farther from God' (op. cit., 214), but lives a life which is defined by a hearty chivalry.

Ivanhoe was hugely popular at the time, with six stage versions circulating simultaneously.[4] It stimulated Thomas Love Peacock's *Maid Marian* (1822) and verse stories by Leigh Hunt, but also allowed Robin and his gang to become a popular figure in the emerging market for 'penny dreadfuls', cheap stories in multiple instalments aimed at children and the working class.[5] Pierce Egan's *Robin Hood and Little John* had 41 instalments from 1838 and sold hundreds of thousands of copies, before becoming a book in 1840. It was translated into French under the title 'The Prince of Thieves'. The 31-part *Maid Marian, the Forest Queen* and the 40-part *Little John and Will Scarlet* followed, with Robin becoming a fixture in boys' weekly papers and annuals by the late nineteenth century. The increasing use of Robin in pantomimes, such as *Babes in the Wood*, often played by a woman, simultaneously develops his fantastical potential as a dashing hero in tights who can be combined with a series of other stock characters from slapstick to supernatural to produce a Christmas play for all the family. Indeed, it might seem that Robin has become an empty swashbuckling hero by this point, less a threat and more a wholesome entertainment for children, along with (as we shall see) the pirate, highwayman, smuggler and so on. So in Howard Pyle's hugely popular children's book (1883), *The Merry Adventures of Robin Hood*, Robin is an egalitarian, but not opposed to King John. In 700 years, Robin Hood appeared to have made the transition from violent myth to jolly good fellow with some jolly good chums. Thighs are slapped and manly laughter echoes through the trees.

In 1881, Alfred Tennyson finished a play called *The Foresters, or Robin Hood and Maid Marian*. It was not performed until after his death in 1892, in New York, with some music by Arthur Sullivan.[6] Widely derided by the critics, some of the song lyrics show us clearly enough just how much the outlaw had changed. Now a gallant and generous patriot living in a sylvan glen, Will Scarlett captures the mood when he sings:

> There is no land like England,
> Where'er the light of day be;
> There are no hearts like English hearts,
> Such hearts of oak as they be.
>
> *(Tennyson 1881)*

And at the end of the play, social order is restored, the chorus sings and dances, and everyone lives happily ever after.

> Now the King is home again, and nevermore to roam again.
> Now the King is home again, and the King will have his own again.
> Home again, home again, and each will have his own again.
> All the birds in merry Sherwood sing and sing him home again.[7]
>
> *(Ibid.)*

The structure of Robin

Though it is clear enough that there have been many Robin Hoods, including Tennyson's dutifully patriotic one, it is evident that Robin does share structural characteristics with many other social bandits and noble robbers. This is not to say that each different outlaw doesn't mean differently in different places and times and to different sorts of people, but rather to enquire as to what is it that allows us to recognize a social bandit and differentiate them from a criminal, a guerrilla or a mad person. This is to ask, what is the 'structure' of the myth of the noble bandit? Here, I want to use this approach to say something about what brings together Robin Hood, Blackbeard, Jesse James and so on. As is obvious, I am hence looking for similarities and family resemblances, rather than the inevitable local differences. Graham Seal, in a study of 100 'outlaw heroes', tries something rather similar (2009). He is not terribly interested in whether a particular element of a story is 'true' or 'false', but rather in the commonalities between different sorts of myths. It is impossible to say whether the story of Robin Hood is true or false, and perhaps it doesn't really matter. What might matter is if we find out that he appears not to be unique, but one example of a much more ubiquitous theme.

In *Primitive Rebels* (1965) and particularly in *Bandits* (1972a), Eric Hobsbawm suggested that there were various common elements to the biography of a social bandit. In what follows, I'm using some of his ideas, but also adding Seal's work on what he has called 'the Robin Hood principle' (2009, see also 1996). Both begin by agreeing that the social bandit has to begin their move to outlaw status by being the victim of some sort of injustice by the powerful. 'A man becomes a bandit because he does something which is not regarded as criminal by his local conventions, but is so regarded by the State or the local rulers' (Hobsbawm 1965: 15). His land may be taken, or his family killed or imprisoned, but unlike most people who are wronged, and who are too afraid to resist, the bandit insists on righting this wrong, as well as others suffered by people ruled by the same power. So we have an oppressed group, with its identity under threat from a power which is in some way alien to it. There is then often an explosive incident of some kind, such as Ned Kelly's outrage at a policeman attempting to rape the Kelly women, or Robin's dispossession from his lands. Locally justified violence then becomes the solution. Who the powerful are clearly varies. It could be the state, church, business interests, a local landowner or industrialist, but they are always arrogant, violent and wealthy. Resistance then necessarily means taking from the rich, and perhaps giving to the poor. 'He is virtually obliged to, for there is more to take from the rich than from the poor, and if he takes from the poor or becomes an "illegitimate" killer, he forfeits his most powerful asset, public aid and sympathy' (Hobsbawm 1965: 20). This isn't merely a truism for Hobsbawm, because of course the rich have the money, but it is a tactical position, too. The bandit is like the guerrilla, in that he needs the support of the people for concealment and resources. Without them, he would quickly be betrayed and captured by the powers that be. So giving to the poor is sensible, in order that he maintains their trust and practical complicity. It also means that he is more likely to kill or injure the rich, and is unwise to do the same to the poor. Schinderhannes, a gang-leader in the Rhineland in the 1790s, advertised that he only robbed Jews, dealers and moneylenders. Whether this was true or not is not really known, but the stories about him became ones that celebrated his courtesy, sense of humour, courage and so on. Such accounts become true, by becoming songs, nursery rhymes and popular clichés.

> Diego Corrientes, the brigand of Andalusia
> Who robbed the rich and succoured the poor.
>
> *(cited in Hobsbawm 1965: 77)*

For Hobsbawm, another important part of the myth is the idea that if the bandit does kill or injure, it is either in self-defence, in which case he has little choice, or a righteous form of revenge or punishment, such as the early Robin Hood's violence towards clerics. The idea of honour, of a moral code, ties all this together. For example, the post-Second World War Sicilian Salvatore Giuliano was a Mafiosi who would allegedly kill members of his own gang if they stole from the poor. The noble robber lives their life by a code which is superior to, or at least the equal of, those in power, so if he lives, he can return to spend a long and happy life in the community he has helped to save. If he dies, it is because of the betrayal of a member of that community, as is the case in later Robin Hood stories. This is often because the Judas figure had been bribed by power, or had their lives and family threatened and were too cowardly to resist. If the bandit is killed in this way, then their nobility is intact, and their legend can inspire people in the future.

It's not only this moral nobility that fascinates though, because the bandit frequently has certain personal characteristics which make them rather attractive, too. They are often young, single and unattached. These are characters that live hard and die young and are sometimes rather handsome, as Guiliano was, or have certain attractive features. Robin, for example, almost always has twinkling eyes and a merry laugh and has been played by generations of virile young men. Bandits are also often described as wearing some rather distinctive clothing, or using a particular type of weapon (Hobsbawm 1972a: 36, 84). They are, in other words, recognizable as a social type, and not merely an anonymous figure with no distinctiveness. This is necessary for their subsequent reproduction as characters, too, since descriptions and images will sell better if they are clear and easily defined. Robin Hood is easy to recognize, with his green hat and his bow, and so it is easy to sing what he looks like, or trade a print of him.

There is a complexity here though because, as I suggested above, the bandit does have trickster characteristics. Robin, for example, often disguises himself to get into Nottingham, or take part in an archery contest. One of the skills that the outlaw possesses is that of disguise or escape. Sometimes this is a function of the landscape that they inhabit – the forest, the sea, the mountains, the backstreets of the city – but it is also often a skill that they demonstrate. This speaks of their cunning, their wit and intelligence. Like the Welsh trickster bandit Twm Sion Catti,[8] they are capable of slipping through the fingers of power, of making the (English)man in the castle look stupid as they disappear laughing into the forest. So the bandit is an extraordinary individual – handsome, intelligent, determined. Someone who is hard not to like, in terms of common evaluations of personality and appearance.

Finally, both Hobsbawm and Seal note that some accounts of the bandit shade over into accounts of magical powers (Hobsbawm 1965: 15). So clever are they at avoiding the authorities, at escaping from overwhelming force or using astonishing skills with the bow, sword or gun, that the only explanation becomes that they must possess supernatural skills. Robin's ability to split an arrow with an arrow might fall into this category, as would stories of Eustace the Black Monk who privateered for England and France in the thirteenth century and could make his ship invisible. The Robin Hood-like Bokkenrijders from the Low Countries had signed a pact with the devil and rode on goats. Kobus van der Schlossen, the leader of a gang from the same part of the world at the end of the seventeenth century, also sold his soul to the devil in exchange for magical powers, but protected poor widows against greedy landlords. The early eighteenth-century Slovak bandit Janosik was supposed to have possessed a belt that made him invincible and a shirt that protected him from bullets.

Summarizing, Seal suggests that the outlaw is 'friend of the poor, oppressed, forced into outlawry, brave, generous, courteous, does not indulge in unjustified violence, trickster, betrayed, lives on after death' (1996: 11; 2009: 74–5). Hobsbawm has a pretty similar list, but adds a seventh idea that we don't find in Seal.

1. He takes from the rich.
2. He never kills apart from in self defence or just revenge.
3. He is supported by the people.
4. If he lives, he returns with honour.
5. If he dies, he is betrayed, and the community grieves.
6. He is invisible and invulnerable.
7. He is not the enemy of the rightful king, but only of their local or temporary replacements.

(Hobsbawm 1972a: 43)

The idea that the bandit supports another authority is important here, because it reflects once again on Hobsbawm's evaluation that these are 'primitive' rebels, proto-revolutionary, but ultimately conservative in their politics. For Hobsbawm, only the party politics of the working class is politics proper, which necessarily places these rebels, and perhaps any cultural politics, in rather an ephemeral position. Interesting, but not that important. This is a theme that runs throughout this book and, as we have seen in the story of Robin Hood, reinforces the division between the idea of the outlaw as dangerous rebel, or ultimately a circuitous support for the status quo. The invention of a noble lineage for Robin Hood, Earl of Locksley, in the seventeenth century reflects precisely this effort to move the outlaw from one position to the other, to inlaw them. Robin is then only a rebel with regard to the unjust order of the time, because when the King comes back, he will bend the knee.

As Seal is clear, these are not only matters of fact or fiction, as Blok (1972) might have it, but questions about the myths that get constructed during and after the period of their adventures. The actual allegiances of real bandits are not the issue, but the way that they get told to contemporaries and following generations. Very useful here is Seal's idea of the 'afterlife' of the hero. They may die bravely, or disappear and go into presumed hiding to return at some future time when the community needs them again. They may live to a ripe old age, but this is less common. Either way, they become elements in mythmaking, in the telling of stories which continue long after they are dead. There is a 'cultural script' at work here (Seal 2009: 79, *passim*). 'When outlaw heroes meet their usually bloody ends, the mythologization intensifies, Folklore, newspapers, artists, dramatists, poets and filmmakers do their work, creating an ongoing afterlife' (op. cit., 80). Seal uses a contemporary example to illustrate the process of making myths, Veerappan, 'The Jungle Cat', a *dacoit* or armed bandit who was killed by the Indian authorities in 2004. There were two films made, and many newspaper and magazine articles. The comparisons used – Robin Hood, Billy the Kid, Osama bin Laden – reflected precisely the cultural script of the noble outlaw. 'This tradition may be so powerful that subsequent outlaws and those who celebrate them will frequently refer back to the real or imagined deeds and to principles of their predecessors as justification and as exemplars for their own actions' (op. cit., 82). In Veerappan's case, reference could also be made to other famous *dacoits*, such as Phoolan Devi, 'The Bandit Queen', or the earlier Sultana Daku, who between 1939 and 1955 was supposed to have committed over a thousand robberies and kidnappings and nearly 200 murders. So the afterlife of the outlaw provides material for both cultural producers, as we will see in much of this book, but also for future outlaws who will refer to themselves in the same sort of terms. Robin Hood is perhaps the best-known example, even used 800 years and half a world away to explain the actions of an Indian *dacoit*. Seal calls this the 'outlaw hero cycle', a sort of arrangement of ready-made plot elements for both the self-justifications of outlaws, but also for those involved in selling cultural representations and newspapers.

The myth is what matters, not whether Robin Hood existed, whether pirates were kind and jolly, or Dick Turpin was chivalrous. 'It is mythology rather than history that validates Hobsbawm's hypothesis' (op. cit., 84). Robin Hood is not only an antiquated children's story, but a figure used in contemporary arguments about politics. So, in a popular book about Robin Hood, the author concludes by supporting the protestors and conservationists who stand against the modernizers who are destroying green England.

> They are vastly outnumbered by the growing numbers of 'Robin Hoods' who in the face of the ecological threats to our forests and disappearing greenbelts, have taken up arms in their own little way to hit a lick against 'Norman' industrialists and developers!
>
> *(Rutherford-Moore 1998: 160)*

Or, in a much more class-inflected fashion, Judy Cox argues that

> Robin is the embodiment of the aspirations of thousands throughout the centuries. He was a symbol of freedom when the majority lived in serfdom, an enforcer of natural justice when most were powerless in the face of tyranny, and hero to revenge the inequality suffered by the poor.
>
> *(Cox 1998: 8)*

In the UK in 2010, when bankers were being paid huge bonuses at the same time that savage cuts were proposed across the public sector, a proposal for a 'Robin Hood Tax' was launched with the support of some very high-profile celebrities.[9] Fundamentally a variation on the Tobin Tax (ul Haq *et al.* 1996), it proposed taking 0.05 per cent from the transactions conducted by global financial institutions and allocating it to poverty reduction measures. The calculation was that this would produce a pot of $40 billion per year, a figure that places the divisions between rich and poor into stark relief, and clearly indicates why the redistributive outlaw is such an attractive character to so many in the first place.

Robin now

I ended the story of Robin Hood with Tennyson, because it allowed us to see just how much the outlaw had changed over 700 years, and also to understand something about the inextricability of the culture industries (broadly and historically conceived) in selling and making the myth. The story of the last century is simpler, in a sense, because it shows us just how the noble bandit became embedded in the production of popular culture in the twentieth century.[10] Along with pirates, smugglers, highwaymen, Western outlaws, Mafiosi, bank robbers and jewel thieves, Robin became a stock figure for selling films. Sherwood also becomes a sort of *mise en scène* for a huge variety of purposes, whether an episode in a cartoon, or the selling of a cheap plastic bow, arrow and hat set made in China.

As Jeffrey Richards notes, in twentieth-century film, Robin became the epitome of the English swashbucking folk hero (1977: 187, *passim*) and he can be found right at the beginning of the industry. The 1908 silent film *Robin Hood and His Merry Men* was the first of five films made by 1914, but the biggest early silent production is the 1922 *Robin Hood* with Douglas Fairbanks Senior as the lead. Budgeted at $1.4 million, this was the most expensive film ever made at the time. Lavish sets, a bunch of merry men who 'skip around like a lot of out-of-work ballet dancers' (op. cit., 195), and a great deal of romantic mediaeval flummery made the film a big hit. The film that really defined the modern Robin was Errol Flynn's 1938 film *The Adventures of Robin Hood* in which Robin leads a Saxon army against their Norman overlords. King John, the Sheriff, Guy of Gisbourne and the rest of the baddies gradually become established as ruthless and arrogant stereotypes, reprised in the Richard Todd film of 1952, *The Adventures of Robin Hood and His Merrie Men*. In many other films, elements of the myth are developed, such as how Robin became an outlaw in the 1967 Hammer film *A Challenge for Robin Hood*, the more mature characters in the 1976 *Robin and Marian* as well as three different films telling the story of Robin's son.[11] The biggest recent films have been the 1991 *Robin Hood: Prince of Thieves* starring Kevin Costner, and the darkly violent *Robin Hood* (2010), with Russell Crowe.

The first TV show aired on the BBC in 1953 as *Robin Hood*, but a much more successful series was the British ITV show *The Adventures of Robin Hood* which gained a big following on both sides of the Atlantic. Starring Richard Greene, it was aired from 1955–60, and 143 half-hour episodes were made. Many TV serials followed over the decades, with the 1980s *Robin of Sherwood* introducing mystical elements and the first example of an Islamic character to join the merry men. The Disney animation of 1973 makes Robin into a fox, a trickster figure who memorably sucks the jewels from the rings of King Richard as he kisses his hand. Robin also occurs countless times as a character in other shows, instantly recognizable in Lincoln green, a forester's cap and carrying a bow. Hundreds of books, both fantasy and history, claim to tell the story, some relocating versions of Robin to other places and times. The first cartoon strip, *Robin Hood and Company*, ran in the Toronto Telegram from 1935 to 1940 and ended up with Robin becoming friends with Blackbeard the pirate. Many comics were released in the late 1940s and 50s, capitalizing on the popularity of Richard Greene's TV show. Robin fights a tiger, apes and wears what looks very much like a superhero costume as 'The Masked Marvel of Sherwood Forest'. He later morphs into DC Comics superhero Green Arrow, who went on to become a member of the Justice League of America. Robin is mentioned in pop songs, becomes the subject of video and board games, pornography and lego toys. He is also used to promote a city, themed tourist attractions and sell cider. There are gay, feminist and green appropriations, and at the time of writing, Robin appears to be becoming a dark character, following the same mutations that happened to many superheroes in the early twenty-first century. The 2009 novels *Hodd* by Adam Thorpe and *Outlaw* by Angus Donald, as well as the 2010 film, contain a great deal of graphic violence as well as an exploration of a tortured character with a twisted moral code. A century on from Tennyson, Robin Hood has become a new kind of gothic anti-hero.

As we will see in the rest of the book, this sort of cultural production is typical of the last century, with all my economic outlaws being exploited in pretty much every single cultural medium. So it seems that it would be easy enough to agree with Jeffrey Richards, and Hobsbawm, in dismissing any notion that he represents political radicalism. Richards is writing specifically about swashbuckling heroes, but his remarks seem to apply more broadly.

> Subordinate functionaries, wicked princelings, faithless ministers may be removed by individual heroic enterprise or even by limited popular upris- ing. But the person of the monarch is sacrosanct. ... There may be changes in the lower tiers of the structure, but the apex of the structure, the throne and all that it implies, is uncorrupt and enduring. With all their fighting, feasting and lovemaking, our heroes never seek to subvert the system.
>
> *(1977: 283)*

This is a valuable caution against assuming that Robin Hood, or any noble robber, has a necessarily radical politics. The many versions of Robin – Robert of Locksley, Robert, Earl of Huntingdon, Robin Goodfellow, Robin des Bois, Robin o' the Hood, Robehod and so on – suggest a much greater mutability than that. Different Robins for different audiences at different times. Yet symme- trically, it also suggests that a judgement which dismisses the possibility that myths of social bandits might be subversive is also premature. Just like any argu- ment about culture more generally, it is difficult to distinguish between a mass culture that numbs, and a counter culture that offers alternatives. Robin seems to be both.

The story of Robin Hood is also one that questions the epistemological status of his representation, and places him on the boundary between fact and fiction. He has a host of origins, perhaps in facts which have been made fiction, and fic- tions which have become treated as facts. In that sense, the 'truth' of Robin Hood is the sum total of culture which takes Robin Hood as its object, and there is no time or place that we can go to that would finally 'fix' his representation as this or that. Seal might be correct in suggesting that '*Wherever and whenever significant numbers of people believe that they are victims of inequity, injustice and oppression, histor- ical and/or fictional outlaw heroes will appear and continue to be celebrated after their deaths*' (Seal 2009: 83, italics in original). Yet this is only the beginning of an oscillation between widely different cultural representations that use Robin, or the setting of Sherwood and the castle, as scripts which justify the inheritance of authority and power, or tell us stories about the violent and practical redistribution of wealth, or simply sell products and make profits.

In the next chapter we will look at a different example. Robin (if he existed) was long dead before the early modern culture industries got their hands on him. He survived for centuries as a largely oral character, only becoming widely soli- dified in print and image by the seventeenth century, by which time he was well on the way to becoming an Earl. The 'golden age' of piracy offers a different timeline. Pirates were entering Seal's 'outlaw hero cycle' at the same time that they were abroad on the high seas, and there is evidence that this made their radical challenges to understandings of business and markets rather more difficult to control. In a strange, but typical, example of intertextuality, in February 2010, it was reported that Somali pirates were intending to donate some of their profits to victims of the Haitian earthquake which took place a few weeks before (Thier 2010). Claiming that the USA have been 'the ones pirating mankind for many years', the Somalis seemed to be adopting the noble robber script with its associated gains in terms of local legitimacy. The title chosen for the piece echoed this beautifully – 'Somali Pirates Say They'll Play Robin Hood in Haiti'.

3

PIRATE UTOPIANISM

(*Text from DVD case of* Pirates of the Caribbean: Dead Man's Chest, *2006*)

Captain Jack Sparrow would probably raise a camp eyebrow at the anti-piracy warning copied above. He would, however, be impressed that the film has grossed well over one billion dollars. Its predecessor, *Pirates of the Caribbean: The Curse of the Black Pearl* (2003), only grossed $733 million, beaten by the third film, *Pirates of the Caribbean: At World's End* (2007), on nearly one billion. At the time of writing, a fourth film is in production. Hardly surprising given the riches at stake. So far the pirates series has made a total of $2,680,308,734, not including income from DVD rentals and sales, sponsoring tie-ups and merchandising. Neither does it include the versions of the films which are sold as pirate DVDs on markets all over the world, or streamed off the internet for private use, or shown illegally in small cinemas in many parts of the globe.[1] The money is important here, just as it always has been with pirates, and the anti-piracy warning reminds us of a few other concepts that matter, too. One is the legal idea of a licence to do business, an agreement from a properly constituted authority, and the other is territorial, simply because authorities tend to govern particular places, and not all places all of the time. In his *Mare Liberum* of 1609, the Dutch lawyer Hugo Grotius had claimed that the sea was no one's territory, and that all should be free to do business there. This was a judgement aimed at challenging the claims of the French and the Spanish, but it also indicated a practical problem in treating the sea as territory. Indeed, it is precisely the spatial limits of authorities that constitute the pirate, and their cousins, buccaneers, corsairs and privateers. The pirate is to the sea what Robin Hood is to the greenwood, the outlaw to the mountain, and the highwayman to the road, and as we shall see below, the comparison was made explicitly on many occasions.

Just like all these other economic outlaws, pirates make money for other people, too, not just themselves. The merchant in the port, the smuggler, the innkeeper, the governor who turns a blind eye, the monarch who accepts the tribute, and there is even mention of a sailmaker's widow in Nassau who made a living stitching Jolly Rogers for Golden Age pirates (Kuhn 2010: 174). Just as important for my argument here are those who made money by popularizing pirate myth. In 1724 Captain Charles Johnson (sometimes supposed to be Daniel Defoe) published the first volume of his *General History of the Robberies and Murders of the Most Notorious Pyrates, and Also Their Policies, Discipline and Government*. The book, with its series of chapters on famous pirates, pretty much defined the symbolism and characterology of this economic outlaw and was a big success. It rapidly went through three editions with each being more enlarged than the last, and a second volume (more fiction and disguised social criticism than serious history) followed in 1728. Since then, there have been seventy editions in four languages (Burl 2006: 265). Much of contemporary piratology comes from this book. Whether the wild-eyed psychopaths, like Blackbeard or Edward Low, or the gentlemen robbers, like Captains Mission, Bellamy, Bonnet and Roberts, the pirate has become both celebrated and reviled. This is a typically ambivalent construction for a description of another way of living, as well as a set of social relations that both inverted and exceeded the cruelties of European imperialism.

This ambivalence shines through in writing about pirates. Whilst there are some who clearly celebrate the romantic outsiders (Rediker 2004, Snelders 2005, Woodard 2007 for example), the majority seem compelled to temper their remarks with episodic moralism. It is as if, suddenly finding themselves carried away, they have to remind us where they stand, just in case there was a misunderstanding. As the writer of *The Pirate Wars* puts it, 'the author of a book such as this one cannot be certain that all his readers will necessarily be on the side of law and order' (Earle 2004: xii). Or Kemp – 'Unlike the pirates of fiction, who are often portrayed as roguish adventurers, the pirates of history were hard, mean men' (2009: 20). Of course, this is not a matter which could be restricted to 'historical fact', as if such an ephemeral court could be the judge of such claims. I want to think about the popularity of Captain Jack Sparrow by tracing representations of piracy and, as with Robin Hood, history and representation are here too intertwined to be disentangled. Giles Lapouge (2004: 19) suggests something similar:

> If we want to penetrate the mysterious heart of the pirate adventure, we
> must therefore observe these evildoers in two lights at the same time – that

> of reality and that of dream. ... The treasure chests of Henry Morgan and
> Rock the Brazilian are real – and this reality is imaginary.

In other words, there is no 'truth' of piracy that is accessible to us, but 400 years
of talking and writing about pirates has opened up some very interesting ways of
thinking about the relation between the state, business and organized crime. Or,
to put it another way, to ask why some forms of making money are legitimate,
whilst others are not. Jack Sparrow holds this question in his raised eyebrow.

This chapter begins by showing how the flexible mercenaries called privateers
were gradually distinguished into pirates and navies. This involved the forging of
an alliance between the emerging mercantile classes and their companies, and the
outlaw figure of the pirate. At the same time, the pirate becomes a character in
the popular imagination, a 'trickster' figure on the side of the people, and against
the authorities that ruled the land. The second section of the chapter moves from
'history' to 'representation' and shows how the image of the pirate moved from a
wild character on the edge of the world, to (again like Robin) a stock cliché for
Hollywood swashbucklers. Following that, I investigate the legacy of radical histories and representations of piracy, focusing particularly on the idea of alternative
organization on the ship and the pirate utopias on the land. The final section pulls
together the historical figure, the stock character and the radical rogue in order to
suggest that the pirate can mean what we want him (and sometimes her) to mean.
Nonetheless, the biggest historical lesson is that the Golden Age pirate emerges at
the beginnings of international business, and is only wiped out when the state and
the businessman strike an alliance that lasts to the present day. But if Hollywood
sells Captain Jack, it opens the possibility that some other histories might get
smuggled in, too.[2]

Histories

There was piracy before, and piracy afterwards, but this chapter concentrates on
Atlantic piracy in the seventeenth and eighteenth centuries. There is no good
reason for this, other than that this is the mythological location for the 'Golden
Age' of piracy, and it begins when, in 1700, Captain Cranby of HMS Poole first
saw the French pirate Emmanuel Wynne fighting under 'a sable ensign with
crossbones, a Death's head and an hour glass' (in Lewis 2006: 228).[3] There were
pirates elsewhere at the same time, such as the largely Muslim Barbary Corsairs
who attacked Christian ships in the Mediterranean, or the Knights of Malta who
opposed them, or Asian and European pirates who took ships in the Indian
Ocean. There are also predecessors to the Golden Age of piracy, such as the early
seventeenth-century Buccaneers (*boucaniers*) based on Hispaniola who preyed
on Spanish shipping and cities in the Caribbean, or the Dutch Sea Rovers or
Freebooters (*vrijbuiter*) from the sixteenth century. Or, we could go back to
Cicero, in his 67 BCE account of Heracleo the pirate who plagued the coast of
Sicily (in Lewis 2006: 22). Or forward to 5th November 2005, when the cruise

ship 'Seabourn Spirit' was attacked by rocket-propelled grenades off the coast of Somalia. But this chapter is not strictly a history of piracy, rather a story about how we get to Captain Jack and the *Pirates of the Caribbean* franchise.

We can't really understand Jack without understanding something about the state – particularly the Dutch, Spanish, Portuguese, French and English states. During the early Golden Age, the device of 'privateering' effectively allowed for an extraordinarily powerful combination of mercenary politics and mercantilism. In Elizabethan England, all the maritime heroes spent some time as state-licensed pirates – Hawkins, Grenville, Frobisher, Raleigh and others.[4] A 'Letter of Marque and Reprisal' (both a legal device and an economic contract) specified the legitimacy of the targets, as well as the distribution of the spoils. Privateering was noble and profitable, Elizabeth referring to Sir Francis Drake as 'my dear pirate'. The device had the further advantage of relieving the monarch of the costs of maintaining a large standing navy, whilst the discipline was seen as an effective training ground for potential navy recruits (Earle 2004: 23). The merchants and gentlemen who financed a privateering trip usually expected two-thirds of any profit, with the remainder being very unequally divided between the captain, officers and crew.[5] On a long sea voyage, what was a legitimate 'prize' and what counted as 'profit' were inevitably flexible. It was quite possible for a gentleman who had exceeded his instructions to be pardoned, and even given public office, as was the case with Henry Mainwaring in 1616 and Henry Morgan in 1675. For merchants, carrying a Letter of Marque was also a form of insurance which diversified the sources of possible profits from a voyage (Kontorovich 2004: 212). If they didn't make a profit legitimately, then the possibility of plunder spread the business opportunities. There was also, in places far from the centres of imperial power, a substantial amount of productive confusion about who was entitled to offer Letters of Marque and pardons. The governors of Jamaica or Tortuga, or the representatives of the trading companies, had some latitude in this regard, and could easily interpret directives to suit local circumstances. At the start of the Golden Age, it seems that the boundaries between legitimate and illegitimate violence, or profit and crime, were extraordinarily unclear, thanks to a device that claimed to produce clarity.

But by the end of the period, the boundary is being enforced most violently. The 1722 trial of Black Bart's crew at Cape Coast Castle on the Royal African Company's Guinea coast of West Africa has been described like this:

> Behind a long table at one end of the chapel sat the judges, naval officers in their blue brass-buttoned uniforms, elegant, three-corner hated governors, powder-wigged, comfortably seated. Atkins, the registrar, was at a separate table, quills sharpened, inkwell filled, notepaper neatly arranged.
>
> At the far end of the hall were the pirates. Guarded by scarlet coated soldiers the men were in rags, filthy from the dungeons, fetters clattering as they shuffled in, unshaven, unwashed, all reeking with dirt, unrecognisable from their days of silken glory.

(Burl 2006: 248)

The pirates may have been unrepentant, and 'walk'd to the Gallows without a Tear' (Rediker 2004: 12), but the alliance between mercantile capital and the state was now clear. Pirates were now an obstacle to state commerce, and hence needed to become *hostis humani generis* – common enemies of mankind.

The interests of the trading companies were key. The French West India Company, the Dutch East India Company, the Royal African Company and many others were initially small investment gambles on a ship and a captain. But they grew to become determinants and instruments of state policy. In England, Earle claims, it was not until the end of the seventeenth century that an alliance between the mercantile classes, state bureaucrats and aristocracy effectively committed them to creating the conditions for the expansion of both trade and the empire.

> The state would provide protection for trade and, in return, would receive a flow of revenue from increased wealth and customs duties and a pool of trained sailors to fight in its naval wars. There was to be no place for pirates in this new world, no place for individualist marauders on the periphery of empire.
>
> *(Rediker 2004: 146)*

Corrupt governors were removed, laws were revised and more ships were sent on station to areas where there was a pirate menace. This coincides with frequent attempts to present merchants, seen by the common people as greedy and duplicitous, as 'most Useful and Beneficial to the Publick' and possessed of 'indefatigable Industry' that nourishes every member of the 'Body Politick' (Rediker 2004: 134).[6] In legal terms, piracy now becomes the benchmark for crimes so heinous that they fall within a universal jurisdiction, and are hence not even subject to the vagaries of state law. In a sixteenth-century version of the Great Chain of Being, God is at the top and rocks are at the bottom, with pirates, thieves and gypsies being just above animals, and just below beggars (Dickens and Ormrod 2007: 23). Merchants were about half way up, but below anyone involved in court, including pages and messengers. Like the outlaw who was declared *caput great lupinum*, a pirate was so far down that they could be detained or killed by anyone, in any part of the globe – and the analogy is still a central metaphor for claims about the universality of international law, and the protection of international trade based on the freedom of the seas (Kontorovich 2004: 230).

But whatever was being pronounced in London or Madrid concerning the barbarities of pirates, there were plenty of people, rich and poor, home and abroad, who were still very happy to support them. Wealthy coastal landowners effectively taxed piracy as a source of income, and also used pirates to oppress and plunder their tenants (Earle 2004: 20). Merchants, shop-keepers and traders profited and, as with smuggling, ordinary people benefited from access to cheap goods. Indeed, it seems that many were attracted to 'go on the account' precisely because of the *popular* notoriety of the pirate. Like Robin Hood, the pirate became a figure who was often celebrated by common people. Though Robin had fought with a pirate called Damon the Monk in one early text, beating him and hanging all his crew from the yard-arm off what is now Robin Hood's Bay in North Yorkshire (Dixon-Kennedy 2006: 139), he effectively became a pirate in the ballad 'The Noble Fisherman'. Henry Avery, the first pirate mentioned in Johnson's *General History*, is described as a 'maritime Robin Hood' and ballads and broadsheets celebrated the bravery and liberty of those who robbed the rich (Rediker 2004: 173). Pirates had already become semi-mythical figures, playing both inspirational and cautionary roles in a variety of contexts. Land sums this up by suggesting that

> even in their own time the pirates were perceived as politically dissident, revolutionary figures and popular accounts of their utopian communities offered a biting tool for the political critic and satirist to attack the hypocrisy and corruption of Church and State.
>
> *(2007: 180)*

Pirates 'developed their project of escaping from history under the protection of history – and they could obviously perpetrate their atrocities more easily in a turbulent world than in a peaceful one. They thrived in the cracks that ran through states' (Lapouge 2004: 90–1). And, of course, the cracks that ran between states. Empty but contested spaces which harboured merchant adventurers, mercenaries and pirates, sometimes all in the same boat. These cracks were also cracks in representation, from the bloodthirsty sociopath to the smiling rogue, and it is to these representations that I now turn.

Representations

Accounts of seafaring robbers are common enough in classical literature. Ancient myth and the writings of Homer, Herodotus, Thucydides, Plautus and Terence provide plenty of accounts of plunder, raids, kidnap and so on. These are either routine acts of state-approved terrorism, or people trying to make a living from foreigners and slavery. Roman literature rather predictably makes pirates into criminals, whilst later mediaeval tales suggest pirates as fantastical, and perhaps possessed of magical powers. Alwilda the Dane was said to have a largely female crew; Eustace the Black Monk privateered for England and France in the thirteenth century and could make his ship invisible; and Johan Stortebecher the German privateer had a hollow mast filled with gold (Rogozinski 1997: 122). But it is not until the beginning of the eighteenth century that a particular condensation of images emerges which largely endures to the present day.

In 1719, Daniel Defoe published *Robinson Crusoe*. Apart from the native 'Friday', Crusoe is shipwrecked alone on the island, and is largely occupied with re-creating the civilization he has left behind. Though there are many different readings of the novel, the majority would focus on Crusoe's conquest of nature, and his construction of a small-scale Arcadian version of paradise. Defoe may well have been influenced by Henry Neville's 1668 'pornotopia' *Isle of Pines* (Bruce 1999), but in its turn the influence of Defoe's book was huge, producing an entire sub-genre of 'Robinsonnades' in the following two centuries. Some were largely derivative versions of industrious Europeans surviving in various forms of wilderness, often accompanied by homilies on simplicity and hard work, such as Johann Wyss's *Swiss Family Robinson* (1813). Others, with more radical intent, began to develop the romantic idea of the 'noble savage' and the original state of nature which fitted so neatly with accounts of Eden and the idea of a Golden Age, and which had been prefigured in de Foigny's *New Discovery of Terra Incognita Australis* (1676). Books, such as Swift's *Gulliver's Travels* (1726) and Diderot's *Supplement to Bougainville's Voyage* (1796), contained ideas about travel to 'virgin' islands where people and creatures were found who showed the manners, politics and institutions of Europe in a distinctly negative light. They were closer to simplicity than their conquerors, like innocent children who ask the most awkward (and revealing) questions.

Rousseau's suggestion that the education of his pupil in *Emile* (1762) should proceed through a reading of *Robinson Crusoe* (in preference to the classical education assumed at the time) underlined the idea of 'natural man' being born free, but everywhere placed in chains. But Robinson Crusoe was not entirely fictional. In 1704, a Scotsman called Alexander Selkirk had been marooned for over four years on Màs-a-Tierra, in the Juan Fernandez Islands off the coast of Chile. He was rescued by a privateer, Captain Woodes Rogers, in 1709, later the author of *A Cruising Voyage Round the World* (1712, see Lewis 2006: 157), which Defoe read. So the author of the *General History*, published five years after *Robinson Crusoe*, could easily have been Defoe, or could have been the Charles Johnson who wrote the play *The Successful Pyrate* first performed in 1712. No one seems to know. It could also have been the author of other accounts of piracy now commonly attributed to Defoe, such as *The King of the Pirates* (also 1719), *The Life, Adventures and Piracies of Captain Singleton* (1720), *Colonel Jacque* (1723), *A New Voyage Round the World* (1724) and *The Four Years Voyages of Captain George Roberts* (1726). As with Robin's misty past, the mystery seems appropriate, and entirely consonant with others who have written of strange lands, outlaw bands in forests and even utopias.[7]

As is common in such accounts, the fiction becomes the fact. Màs-a-Tierra was renamed Isla Robinson Crusoe, and 'Captain Johnson' became the inspiration for a thousand books and films. Not that *The General History* is the first pirate book. Alexander Exquemelin's *The American Sea-Rovers* was published in Dutch in 1678 and is both a travel book and an account of the extraordinary cruelty and violence of the buccaneers. Exquemelin tells us about 'spiders with a body as big as an egg', jungle people with claws like monkeys that allow them to climb trees, and describes prisoners being hung by their genitals or gradually hacked to death (2000: 44, 97, 151). Within eight years the book had been translated into five languages.[8] William Dampier's *New Voyage Round the World* (1697) covered similar territory, became a best-seller and brought him some fame as a naturalist. After publishing his follow up, *A Voyage to New Holland* (1703), Dampier and another ship, the *Cinque Ports*, went on a privateering voyage to South America. The ships parted in Panama in 1704, and after the death of its captain and a series of arguments, it was the *Cinque Ports* that marooned Alexander Selkirk. On a later voyage, Dampier was accompanying Captain Woodes Rogers when he rescued Selkirk (Rogozinski 1997). So stories of amazing animals, the odd customs of native people and accounts of robbery bring together elements of travel journalism and diaries, science and utopian literature. But (after something of a silence in the second half of the eighteenth century), the re-reading and writing of the *General History* throughout the nineteenth century largely erased these variegated origins, and began to construct an archetype of setting, imagery and behaviour, a *mise en scène* which could be re-presented in some highly profitable ways. In part, this involved the creation of the historical romance, particularly the novel, as a vehicle for popularizing the pirate.

The first modern 'fictional' pirate is probably Arviragus in Charles Johnson's play *The Successful Pirate* (1712). He appears to be a disguised version of Henry Avery, later also to appear in Captain Johnson's work, though there seems to be no relation between the two Johnsons. Pirates were very commonly featured in the press, which certainly inspired many of Defoe's accounts (Backscheider 1989: 478), but there is little else in fiction until James Cross's play *Blackbeard; or, the Captive Princess* ('a serio–comic ballet of action, in two parts') was presented in 1798 (Cordingly 1999: 233). This play was revived continually during the nineteenth century, but it is Byron's poem *The Corsair* (1814) that was the first really influential fictional account of the loneliness and mystery of the pirate, an ambiguity which allowed the character to be simultaneously villainous and noble. It sold 10,000 copies on its first day of publication, and installed the corsair as a Byronic hero, though in this case an 'oriental' not a Caribbean pirate. Supposedly inspired by Jean Lafitte, a French privateer who fought the English at the battle of New Orleans, Byron's Conrad was 'Lone, wild, and strange, he stood alike exempt / From all affection and from all contempt.' The title of the poem was borrowed for Berlioz's overture of 1844, Verdi's opera of 1848 and Adolph Adam's ballet of 1856 (revived and revised in various versions). Two years after *Ivanhoe*, Walter Scott published *The Pirate* in 1822, Edward Fitzball wrote the play *The Red Rover, or the Mutiny of the Dolphin* in 1829, and Charles Ellms partially plagiarized Defoe for his *Pirates Own Book* in 1837, with at least nine subsequent editions. By the mid-nineteenth century, the pirate begins to become a stock character in fiction with stories by Captain Marryat, Charles Kingsley, Washington Irving, James Fenimore Cooper, Edgar Allen Poe, Robert M. Ballantyne and many others, as well as Gilbert and Sullivan's 1879 operetta *The Pirates of Penzance*. Robert Louis Stevenson's *Treasure Island* of 1883 is hence, despite its supposed seminality, quite a late work, and one that borrowed heavily from *The General History*, as well as the authors mentioned above. J. M. Barrie's 1904 play *Peter Pan* became a book in 1911, and the contemporaneous fiction of Howard Pyle,

Samuel Walkey and Rafael Sabatini articulated a version of the evil Spaniard, and (again like Robin) the noble born or honest pirate. In a century, the pirate had moved from Byron's romantic and dangerous icon to children's book cliché and bare-chested swashbuckler.

These rather de-politicized images then go on to define pirates in twentieth-century film. Parish could summarize the plots of 137 pirate films in 1995, and characterize them as 'a man fighting for the right in a world that does not understand the right as he sees it' (1995: 3). Sabatini's novels were adapted for films with Douglas Fairbanks senior and junior, Errol Flynn, Tyrone Power and others. Part of the wider genre of swashbuckling films, sword-play and bare chests are pitted against evil pirates or evil Spaniards in *Captain Blood* (1926), *The Sea Hawk* (1940), *Captain Kidd* (1945) and so on. There was something unthreatening about many of these films, with good and evil being so clearly marked. The reviewer of *The Black Pirate* of 1926 in the *New York Times* puts it well: 'This is a production which marks another forward stride for the screen, one that the boy and his mother will enjoy and one that is a healthy entertainment for men of all ages' (in Cordingly 1999: 203). Many of these films required that the whole-someness of the pirate was maintained by having him be an outlaw aristocrat, or falsely accused of a crime, or disguising himself for the purpose of vengeance, or simply a privateer for England and the Queen. Richards suggests that the core of these films is 'male beauty' and 'a joyous love of adventure'. 'The values are the values of the knightly class, as embodied in the chivalric code' (1977: 4). The object of the hero is not revolution, but restoration, or the extermination of a general evil such as slavery, or a specific pirate or governor. These films do not endorse piracy or spend much time presenting the social relations that created the pirate.

> Even when the heroes are unequivocally pirates, they are not criminals. They are rebels with a cause, the fulfilment of which leads to their retire-ment. They seek revenge for a father/mother/brother or they campaign against slavery and oppression or, most often, they represent the forces of truth and justice against the universal enemy, Spain, opponent of liberty, overlord of slavery, grim graveyard of freedom.
>
> *(Richards 1977: 268)*

By the second half of the twentieth century, even the thin politics of the swash-buckler is beginning to fade, and the pirate film begins to become a vehicle for the children's romance or the comedy pastiche. *Abbot and Costello Meet Captain Kidd* (1952), *Yellowbeard* (1983), with many of the Monty Python team, and *Hook* (1991) become fairly representative of the development of the genre, with the occasional attempt to bring a little sword-play back in with films such as *Pirates* (1996). To a certain extent, Jack Sparrow inherits this set of marketing clichés, as well as this target market. We seem to have moved a long way from the idea of the pirate as a revolutionary figure, as a character who problematizes the state monopoly over violence for political and commercial gain. But there are other histories of representation that can be told, too, and perhaps Jack still contains faint echoes of these other ways of being. Pirates were not merely romantic heroes, but actively constructed a different set of institutions and opened a space for the political imagination.

Alternative organization

In the seventeenth century, navy and merchant ships were vicious and unsanitary places. Discipline was cruel and violent, with officers often justifying sadism in support of discipline. The food was bad and the pay poor. These conditions of labour, combined with continual mortality, meant that ordinary seamen were often 'pressed' into service, either from British or foreign ports. Such a recruitment policy was necessary simply because one in four of the crew on a slaving ship would die on the voyage (Earle 2004: 167). Land quotes a series of figures that could be summarized by suggesting that if half a crew returned the ship had done rather well (2007: 174). If this was 'normal' seafaring work, then the life of a pirate must have seemed like rather an attractive option. Indeed, the abuse suffered under state-sanctioned regimes is often cited as a mitigating factor for piracy during trials and confessions (Rediker 2004: 4). But as we will see below, pirates also developed radical alternative forms of work and economy, and it is easy to imagine the stories concerning the proto-democratic and egalitarian practices circulating on board navy and merchant ships. These became central to early representations of piracy.

It is with the buccaneers that we first begin to see stories about the emergence of a radical collective identity. This was a community of exiles who developed the 'custom of the coast', the 'Jamaica Discipline' or the 'Law of the Privateers'. Nicknames replaced birth names, and it was forbidden to speak of a man's origins (Earle 2004: 101). Many historians have suggested that there was a real radicalism here, a class hostility combined with a peasant utopianism that constructed an image of a 'revolutionary Atlantic'. This, in part, was driven by a brutalized experience of labour, but also by political currents inherited from the English Revolution. Members of the New Model Army, Ranters, Diggers, Levellers and radical Protestants provided the history for an anti-authoritarian politics (Hill 1978, Lamborne Wilson 1995: 20; Linebaugh and Rediker 2000, Rediker 2004: 61, *passim*; Parker *et al.* 2007). Adding to this political undercurrent were slave rebellions which happened throughout the seventeenth century, as well as uprisings of indentured white servants (Do or Die 1999). On board the ship, the influence of the increasing numbers of ex-merchant seamen is important as 'pirate ideology now began to reflect the grievances of the lower deck as well as the ideals of the buccaneers' (Earle 2004: 166). It may well also reflect the socially isolated yet collective and synchronized experience of seafaring labour (Linebaugh and Rediker 2000, Rediker 2004: 25). These contexts set the scene for the political economy and organization of piracy during the early eighteenth century.

Written 'articles' were a form of social contract, a collectively agreed description of the boundaries of legitimate authority. They were used by buccaneers (see Exquemelin 2000: 71), but become more fully developed with the pirates of the Golden Age. Those drawn up by Captain 'Black Bart' Roberts were similar to those of contemporary Captains Lowther and Philips, so we can assume that their substance was transferred between pirate ships, with amendments to cope with the desires of particular captains and crews. Roberts's 11 articles gave each man a vote, most an equal share of stores and plunder, and rewards for being one of the boarding party on a prize. The few who benefited unequally were the Captain and Quartermaster (two shares each), the Master, Boatswain and Gunner (one and a half shares each), and other officers (one and a quarter). In comparison with the unequal shares and wages on merchant and navy vessels, this was remarkably egalitarian, but this didn't mean that the boat was free from violent authority. Punishments were to be enforced for theft, desertion or fighting on board, and there was to be no gaming for money. Lights were to be put out by eight o'clock, and drinking could be continued only on deck. All pirates were to keep their pistols and swords clean, and no boys or women were allowed on the ship. Compensation for injury was established, depending on the severity of the injury, and any musicians were allowed Sunday off (Burl 2006: 103–12).

Roberts's articles make for a remarkable document. It contains both considerable rewards and a graded set of punishments – being set ashore somewhere where hardships would ensue, slitting the nose and ears, a slow death by marooning on an island or a quick death on board. The details of different articles are interesting, but they are all unified by the absolutely radical idea that authority depended on consent. Articles were usually sworn on a Bible, though Captain Philips used an axe, and consent was signed or marked on the articles themselves and solemnized by heavy drinking. Importantly, the captains themselves were also voted for, often with the advice of the 'lords', the senior members of the crew. Charles Ellms quotes one lord addressing the others on the election of Captain Roberts in 1719:

> [T]he good of the whole, and the maintenance of order, demanded a head, but that the proper authority was deposited in the community at large; so that if one should be elected who did not act and govern for the general good, he could be deposed, and another be substituted in his place.
>
> *(in Lewis 2006: 230)*

The Captain only had absolute authority during conflict. At all other times, he was subject to consent, even over the use of his cabin, and his manners, which were not supposed to be too 'Gentleman-like' (Rediker 2004: 65).[9]

But pirates were not simply inhabitants of separated floating polities. Rediker (1987) argues that the connections between crews and boats were strong during this period, and that there was a certain co-operation between ships, and that they sometimes operated collectively. The epitome of such co-operation is the idea of the proto-democratic community moving onto the land. This is not an idea that was restricted to the Golden Age or the Caribbean. Accounts of cities such as Rabat-Salé on the Atlantic coast of what is now Morocco (Earle 2004: 44) suggest a self-governing and multi-ethnic city-state which was economically reliant on piracy and slavery. Lamborne Wilson's book on the Sallee Rovers pays particular attention to the 'renegadoes', Christians turned Muslim, and the pirates (1995). Though the mercantile relationships in Algiers, Tunis and Tripoli were better described as small business capitalism, the Corsair captains enjoyed a summer of piracy and a winter of entertainment, seemingly rather untroubled by the nominally Islamic nature of the city. In Salé, the division of the spoils was much more communistic, and the regulation of behaviour was anarchistic, leading Lamborne Wilson to conclude that, though not a pure pirate utopia, 'it was the *only* state ever founded on these principles' (1995: 146).

If not founded on radical principles, there were certainly other pirate towns (Kuhn 2010; 136 *passim*). Places like Tortuga off the north-west coast of Hispaniola (now Haiti and Dominica), Port Royal in Jamaica, New Providence in the Bahamas (now Nassau, see Woodard 2007) and St Mary's (Saint-Marie) off the north-east coast of Madagascar might be described as pirate republics, but were probably better imagined as frontier towns with all the excitements which that might bring. In 1891, Howard Pyle – the author and illustrator of a collection of Robin Hood stories – rather excitedly described Tortuga as 'a center of inflammation, a burning fire of human wickedness and ruthlessness and lust' (in Lewis 2006: 26). Other, less well-evidenced utopias existed, too. According to Defoe, in *The King of the Pirates* (1719), Captain Avery settled for a while on Madagascar, as the mock king of a libertarian settlement. A Captain North also established a temporary settlement in Madagascar (Lamborne Wilson 1995: 193), and John Plantain claimed to have established a settlement at Ranter Bay on the same island in about 1720. The 'King of Ranter Bay' is often enough referred to as Ranters' Bay, though there is no evidence of any connection to the mid-seventeenth-century English radicals.

The most inspiring pirate utopia is almost certainly a fictional one. In the fourth edition of the *General History* we can find an account of 'Libertalia',[10] supposedly established by Captain Mission and claimed by Johnson to be translated from a French work. Mission's community was allegedly inspired by the radical (and defrocked) Dominican monk, Carracioli, who was intent on remaking Eden in the Bay of Diego-Suarez, again in Madagascar. Libertalia was based on equality of ownership, a democracy that only elects councillors for three months at a time, and Mission himself was elected 'Lord Conservator' for three years. Money was put in a common chest, there were no hedges between fields, property was distributed to all and the slaves on captured vessels were freed. All decisions were to be the subject of a general vote by the 'Liberi', there was no death penalty, and complete religious tolerance. Johnson, in thoroughly radical style, has Mission say that he has not 'asserted his own liberty to enslave others'. All races mingled freely, there was an attempt to construct a common language and, at the beginning, an attempt to impose chastity. This gave way to polygamy. It lasted for a few years, with up to 400 inhabitants (Earle 2004: 129, *passim*; Lamborne Wilson 1995: 193, *passim*; Lapouge 2004: 131–8). Even if fiction, it lives on as inspiration, with Lamborne Wilson insisting that there is no reason to suppose that Libertalia did not exist, and many reasons to think that it might have done. Indeed, the novelist William Burroughs was so impressed with Captain Mission that he proposed him as an example for the dispossessed of the world. Mission's was a 'retroactive utopia', a moment when history could have been different, and a world of communes could have opened up 'freedom from the tyranny of government'. For Burroughs, 'Your right to live where you want, with companions of your choosing, under laws which you agree, died in the eighteenth century with Captain Mission' (1999: 416).

The question of who those companions might be is also important to Captain Johnson, though perhaps his concerns were more to do with marketing his book. In the first edition of the *General History* there was a fold-out picture of Anne Bonney and Mary Read, the most famous female pirates. According to the narrative, Bonney was born illegitimate and raised as a boy. She joined Calico Jack Rackham's crew in the Caribbean where she met Mary Read. Read was also illegitimate, and was dressed as a boy by her mother. She disguised herself as a man and fought in Flanders and the Netherlands, eventually joining pirates in the West Indies. Famously, she fought a duel defending her male lover's honour, and killed the man who had challenged him. These accounts of Bonney and Read now play centre-stage in a wider story of women, violence and the sea. The two most famous pirate women are inserted into a history that stretches back to Queen Artemesia from the Persian Gulf in 480 BCE, Queen Teata from the Adriatic in the third century BCE, the legendary Alfhild or Alwilda the Terrible in ninth-century Scandinavia and Jeanne de Belleville from Nantes in the mid-fourteenth century. If the male pirates' stories often tell of a release from wage slavery, the stories of female pirates tell of escapes from subordination to a gender role. Icons include Grace O'Malley and Elizabeth Killigrew, both from Ireland in the 1560s, as well as the sixteenth-century Englishwoman Charlotte de Berry, who led a mutiny and became Captain Charlotte. Mary Harley and Mary Crickett were from Virginia in the early eighteenth century, and the English Ann Mills cut the head off a Frenchman after running him through with a sword. Maria Cobham was a Plymouth prostitute who married and went to sea with Captain Thomas Cobham. Mary Ann Talbot dressed in men's clothing at the compulsion of her 'guardian' Captain Essex Bowen, and the brave Hannah Snell ran away to sea in search of her husband (Do or Die 1999, Lapouge 2004: 158, *passim*; Burl 2006: 108; Rediker 2004: 113).

The idea of the female pirate marked twentieth-century fiction, too. In Fryniwyd Tennyson Jesse's *Moonraker* (1927), the handsome, fearless and tortured Captain Lovel turns out to be a woman with some strong opinions about female liberty. Women were sometimes seduced by the dashing pirate, such as Joan Fontaine in the film *Frenchman's Creek* (1944), but could also be beautiful and mysterious pirates themselves, such as Jean Peters in *Anne of the Indies* (1951) or Geena Davis in *Cutthroat Island* (1995). Jo Stanley's edited collection *Bold in her Breeches* (1996) brings together essays which insist that the sea was a place of relative freedom and tolerance for women who wished to live differently, and begins to construct the pirate as a feminist icon, as well as an anarchist one. However, the 'truth' of such depictions is simply unavailable, and even those with radical sympathies have to acknowledge that women were more often objects of considerable violence and much superstition (Rediker 2004: 110; Kuhn 2010).

But the radicalization of pirate imagery doesn't end there. Barry Burg's *Sodomy and the Pirate Tradition* (1985) marks a current of writing that suggests a libertarian attitude to sexuality onboard ship. Inducing from various pieces of evidence, Burg and others suggest that homosexuality, particularly in the form of junior companions, was common (Earle 2004: 107). Lamborne Wilson simply notes, citing Foucault, that a specific form of sexuality between men, or men and boys, was not named at that point, and hence that there is a danger in importing nineteenth-century categories to an earlier context (1995: 185). Polymorphous sexualities may have been unmarked and routine, and it is this sense of libertarian sexual tolerance and a certain kind of dandyism that also gets celebrated by William Burroughs in his writings about the city of Tangier, and the accounts of Captain Mission and the Cities of the Red Night (Burroughs 1999). Hardly surprisingly, added to this sexual diversity is the idea that pirate ships were racially heterogeneous, too. One source suggests that 30 per cent of pirate crews were of African descent, though Earle believes this to be something of an exaggeration (2004: 171). Cordingly records a series of examples of black seamen on pirate ships, but notes that they were probably used as slaves (1999: 27). Rediker is much more optimistic, recording examples of 'free negroes'. Partly supporting such descriptions is evidence about the national origins of pirate crew. Black Sam Bellamy's crew of 1717 included British, French, Dutch, Spanish, Swedish, Native American, African American and African sailors (Rediker 2004: 53–4).

Whether Captain Jack Sparrow can bear the weight of such progressive representations is questionable, but they reveal an account of piracy which connects the pirate to seventeenth- and eighteenth-century radicalism, and also reflects twenty-first-century concerns. Jack may be a rogue, but he dresses with a camp dash, and is not (at heart) racist or homophobic. Further, his sexism is of such a transparent and playful form that it is difficult to take seriously. In the radical imagination, the pirate crew, male and female, straight and gay, black and white, is re-cast as a democratic assembly of equals – with even a suggestion that attitudes to disability were more inclusive (Kuhn 2010: 80). Pirate scholarship over the past 40 years seems to have made this group into revolutionaries in their constitutions and practices, a model of alternative organizing and identity that can be projected from a romantic past in order to inspire a different future.

Pirates and the radical imagination

> In an honest service there is thin commons, low wages and hard labour. In this, plenty and satiety, pleasure and ease, liberty and power. And who would not balance creditor on this side, when all the hazard that is run for it, at worst, is only a sour look or two at choking? No, a merry life and a short one shall be my motto.
>
> Damnation to him who ever lived to wear a halter.
>
> *(Black Bart Roberts, 1670?–1722, in Burl 2006: vii)*

Roberts wore fine clothes, drank tea from fine china, and enjoyed listening to pressed musicians. His ship sometimes fired 'a miscellany of smallshot, pellets, broken bottles and nails' that could 'ravish a living body into a carcass of disentangulated flesh and scarecrowed bone' (Burl 2006: 130, 163). Captain Low was alleged to have cut a man's lips off, fried them, and then made him eat them whilst they were still warm (Kemp 2009: 11). This pornography of butchery sits alongside the demand for freedom. The violence and sadism of pirates is well documented (Cordingly 1999: 3, 157), but so are the cruelties of merchant and navy captains (Rediker 1987, 2004), as well as those of the legal and ecclesiastical systems at home and in the colonies. Drowning, pressing, burning, hanging and strangling were all legitimate death penalties, not to mention the tortures applied by various inquisitions. So perhaps the violence can be set aside as historical context, and the sort of decoration that many readers (and writers) enjoy. Pirates were not unique, or even unusual, in being cruel to their enemies, but the violence certainly helped authors, from Exquemelin onwards, to sell work which revelled in tales of wild outsiders. In 1734 the same Captain Johnson who had popularized the pirate added further sensational characters to the mix with his *A General History of the Lives and Adventures of the most famous Highwaymen, Murderers, Street Robbers, &c. to which is added a genuine account of the Voyages and Plunders of the most notorious Pyrates.*

So the pirate combined a swaggering marketability with a sense of danger. The character seems to embody a challenge in terms of the organization of labour and the distribution of reward, and to occupy a historical moment when the legitimacy of states, merchants and international trade was not yet fully established. This gap, this power vacuum, even today provides iconography for imagining freedoms beyond those that market managerialism allows, and perhaps even forms of re-distribution that erase hierarchies of status and reward. According to one of their prisoners, the pirates Bellamy and Lebour 'pretended to be Robbin Hood's men'. Captain Johnson, in one of the later and probably more fictionalized editions of his work, suggests a speech for Bellamy to the captain of a captured navy ship:

> [D]amn ye, you are a sneaking Puppy, and so are all those who will submit to be governed by Laws which rich Men have made for their own Security, for the cowardly Whelps have not the Courage otherwise to defend what

they get by their Knavery, but damn ye altogether: Damn them for a Pack of crafty Rascals, and you, who serve them, for a Parcel of hen-hearted Numskuls. They vilify us, the Scoundrels do, when there is only this Difference, they rob the Poor under the Cover of Law, forsooth, and we plunder the Rich under the Protection of our own Courage.

(Rediker 2004: 116)

No wonder that so many contemporary radical scholars continue to use the pirate to raise questions of legitimacy (darkmatter 2009, Kuhn 2010), particularly in a context when the trading companies that precede the global businesses of the present day can so easily be seen as instruments of greed, class interest and naked imperial power. Lamborne Wilson suggests that Hobsbawm didn't include the pirates in his classification of social banditry because they didn't represent the peasantry (1995: 145), but dismisses such a distinction as unhelpful, largely because the pirates did represent an example of alternative social organization, and not only a relationship to a particular group of oppressed people.[11] The pirates' interest was not primarily wealth, because 'Pirates did not hide wealth. They wasted it' (Burl 2006: 239). They drank, they destroyed, they ate – they created a carnival which was entirely excessive in terms of an emerging culture of 'time is money' and returns on investment. The money they made they spent in harbour as quickly as they could – gambling, drinking, whoring – until they had nothing left, and had to go to sea again (Kuhn 2010: 36). In so doing, in denying the legitimacy of property, and dominion over the seas, they 'declared War against all the World', just as the world had declared war against its common enemies. This, to restate, was a time in which states and merchants were closing all the gaps, and demanding that their legitimacy was recognized through the use of violence, too. If the sea had been a global commons, it was now subject to enclosure on behalf of states, in turn acting on behalf of an emerging capitalist class. Judge Nicholas Trot Esq, at the 1718 trial of Stede Bonnet and his crew, claimed that 'the sea was given by God, for the use of men, and is subject to dominion and property, as well as the land' (in Lewis 2006: 169). But pirates had no country because they came 'from the seas' (Rediker 2004: 8, 72). For the authorities this meant that pirates, like wolves, were imagined as a wild part of nature, separated from civilized culture. This sort of representation then neatly sidesteps the notion that piracy was actually an alternative form of organizing, one based on face-to-face legitimacy and the satisfaction of immediate needs.

The trial of Black Bart's crew in 1722 that acted as the beginning of the end of the Golden Age of piracy was a symbolic defeat for a certain sort of organization, and a clear victory for another. John Atkins, the surgeon on *The Swallow*, the navy ship that had killed Bart himself, summarized one view of the matter rather nicely:

Discipline is an excellent path to victory; and courage, like a trade, is gained by an apprenticeship, when strictly kept up to rules and exercise. The pirates though singly fellows of courage, yet wanting such a tie of order and some director to unite that force, were a contemptible enemy. They neither killed nor wounded a man in the taking; which ever must be the fate of such a rabble.

(Earle 2004: 198)

Discipline, in this context, merely suggests that autocratic and bureaucratic organizational forms might be more effective in the context of battle. But there is a further dimension to the condemnation of piracy, because if this was merely a choice between organizing principles, it could be deemed a contingent matter that any human being might make a choice about. So it had also to be a question of morality. Note Judge Trot, in his speech that pronounced a death sentence on Major Stede Bonnet, a gentleman pirate in 1718:

[T]he Principles of Religion that had been instilled into you by your Education, have been at least corrupted, if not entirely defaced, by the Scepticism and Infidelity of this wicked Age; and that what time you allow'd for Study, was rather apply'd to the Polite Literature, & the vain Philosophy of the times, than a serious Search after Law & Will of God, as revealed unto us in the Holy Scriptures ...

(in Lewis 2006: 174)

It seemed that the will of God was on the side of law, and the state, and the East India Company.

Between 1716 and 1726 something like 500–600 pirates were hanged. The last pirate captain of the Golden Age, Olivier La Buse, was hanged on the beach on the island of Bourbon in July 1730 'before a cheering crowd' (Earle 2004: 206). But this doesn't mean that piracy is now merely a historical matter, indeed, it is still rather common, and has been a consistent feature of maritime trade, international relations and popular representations. When the USA needed a navy for its war against Britain in 1812, it issued Letters of Marque to smuggler pirates such as Jean and Pierre Lafitte, the latter of whom is still the subject of many legends surrounding buried treasure around the Gulf of Mexico and was possibly the inspiration for Byron's corsair. Thomas Jefferson wrote in a letter that he wanted to 'encourage those privateers to burn their prizes and let the public pay for them ... they will make the merchants of England feel and squeal and cry out for peace' (in Mitchell 2006: 320). At roughly the same time, the Puerto Rican pirate Roberto Cofresi was tolerated for a long time by the Spanish government of the day largely because his targets were US ships. He was eventually executed in 1825, after turning to attack Spanish shipping, too, but has since been depicted as a noble gentleman who became a pirate from necessity, an example of nationalist resistance, as well as being possessed of magical powers and able to make his boat disappear. Recent women pirates, such as Ching Yih Saou (China in 1807–10) and Lai Choi San (Macao in the 1920s) still inspire stories of sorcery and cunning.

The beginning of the twenty-first century saw an increasing interest in pirates, now poor young men from poor countries and bankrolled by business interests. More interested in ransom of people and boats than plunder, they use small fast boats and machine guns in order to hijack slow tankers and wealthy yachts. According to the International Maritime Bureau's 'Piracy Reporting Centre' in Kuala Lumpur, in 2010 there were 445 reported attacks, up from 239 in 2006. This involved well over 1,000 hostages being taken and eight people being killed (ICC 2011). The most dangerous waters are those around Somalia, with Indonesia, Nigeria and Bangladesh having hostile coasts, too. There is also a growing literature on the problem, with quite a few books providing advice for smaller boat owners, and painting the open seas as a place which is still populated by dangerous outlaws (Burnett 2003, Hympendahl 2003, Langewiesche 2006). Larger attacks are sometimes mounted on giant cargo ships and cruise liners, using rocket-propelled grenades and folding ladders in order to bring back huge wealth and celebrity to their local communities. The selling of representations of pirates continues, too, with Ross Kemp, a celebrity from a BBC soap opera, making a film and (surprisingly good) book about the economic and political conditions that produce piracy in Somalia, Nigeria and Indonesia (Kemp 2009).

Symmetrically, neither should we assume that the link between the state and profitable violence is broken. This may be a Golden Age for the new privateers, too – mercenaries, security services and private armies. The USA and the UK are at the forefront of privatizing contemporary war to companies such as Blackwater, DynCorp, Executive Outcomes, Spearhead Limited, Military Professional Resources Inc and so on (Chwastiak 2007, Armstrong 2008). The implications for foreign policy would be easily recognizable to Elizabeth I, whilst the rape and plunder would not offend Francis Drake. Kontorovich (2004), in his commentary on the universality of piracy as a heinous offence, nicely shows how privateering and piracy have always been porous categories. The 'licensed privateer' principle brings into doubt the 'common enemies of mankind' principle, which suggests that neither is actually a principle at all, but a position which depends on which way the money is moving. In other words, moralizing about pirates has a long pedigree, but so does putting a certain distance between the state and the mercenary.

So the loot is important, just as it always has been with pirates, and economic outlaws in general. Other people have made a lot of money by employing them, by condemning them, and by representing them. In 1960, the Italian film *Robin Hood and the Pirates* appears to have attempted to double its chances of making money by assuming that two bets were better than one. Osborne (1998) recounts how the North Carolina Maritime Museum was planning a new multi-million dollar exhibition on piracy after the discovery of the wreck of Blackbeard's *Queen Anne's Revenge* off the coast in 1996. He noted that 'politicians ecstatically foresee Blackbeard motels and restaurants sprouting up like mushrooms, and a mock cannon battle known as Blackbeard's Bounty Festival has been staged'. Captain Jack Sparrow has made his way onto lunch boxes, the Oakland Raiders American football team use pirate imagery, and Captain Charles Johnson's book has rarely been out of print for almost 300 years. Perhaps even more remarkably, pirates are now being used to teach rational choice economics, with Leeson's book *The Invisible Hook* suggesting that Adam Smith's 'hidden hand' best explains pirate behaviour. Leeson suggests that the principal agent problem lies behind pirate democracy, that the Jolly Roger was a market-signalling strategy, with stories of torture helping to establish the brand. He concludes by suggesting a business-school class on 'The Secrets of Pirate Management' (2009: 176) which would demonstrate that 'greed is good' and the profit motive explains everything. As with Robin Hood *et al.*, capitalism markets what it can sell, even accounts of why capitalism is the single best way as taught by US business school professors. The irony is that, rather often, it can also end up selling some things which have histories that can easily be turned to other purposes.

Chris Land, writing about the links between piracy and anarchism, is well aware that pirates can mean different things. On the one hand, he suggests that Jack Sparrow is 'the embodiment of liberated, post-modern subjectivity, ruled by his desires and completely at odds with the staid world of work and civilization' (2007: 170). So perhaps he is merely an escapist figure, a character from a fantasy sold to us by the marketers running the dream factory. Yet, Land and many others also want Jack and his gang to mean more than this. Perhaps, he hopes, the 'popularity of all things piratical may speak to something enduring in the popular imaginary: a desire for freedom and democracy … an insurrectionary current to the present day' (183). The skull and crossbones was supposed to have fluttered over the Alamo as Davy Crockett died; appeared as a revolutionary symbol in the Paris Commune, where a daily paper called *Le Pirate* was published for a while; and now unites anarchists and those cultural producers who embrace the piracy of intellectual property in the name of the virtual commons. It inspires the underworld, too. Dickie tells us that threatening letters from the Mafia in Sicily in the late nineteenth century would often demand money and be marked with a skull and crossbones (Dickie 2004: 114). *Mano nera* (Black Hand) letters in New York in the early twentieth century were marked in the same way (op. cit., 207). The image also gets used by pro-capitalist entrepreneurial authors who want to sell a book about 'how hackers, punk capitalists, graffiti millionaires and other youth movements are remixing our culture and changing our world' in the horrible subtitle to Matt Mason's *The Pirate's Dilemma* (2008). It seems to me that the very strength of images of piracy has been these entanglements of history and fantasy, in which the radical possibility of freedom can be turned into a lifestyle choice and a particular sort of hat.

Yet even in Mason's breathless world of trend-spotting for fun and profit, the pirate is against the certainties of power. Indeed, outlaw figures can be used to signify both entrepreneurial resistance to established monopolies and business models, as well as anarchist resistance to state and commercial power. Both dissolve the established order, even if one usually wishes only to replace the established tycoons in the corner office. For the more radical version, from

Exquemelin onwards, a utopia which resembles a state of nature has been articulated against the emergence of the venal mercantile state. An aquatic or island Arcadia, populated by authentic characters, is contrasted with the hypocrisies of self-righteous imperialism. It might be said that this is 'bad' history, because it clearly confuses the 'reality' of piracy with the stories of Captain Johnson. But, as I have shown, these confusions go back to the earliest accounts and so,

> perhaps we should be wary of over privileging the economic and 'real' history? In the creation of a moral economy and a distinctly radical culture, the pirates' political legacy has been long lasting and has made a significant contribution to the development of the contemporary culture of radical, anti-capitalist and anarchist dissent.
>
> *(Land 2007: 190)*

I agree, but I would add that he has made a lot of money for Disney, too. The dialectical point is that the 'pirate is malleable and plastic: villain, rebel, seducer, barbarian, man of the people, idealist, and sadist. He is what we want him to be' (Osborne 1998).

Just as piracy grew in the gaps between states, so do images of piracy reflect diverse interests. Exquemelin describes sadists, Captain Johnson prefers libertarians, romantic authors seemed to enjoy the mystery of the outsider, while twentieth-century film moved from swashbuckling hero to comedy villain. Captain Jack adds the rock-star swagger, and a metrosexually knowing smile. All these images are interesting enough, since they ask questions of identity, but the original context of the pirate also asks a question about the relation between the individual and the state, and the legitimacy of trade. It is perhaps no surprise that, in the third *Pirates of the Caribbean* film, Jack's enemy is the East India Company itself, one of the world's first global corporations, and the possessor of its own army and navy. These are issues that, in an era of international business and privatized war, have perhaps become even more urgent than ever. The fact that the Disney corporation makes so much money from Jack Sparrow isn't really an irony, but the culmination of four centuries' work on turning boatloads of privateers into these global corporations. Jack Beeching, in his introduction to Exquemelin's violent utopian travelogue, captures a similar sentiment: 'Anarchistic, untrammelled, extravagant, sadistic, a crack shot and wildly courageous, the buccaneer is a gay dog amongst Protestant paladins – not only a fantasy figure for today's cautiously ethical businessman, but his exact historical progenitor' (2000: 20).

In the next chapter I will explore a series of figures that followed over the next century, and did on the land what the pirates did on the high seas. Robbers, banditti, smugglers and highwayman – all characters that gradually became understood through the lens of European romanticism, and allowed the outlaw to continue their progress from the greenwood to the industrializing city.

4

ROBBERS AND ROMANTICS

As should be fairly clear from the story of the pirates, as well as that of Robin Hood, by the late eighteenth century both figures are becoming part of a much more generalized celebration of the bandit in the culture of north-western European societies. They both make and are made by the gradual congealing of Seal's 'cultural script' and 'outlaw hero cycle' (2009). In other words, pirates can be understood as Robin Hood, and images of Robin Hood are shaped by ideas about piracy. In a wide range of popular media of the time, the outlaw is gradually becoming a figure that condenses a range of social issues and problematizes aspects of the inequalities of the beginning of the modern period. This chapter will review a parade of these characters, concentrating roughly on the period 1600–1850, but noting the moments when they enter our present, too.

Bear in mind that this is a period when industrialism and urbanism are sweeping across Europe. Huge cities are growing, making the countryside into an imaginative landscape which is clearly distinct from the town. Indeed, Raymond Williams notes that the etymology of 'country' is first from *contra*, against, in the sense of land which is spread out, facing the observer (1976: 81). The country, as the place of the bandit, becomes strange when seen from the town. It becomes another place, a place of secrecy, threat and freedom, and a landscape of turnpikes, rocky coves, mountains and gorges which holds the promise of a certain sort of otherness. It is often what James Scott calls a 'nonstate' space, a 'wild, trackless, labyrinthine, inhospitable' place where the population is dispersed or migratory and is far away from the surveillance of the centre (1998: 187). And as the city grows, so does the work of the city become industrialized and enclosed. The wage slavery of the factory and mill, or the experience of labour at the desk, make spatial mobility and economic self-reliance into experiences that might be mused upon when staring out of the grimy window. The popular idea of the outlaw is in this sense predicated on a fundamental estrangement from most people's everyday experience. To put it another way, the distinction between the bandit and their audience becomes sharper as urbanized capitalism replaces feudalism and mercantilism.

At the same time, the development of romanticism in the late eighteenth century (itself an outcome of the same currents) provided a way for the outlaw to be understood as noble, authentic and passionate. If the wild country was what lay outside or before civilization, then the virtues of the outsider are precisely that of nature – honesty, violence and beauty. Like Byron's corsair, the romantic hero gazes to the far horizon, braves the elements and laughs in the face of thunder and lightning. If most people are creatures of the mass, timidly occupying themselves with their lives within the town, then the romantic hero stands on top of a mountain and allows the wildness of the elements without to mirror the strengths of the emotions within. They are spatially removed from civilization, somehow closer to nature, and less constrained by social convention and mere manners. Perhaps they ask the questions we are afraid to ask, and do the things that we really want to do.

The relation between actual social bandits, such as Janosik or Diego Corrientes (Hobsbawm 1965: 13), and the activities of romantic bandits is a complex affair. If we take the example of the highwayman, Louis Dominique Bourguignon, otherwise known as Cartouche, then the history tells us little. He was born in 1693, worked the roads around Paris, and was executed by breaking on the wheel in 1721. But the myth that coalesced around his name was transmitted through ballads and prints, bodice-ripping novels, films in 1911, 1934 and 1954, a cartoon in 2001 and TV movie in 2009. The best-known film is probably the 1962 version, starring Claudia Cardinale and Jean Paul Belmondo. In the film, Cartouche transforms into a noble robber because a gypsy girl called Venus sacrifices her life for him. My point is, once again, that the afterlife of Cartouche is as important, if not more important, than the facts about a Parisian robber. His name provides a hook for the machinery of myth-making to construct a witty swashbuckler who could evade the clods of the *ancient régime*. Or, to take another example, Marco Sciarra, the Neopolitan brigand from the 1590s who may have described himself as 'Scourge of God and envoy of God against usurers and the possessors of unproductive wealth' (in Hobsbawm 1972a: 98), but he may not. It doesn't really matter for my purposes whether he did or didn't, though I would understand if historians were not entirely impressed with such a cavalier attitude to the difference between fact and fiction.

Robbers and banditti

In 1631, at the age of sixteen, the Neapolitan painter Salavator Rosa left home and took to the hills. It was said that he had joined a bandit gang. Whether this is true or not is hard to say, but it doubtless helped when he began trying to sell his landscape paintings in Rome a few years later. Rosa is generally regarded as a painter with an early gothic sensibility, in which crags and precipices are decorated with twisted trees and populated by banditti and witches. His outlaws are an enchanting but cruel part of nature, and these images were sold to tourists from northern Europe as mementos of their grand tour (Davenport-Hines 1997: 22). Attacks by bandits did happen, often for ransoms, but in a painting like 'Attack by Bandits' (1670), Rosa is making the robbers into decorative figures in a wild landscape, not merely thieves. These are paintings intended to sell, so this is what he produced and – like a volcano, a storm or a flash of lightning – the bandit is one of the dramatic sights that a civilized European might meet on their travels. For the third Earl of Shaftesbury, Rosa's figures in a landscape were examples of the aesthetic of the sublime – 'wild savage figures of banditti, wandering gypsies, strollers, vagabonds, etc., at which he was so excellent' (in Davenport-Hines 1997: 29).

For this emerging gothic sublime, nature was illuminating civilization. These exotically dressed inhabitants of the wild places of the earth were capable of shaking the blasé indifference of the cultured, and showing the aesthete naked truths which could not be found in the town or the country estate. In part, these were truths which concerned the relation between the human and the wilderness but, like the noble savage on a palm-fringed distant island, they were potentially capable of transmitting political truths, too. The wisdom of the bandit might be in their resistance to modernization or cruel rulers, their deep knowledge of the mountain and ravine, and in their understanding of tradition and natural law. Stories about Stenka Razin, the seventeenth-century Cossack who rebelled against the Tsar, the *hajduk* outlaws of the Balkans who resisted the laws of the Ottoman Empire or the brigands of Spain and Italy, could be understood as examples of principled resistance to illegitimate power. Again, this is not to say that these were historical truths, but that it became a way for forms of nationalism to be combined with a romantic sensibility which celebrated a passionate impulsiveness and a relation to the land.

In 1782, a play called the *The Robbers* was performed in Mannheim. Sensational reviews followed, as well as the arrest of its author. It was written by Friedrich Schiller when he was at school in the late 1770s, and concerns the story of two brothers, Karl and Franz Moor. The elder, Karl, a handsome melancholic idealist, takes a band of rebellious students into the forests of Bohemia and fights against the corruption of the authorities, including his father Maximilian. He demands freedom, something that requires bursting from constraint:

> Am I to squeeze my body into stays, and straitlace my will in the trammels of law? What might have risen to an eagle's flight has been reduced to a snail's pace by law. Never yet has law formed a great man; 'tis liberty that breeds giants and heroes.
>
> *(in Duncan 1996: 82)*

Some of his young robber band are dreamers, too, but others (particularly the unscrupulous Speigelberg) are motivated merely by violence and money. Karl's ugly younger brother Franz stays at home, scheming to inherit his father's estate. Franz is a cold rationalist, driven by the need for power, and logically convinced that reason, not passion, is the basis for government. However, our sympathies are with warm-hearted Karl, though we see the dreadful things that a robber ends up doing in the name of justice. Tortured by guilt, he eventually turns himself in to the authorities after the death of his father.

Schiller seems to be telling us that someone outside society, an outlaw, could have motives that are nobler than those within, even though in the preface to his play he denies that he is trying to make criminals praiseworthy. There are more noble reasons for describing the allure of the criminal. 'If I would warn mankind of the tiger, I must not omit to describe his glossy, beautifully-marked skin, lest, owing to this omission, the ferocious animal should not be recognised until too late' (in Duncan 1996: 67). Despite Schiller's protestations, like William Godwin's novel *Caleb Williams*, published in 1794, the central conceit in *The Robbers* is that the fugitive might be on the run as a result of injustice, and that individual freedom is the only guarantee of living an authentic life. Mr Raymond, a character in Godwin's novel, declares, 'We, who are thieves without a license, are at open war with another set of men, who are thieves according to law' (in Spraggs 2001: 236). Schiller's play is a little more complex than this, because the tension between the brothers also reflects the tensions between Karl's instinct and Franz's reason, as well as the tragedy that follows if one is followed at the expense of the other. Nonetheless, both Schiller and Godwin are reflecting one of the central tropes that begin to structure ideas about the romantic outlaw, a heroic yet tragic figure whose bravery is matched by his (because it is almost always a he) passion for a good cause or a beautiful woman.

The Robbers was made into an opera by Verdi in 1847, and again by Giselher Klebe in 1957, as well as films in 1913 and 1940. It can be seen as an early example of the influence of European romanticism on understandings of the outsider, but is now effectively submerged by the torrent of contemporaneous economic outlaws – pirates, smugglers, highwaymen and so on. The outlaw could be located anywhere beyond civilization, and early nineteenth-century British authors could sometimes articulate that as the highlander, the wild man of the North, a creature of mountains and simple tastes. Walter Scott's *Waverley* of 1814 has the clan Mac-Ivor, loyalists to Bonnie Prince Charlie during the Jacobite Rebellion, whilst his 1817 *Rob Roy* continues the same theme, loosely basing a plot about an outlaw who demands protection money on a Scottish landowner who fought against the English in the seventeenth century. Like Robin Hood in Scott's *Ivanhoe* of 1820, these are rebels in the name of an older legitimate authority. William Wallace, for example, who resisted the English army in the early fourteenth century, was the subject of a short essay by Scott, 'The Exploits and Death of William Wallace, the "Hero of Scotland".' Like Schiller's gang, these are not robbers in the simple sense of stealing for their own benefit; they are rebels from beyond the borders of civilization, and they resist in the name of justice.

At the same time, Byron's four 'Oriental Tales' (published in 1813 and 1814), of which *The Corsair* was one, underlined the idea of the outsider as someone who inspires admiration from visionaries and contempt from narrow-minded conservatives. These were best-sellers for their time, relying on the exoticism of the orient, a beautiful woman and a passionate man. The first, *The Giaour*, sold ten thousand copies on its first day of publication, and resulted in 14 new editions by 1815. Swaggeringly handsome but always lonely, Byron's heroes, like Don Juan in his uncompleted epic poem, are (as was said of Byron himself by Lady Caroline Lamb) 'mad, bad and dangerous to know'. Their moral or political stances, their passionate romances or their nomadic lives, always place them at odds with the society that they find themselves in. They are tragic figures, in the sense that we often know that things will not end well for them, but they cannot really help themselves. Just as Byron himself was represented as a restless wanderer, driven by his passions for people and revolutionary ideas, so did the various heroes of his poems resist injustice and cruelty, fall in love with unsuitable people, and show a general disregard for social conventions, particularly the institutions of the powerful. Sometimes, the lack of regard for convention turns into a brooding mystery, or an active contempt for the small people who pass their days in such small ways.

As I suggested a few pages ago, one of the most important issues here is the idea that being 'outside' is a position that provides a certain integrity.[1] If following the rules is the way to a safe and pleasant life, then bending, breaking or simply ignoring them courts personal danger but at the same time opens vistas of freedom that most people will never experience. The intensity of experience, unity of action and belief, and personal magnetism of the romantic hero becomes a way to understand anyone who lives outside the law – and Robin Hood and pirates would fall easily into this category. Not that all criminals would be immediately imagined as noble robbers, but this 'cultural script' was well established by the 1820s. Implied in all this was some sense that the authorities, the powers that be, were corrupt and unjust. Logically of course, in order for the outlaw to have any moral or political legitimacy, the present order must be morally, economically or politically illegitimate. This moral high ground might then be used to question the spiritual authority of the church, or the political authority of a sheriff or a king, as it was with Robin. Or it could be used to comment on the cruel practices of navies, and the geopolitical claims of states, as was the case with pirates. Yet in a more everyday manner, it often also came down to taxes, perhaps the first and most direct way that states impinged on the lives of ordinary people. As I suggested in the previous chapter, the popular support of pirates in some coastal communities was related to their trading activities. Piracy was the first step in an economic system that resulted in cheaper goods for ordinary people. In practice, armed theft at sea was actually a minor part of this trade because it was smuggling that was for centuries much better organized than piracy, much more widespread and often just as celebrated.

Smugglers

The Smuggler Captain's Song

'Fire on, fire on,' says Captain Ward
'I value you not a pin;
If you are brass on the outside,
I am steel within.'
'Go home, go home,' says Captain Ward
'And tell your King from me,
If he reigns King upon dry land
I will reign at sea.'

(Old song, cited in Quinn 1999: 165)

Though the period 1700–1850 marks something of a high point in the Western European idea of smugglers as brave individuals resisting the state, this doesn't mean that smuggling was new in 1700 or that it ended in 1850. The popularity of images of the smuggler tells us as much about popular attitudes to taxation and the state as it does about the practice itself. Just as the story of the Golden Age of piracy tells us something about the abilities of states to regulate international commerce, so does the story of this 'golden age' of smuggling reveal the ways in which the state was attempting to regulate its internal tax-raising powers, often in order to pay for wars. Since the administration and surveillance functions of the state were relatively weak at this time, taxes on incomes or expenditures were relatively easy to underpay by concealment. However, the importation or exportation of goods was a different matter since it involved the physical movement of materials across boundaries. Land boundaries were difficult to police, especially if they were long or cut across marshy or mountainous areas, but coasts could be imagined as actual edges of a state, as lines where entry and exit could be controlled and commerce made visible. The idea of controlling movement was hence both the assertion of sovereign power over territory and a way to raise money for a state through the collection of 'duty' or the exercise of 'custom'.

Despite the moralizing and naturalizing terms used by governments, most people in Western Europe did not see taxes on the export of wool, or the purchase of alcohol, lace, tobacco, tea, silks and so on as legitimate, and it is not surprising that they attempted to evade them when they could. A British parliamentary committee of the 1740s was told that 'the generality of people on the coasts are better friends to the smugglers than they are to the Custom House Officers' (in Winslow 1977: 147). Christopher Hill describes smuggling as a 'national sport' in the eighteenth century, with both illegal imports and exports in key commodities often being as large in volume and profitability as the legal ones (1969: 238). Purchasing something cheaply, in the knowledge that some smugglers were making a profit, was often not even regarded as a crime. Both the activity of smuggling and the resistance to excise men were commonly regarded as legitimate activities, and increasingly romantic ones, too, as images of rocky cliffs, boats slipping across moonlit coves and gnarled seamen in coastal taverns came to represent this particular form of economic exchange. Most of my examples in this section are from Britain, but there is plenty of evidence that other coastal (and inland) communities valued the smuggler, too.

There was a lot of money to be made by moving things from one place to another, particularly if rates of comparative taxation were different, the borders were difficult to police, or poverty and low wages for ordinary forms of employment made becoming a 'Gentleman of the Night' an attractive option. Neither was this an economic decision restricted to the impoverished working classes. Local merchants and gentry might become 'venturers' who would put up the capital for smuggling runs, whilst others (often shopkeepers) would be part of a supply chain which stored and distributed smuggled goods far inland, often with the members of the revenue service taking a small consideration to look the other way (Morley 1990: 13–14). The differences between the venturers who speculated on smuggling runs, and the merchant adventurers who speculated on privateering and overseas trade was probably merely a question of scale.

The term 'Free Traders' was also often used, suggesting a contradiction between liberty and protectionism or taxation which doubtless helped to portray the smuggler as involved in resistance rather than crime. Even Adam Smith, commonly positioned as the father of free-market capitalism, saw little distinction between trade and smuggling. He suggested that the smuggler 'would have been, in every respect, an excellent citizen had not the laws of his country made that a crime which nature never meant to be so' (in Hill 1969: 238). Smuggling required courage, involved action against the entrenched interests of the powerful, and hence had connotations of class resistance, as well as exhibiting characteristics which would be valued in other contexts. Captain Dore, an early nineteenth-century smuggler into Sussex, was 'full of what Englishmen admire, pluck and daring, and he declared he would never be taken' (Quinn 1999: 53). So for many people it was the policies of the state that produced the 'owler', 'mooncusser' or 'moonraker', and not some failing in the characters of individual citizens. The authorities who attempted to stop the smugglers had names attached to them that suggested less fondness – preventers, philistines, blockademen, searchers, gaugers and so on. They were often involved, too, of course, either by turning a blind eye in return for bribes or informing and collecting rewards – often in excess of the value of the property – which could then be shared.

Though smuggling has not produced individual names like those associated with piracy, it is clear that famous smugglers and gangs were certainly the subject of heroic stories at the time, some of which did receive national publicity. Isaac Gulliver and Tom Johnston from Dorset were famous in the region, and accounts of their exploits have a rather trickster-like quality to them. Gulliver was officially an inn-keeper, but managed 15 smuggling ships. His custom-built house had many secret rooms, and the whole village of Kinson (now part of Bourne-mouth) was honeycombed with underground passages. He seems to have built his business largely on bribery, but there are also stories of a false death and burial to evade capture, and an escape in an empty cask (Morley 1990: 140, *passim*). Johnston's career is even stranger. He was described as handsome and humorous, as well as being capable of dressing in disguise, escaping from pursuers and captors and even jail. 'Captain Johnston', a name which nicely echoed piracy, travels between England, France, the Netherlands and the USA, his adventures culminating with a hopeless attempt to captain a submarine to rescue Napoleon from St Helena. Napoleon died before the rescue could be attempted, and the submarine sank in the Thames in 1822 whilst Johnston was trying to sell it to the Spanish (Morley 1990: 34, *passim*).

Though histories of smuggling document what Winslow describes as a 'guerrilla war' (1977: 119) with substantial violence and cruelty on both sides, the archetypal smuggling story is one in which the brave common man evades the massed excise men by hiding in a cave or clinging to a ledge. Brandy is hidden in a coffin, cigars in broomsticks and tobacco is made into ropes. The searchers poke a corn stack with their swords, but fail to find the contraband hidden within. Quick wits and cunning are pitted against superior force, all lit by moonlight or during a crashing storm, and the smuggler usually escapes, leaving the excise men scratching their heads or cursing.

> The smugglers themselves, far from being reviled as criminals, were celebrated as local heroes. They were genuine Robin Hood figures who, if they didn't quite take from the rich and give to the poor, at least made sure that the poor could afford luxuries that would otherwise have been the exclusive preserve of the rich.
>
> *(Quinn 1999: 9)*

If the smugglers were presented as honourable men motivated by ties of family and community, then the excise men were lonely, cowardly or stupid. If they were successful, it was because they were cold-blooded and heartless, capable of deploying their superior force with no regard for persons or context. This is often a very straightforward morality tale, with right and courage on the side of the weak. Stories are even told of smugglers rescuing excise ships that have got into trouble due to lack of local knowledge, or agreeing to spy for the state against the French because of their easy access to channel ports. Though there are accounts of Mafiosi-like gang violence, such as that of the Sussex Hawkhurst gang in the mid-eighteenth century (Winslow 1977: 133; Quinn 1999: 79), they have tended to have been erased by the idea of the romantic smuggler hero – later amply documented by authors like Athol Forbes in his 1909 collection of stories, *The Romance of Smuggling*.

A hundred years before Forbes, in the late eighteenth and early nineteenth centuries, there were common popular ballads such as 'The Smuggler's Boy', 'The Smuggler's Bride' and 'Will Watch: The Bold Smuggler'. The latter was immortalized as a Stoke-on-Trent pottery figure celebrating an outlaw who was killed by the Royal Navy whilst evading arrest. Watch is wearing improbably brightly coloured and swaggering clothes, just like those of the characters found in the work of artists such as George Morland, Sir Francis Bourgeois, Sir David Wilkie (Painter to the King from 1830) and Henry Perlee 'Smuggler' Parker. In a painting like *Teignmouth by Moonlight* by Thomas Luny, a ship and a watchtower are outlined against the moon in the distance whilst some suspicious-looking characters have their faces lit by a fire on a beach in the foreground. Many sketches and paintings were turned into popular prints, often showing men and women dressed in seagoing rustic with barrels, or in rooms hiding or counting things, as in the print *Smugglers Alarmed*, or Wilkie's best-seller *The Smugglers Intrusion* (Morley 1990: 180, 206). Henry Parker's paintings, including one of Isaac Gulliver, have more than a trace of oriental banditti about their clothing. Other prints show pitched battles between smugglers with odd hats and blue-coated excisemen, with swords raised over casks on beaches, or attempts to board boats in the middle of a titanic storm.

Unlike many of the economic outlaws covered in this book, women also seem to have played a common part in representations of smuggling. Stories and paintings commonly show women receiving and hiding smuggled goods, and often being involved in deceiving the customs men when they search the home. Their cunning is generally gendered, in the sense that they are depicted as being able to hide casks of brandy in their skirts where they would not be found, flasks in their garters or putting the baby's cot over the trapdoor where the contraband was stored. There are also accounts of women being centrally involved in the trade itself, in which case they might dress and act as a man on occasion – such as Bessie Catchpole who took over her dead husband's boat in the early nineteenth century and used the Suffolk coast to smuggle brandy and tobacco (Quinn 1999: 27, *passim*). As we saw with pirates in the previous chapter, the female figures can also be possessed of a form of magic, like Bessie Millie, the witch who assisted smugglers in Orkney. Magic was not always gendered though, as evidenced by the example of Yawkins, captain of the *Black Prince* which was involved in so many hair-raising escapes that it was said he had made a bargain with the devil, who in consequence now took 10 per cent of his crew for every voyage (op. cit., 40, 43).

Throughout the nineteenth and twentieth centuries, stories with a smuggling background form a small but important part of the idea of the historical outlaw. R. D. Blackmore's 1869 *Lorna Doone* is a novel which relocated the highlander to Exmoor in the early eighteenth century and depicted the irresistible depravities of the Doone family, once noble, but now engaged as bandits, highwaymen and smugglers. A few decades later, J. Meade Falkner uses a thinly disguised 1750s Dorset coast in the south of England to set his *Moonfleet* (1898), a story about an orphan, a diamond, Blackbeard's ghost and casks of wine. The seven Doctor Syn novels by Russell Thorndike (from 1915 to 1944) depict the adventures of an eighteenth-century Oxford scholar who becomes a pirate and then later settles down as a smuggling vicar. At night, he takes on the guise of 'the scarecrow' who leads a smuggling gang called 'the night riders', with his motivation being generally (and rather vaguely) to take revenge on an ex-friend who ran away with his wife. Helped sometimes by the local highwayman, Jimmy Bone, the local witch, Mother Handaway, and a black stallion called Gehenna, the Doctor Syn series combines a gothic sensibility with a trickster's skill at evading the authorities. But it is Daphne du Maurier's *Jamaica Inn* (1936) which is probably now the defining novel of this genre. Set in Bodmin Moor in 1820, the inn of the title provides a hiding place for a ruthless gang of wreckers led by an albino vicar.

The smuggler has now become a distinct part of the myth of the economic outlaw, with the moonlit bays of nineteenth-century paintings being translated into haunting representations of quiet villages, mysterious pubs and thin-lipped excise men. *Lorna Doone* was made into film first in 1911, with six more made by 1953, as well as inspiring at least four TV series and TV films. *Moonfleet* was made into a film in 1955, and has been used as the basis for at least two TV series. The Doctor Syn series has been made into three films as well as various radio plays, and also turns up in a comic book. *Jamaica Inn* was filmed by Alfred Hitchcock in 1939, as well as being adapted for TV and the stage. Like the pirates and outlaws before them, the smugglers are characters who routinely resist the state. At the same time, they show an entrepreneurial sensibility and justify their activities with a fog of romanticism and an argument about redistribution. Rudyard Kipling's 1906 poem, 'A Smuggler's Song', framed as advice to a young girl, catches the sense well:

> If you wake at midnight and hear a horse's feet,
> Don't go drawing back the blind, or looking in the street,
> Them that asks no questions isn't told a lie.
> Watch the wall, my darling while the Gentlemen go by!
> Five and twenty ponies,
> Trotting through the dark –
> Brandy for the Parson,
> 'Baccy for the Clerk;
> Laces for a lady; letters for a spy,
> And watch the wall, my darling, while the Gentlemen go by!

Highwaymen and the turnpike

The social historian John Rule argues that popular attitudes towards a whole series of eighteenth-century crimes in England can be understood as struggles over the legitimacy of developing conceptions of property. In many contexts, smuggling, poaching, pilfering, wood-collecting, beachcombing and even wrecking were not considered criminal at all, but part of a struggle between the classes, in which natural justice was on the side of the poor whilst force was on the side of the rich (1977, Hobsbawm *et al.* 1972). This formulation of 'social crime' neatly echoes and expands elements of the idea of the social bandit, but there are also some much clearer examples in which the definition of crime is at stake, and in which the villain becomes articulated as a romantic hero.

In 1714, someone called Alexander Smith was credited as the author of another 'General History'. This time it was entitled *A General History of the Robberies and Murders of the Most Notorious Highway-Men, Foot-Pads, Housebreakers, Shop-Lifts and Cheats of both Sexes, in and about London, and in other Places in Great Britain, for above forty years past* (Sharpe 2005: 60). He followed this with a dictionary of the grammar and cant used by thieves, as well as accounts of bailiffs and court intrigue. In 1734, this was republished, with a few pirates added, and credited to the same Charles Johnson who wrote the general history of pirates that we encountered in the previous chapter (Burl 2006: 265). No wonder Martin Parker the poet was keen on the London Stationers' Register, when attributions of authorship (and hence reward) were so flexible. Johnson's book attests to the general fascination with robbers on land, as well as the sea. As the turnpike roads began to stretch across the wild country, their rich pickings paralleled that of the boats that sailed across the seas. Both trade routes gathered predators who were often seen as very similar in nature. Earle, for example, in his book on pirates quotes *The Times* in 1819 complaining that 'this villainous mass of ocean highwaymen are the very ejectment of the four quarters of the globe' (2004: 214).

Gillian Spraggs, in her 600-year survey of the English 'cult of the robber', shows that the celebration of outlaws and highwaymen has been a longstanding fascination in popular culture and literature. She suggests that there are a series of issues being articulated here – about gender,[2] character, social class and national virtue – which gave particular types of robbers and robbery a form of social endorsement:

> Robbery, then, was widely regarded as a way in which a mettlesome fellow might provide for himself whilst making a point about his manhood, while the penniless young gentleman who took a purse on the highway, or even burgled a house, was showing the pride and courage he had inherited from his ancestors.
>
> *(2001: 7; see also Pearson 1975: 205)*

Popular representations of these 'Knights of the Roades', or 'High-Way Lawyers', suggested that they did no manual work, dressed well, rode good horses, and always had money for a drink. William Nevison, 'Swift Nicks', was sung about in the ballad 'Bold Nevison'. Smiling at the judge and jury he says,

> I have now robbed a gentleman of tuppence.
> But I've never done murder nor killed.
> But Guilty I've been all my lifetime.
> So gentlemen do as you will.
> Now when I rode on the highway

I always had money in store.
And whatever I took from the rich,
Why, I freely gave it to the poor.

(in Seal 1996: 51)

Like a gentleman, the robber could enjoy leisure, and live a life of courage and honour. Of course, as with pirates, smugglers and so on, experience and practice were probably less glamorous and a great deal more violent, but that didn't prevent the highwayman from being elevated above the common criminal in popular culture.

The idea of 'gentlemen thieves in velvet coats' (Spraggs 2001: 103) was one element in a growing literature of accounts of criminal careers, last speeches, repentances and confessions, and descriptions of hangings. For example, in *The Life and Death of Gamaliel Ratsey* of 1605 we learn various anecdotes about a generous and quick-witted ex-soldier who had a brief career as a highwayman. Based supposedly on conversations with friends before his hanging in 1605, it is in fact substantially plagiarized from *Luke Hutton's Repentance* published in 1595. *The Life and Death* sold well, and was followed by a sequel, *Ratseis Ghost*, in which he robs a lawyer, amongst various other adventures. The lawyer is described as a miserly covert thief 'who fleeces his victims within the law's protection', whilst Ratsey is a robber of the open road – brave, honest and only concerned to spend his winnings on having a good time (op. cit., 115). Others who deserve to be robbed are cattle dealers, clothiers, a conjuror and a troupe of actors – all characters who benefit from different forms of deceit. Like Falstaff in Shakespeare's *Henry V*, Ratsey is a 'good fellow', an honest thief who looks after his friends and keeps his promises. Alexander Smith, in his 1719 *Complete History of the Highwayman*, even tells us about an oath sworn when admitting a new member to the company which threatened dire punishments for disloyalty and cowardice (Spraggs 2001: 151). Highway robbers display bravery, comradeship and sometimes even make chivalric decisions about who can afford to be robbed and who can't.

The connection between the myth and actual practice was again rather vague, and driven by the desire to sell pamphlets, books, prints, songs and so on. Take, for example, James Hind, a Royalist soldier who was hung, drawn and quartered in 1653. Imprisoned in Newgate in 1651 immediately after the English revolution, he was rapidly fictionalized as a Royalist gentleman robber who gave twenty shillings to those who were for the King and robbed those who were not. In biographies like *Hind's Ramble* and *Hind's Exploits*, he was presented as a merry prankster who never shed blood. A chapbook[3] titled *No Jest like a true Jest: being a compendious Record of the merry Life and maddest Exploits of Capt. James Hind, the greatest Robber of England* was reprinted five times (Sharpe 2005: 54–5). It seems fairly clear that, at the time, Hind actively participated in the construction of himself as someone who deserved leniency from the court on the grounds that, as it is said towards the end of *Hind's Ramble*, he was 'charitable to the poor ... a man that never murdered any on the Road; and always gave men a jest for their money' (in Spraggs 2001: 164). The same might be said of Claude Du Vall, hanged in 1670 and renowned for his politeness, charm and abilities in playing the flageolet. A much-reprinted account has him dancing beautifully with a lady after she has dismounted from her coach. He, like James MacLaine ('the Gentleman highwayman'), was visited by many society ladies and associated celebrities whilst in prison. In the mid-eighteenth century, highwaymen were very fashionable indeed, seemingly amongst those in polite society as well as the common people (Moore 1997: 133).

Though the key elements of the charm of the highwayman were well established in the eighteenth century, it is William Harrison Ainsworth's later gothic romance *Rookwood* (1834) that provides the most well-known popularization of the myth.[4] Dick Turpin, a violent and unpleasant robber of the 1730s (Seal 1996: 52; Sharpe 2005: 137), here becomes a chivalrous hero, and the story of the ride to York and the death of his loyal steed Black Bess is now very often assumed to be true. There is no evidence that it is, though stories presenting Turpin as a Robin Hood character and a joker were in circulation from 1737 onwards:

He only taketh from the rich
what they well can spare;
And after he hath served himself,
he gives the poor a share.

(in Spraggs 2001: 253)

In later versions of the Turpin ballad, he robs a lawyer, an exciseman, a judge and a moneylender – all characters who deserve the justice he metes out to them. He was by no means a famous figure at the time, but one of many whose name appears on multiple plagiarized semi-fictions throughout the eighteenth century. Ainsworth's Turpin reworks these traditions for an audience familiar with Scott's historical romances, the figure of the banditti and the idea of the Byronic hero:

Like our great Nelson, he knew fear only by name ... Turpin was the *ultimus Romanorum*, the last of a race which (we were almost about to say we regret) is now altogether extinct. ... With him expired the chivalrous spirit which animated so many knights of the road; with him died away that passionate love of enterprise, that high spirit of devotion to the fair sex.

(in Sharpe 2005: 152)

The book was a huge best-seller, and versions of the story were produced for the stage, the mass-market cheap novelette, and the children's toy theatre. Turpin became the defining figure of the English highwayman, and the vogue for highwayman romance continued for several decades afterwards with huge numbers of tellings and retellings of the stories from a century before. Whether in novels, penny theatres or penny dreadfuls (sometimes called 'penny bloods'), variations on

Turpin became common. The penny dreadfuls collected highwaymen together with pirates, Sweeny Todd the demon barber of Fleet Street, vampires and urban gangs – such as the 105-issue *Wild Boys of London* which started in 1860 (Sharpe 2005: 177, *passim*). By this point, the robber was moving into the city and a new mythology was beginning to develop.

The underworld

The highwayman was not only a creature of the roads, he was also connected to the urban criminal, since the city was the origin and destination of both highwayman and prey, yet attitudes to the urban underworld tended to be much more ambivalent. It was a source of considerable fascination, 'a freemasonry of crime', with published accounts of the practices, organization and language of pick-pockets, swindlers and prostitutes being common from Tudor times onwards (Agnew 1986: 65; Spraggs 2001: 96). The tone, of course, was condemnatory, but a lot of 'cony-catching pamplets' were sold. By the early eighteenth century, there was a common perception that London was rife with criminality, and broadsides, pamphlet accounts of lives, as well as publications like *The Ordinary of Newgate, His Account* and the *Old Bailey Sessions Papers* fed a public seemingly fascinated by the salacious details of any crime (Backscheider 1989: 477). It seems to be at this point that the scale and labyrinthine geography of the city begins to make it into a metaphorical wilderness, too, one of James Scott's 'nonstate' spaces (1992). In a strange inversion, London becomes a jungle within civilization, a move which prefigures many of the ideas about the Mafia and organized crime we will discuss in chapters six and seven. As the novelist and magistrate Henry Fielding wrote in 1751:

> Whoever indeed considers the cities of London and Westminster with the late vast addition of their suburbs, the great irregularity of their buildings, the immense number of lanes, alleys, courts and bye-places; must think that, had they been intended for the very purpose of concealment, they could scarce have been better contrived. Upon such a view, the whole appears as a vast wood or forest, in which such a thief may harbour with as great security, as wild beasts do in the deserts of Africa or Arabia.
>
> *(in Sharpe 2005: 95)*

Daniel Defoe, as well as writing many books about pirates, also demonstrated this moralizing fascination with the urban criminal in many essays and books, such as *Colonel Jack, Moll Flanders* and *Roxana*. A particularly remarkable example of such a creature was Jonathan Wild, the 'Thief-Taker General of Great Britain and Ireland', who managed to both run a criminal empire and retrieve stolen goods in return for a fee (Moore 1997). Styling himself as the proprietor of the 'Office for the Recovery of Lost and Stolen Property', he was finally executed in 1725, and there were few who mourned his demise. In works like John Gay's musical play *The Beggar's Opera* (1728) and Fielding's *The Life of Jonathan Wild the Great* (1743), Wild[5] is used as a figure of corruption and avarice, and implicitly compared to businessmen and politicians.[6] The former was a huge success, making Gay a lot of money, and leading to the production of *Beggar's Opera* playing cards and fans (Moore 1997: 227). However, these were works with no heroes, just gargoyles coloured in shades of grey. Heroic accounts of urban robbers are rare until we get into the twentieth century, but an early exception was the eighteenth-century housebreaker Jack Sheppard, largely due to the fact that he escaped from jail four times in 1724 and appears to have displayed a rather insouciant attitude towards freedom, captivity and even death. Defoe wrote two best-selling pamphlets in 1724 in which Sheppard became a clever jester, but the most successful retelling of his story was again by Harrison Ainsworth who made him (and Jonathan Wild) characters in his 1839 novel, *Jack Sheppard*. Seven adaptations for theatre opened in the month of publication, and in one theatre 'Sheppard-bags', 'containing a basic housebreaking kit – several picklocks, a screwdriver and a crowbar – were hawked to the audience in the lobbies' (Spraggs 2001: 241).

The figure of Turpin, with his easy charm and nostalgia for a chivalric form of masculinity, appears to have been easily accepted by a readership charmed by the galloping romantic hero, but the lionization of Jack Sheppard and his ilk provoked considerable protests. Turpin's exploits clearly took place in the past, and outside the city, and though Ainsworth's versions of both Turpin and Sheppard presented men of daring, generosity and a hint of noble blood, it was the housebreaker who was accused of being an incitement to the corruption of public morals. The highwayman and the pirate could be portrayed as gallants, whilst the romanticization of urban crime was far more troubling. In the 1720s, Defoe had railed against the dangerous influence of *The Beggar's Opera* even as he sought to sell his books on pirates and thieves, and wrote *Moll Flanders*, a best-seller about the adventures of a marvellous prostitute (Duncan 1996: 89). Fielding's 1751 *Enquiry into the Causes of the Late Increase of Robbers* expresses a similar concern about the moral downfall of the common people less than a decade after he had been writing about Wild himself (Pearson 1983: 33). Defoe and Fielding's rather pious concerns were echoed a century later in the scandals over the so-called 'Newgate novels' in the 1830s – a category that included authors of highwayman stories such as Edward Bulwer-Lytton and Harrison Ainsworth – which were predicated on the idea that impressionable young minds might find the glamour of crime too much to resist. From the *Penny Satirist* of 1839 we have the following fictional exchange, after they have seen one of the many Jack Sheppard plays:

FIRST JUVENILE. – I say, wasn't it well acted?
SECOND JUV. – I believe you. I do likes to see them sort o' robber pieces.
  I wouldn't give a tizzy to see wot is call'd a moral play – they ar so precious dull. This Jack Sheppard is worth the whole on 'em.
THIRD JUV. – How I should like to be among the jolly cocks; plenty to eat, drink, and spend – and every one has his *mott* too.

FOURTH JUV. – Ar; shouldn't I like to be among 'em in real arnest. Wot jovial lives they seem to lead; and wot's the odds so long as you 'ar happy? Only see how such coves are handled down to posterity, I thinks it's called, by means of books, and plays, and pictures!

FIFTH JUV. – Blow'd if I shouldn't just like to be another *Jack Sheppard* – it only wants a little pluck to begin with.'

(in James 1978: 271–2)

There is a theory of media influence here, as well as assumptions about class, gender and education. C. W. Cornwallis, in his 1853 *On the Treatment of the Dangerous and Perishing Classes of Society*, suggests that Turpin, Sheppard and Duval 'inculcate the same lesson, exhibit to admiration noted examples of successful crime [and thereby] attract the attention and ambition of these boys, and each one endeavours to emulate the conduct of his favourite hero' (cited in Pearson 1983: 165). Dickens and Thackeray shared this sense of unease and tried to turn it into a dark characterization of the criminal that allows little space for conceptions of the romantic hero, let alone revolutionary redistribution. Dickens, for example, in his preface to *Oliver Twist*, a book which was outsold by *Rookwood* at the time, clearly distances himself from moonlight-robber romance, and his criminals are grubby, uneducated characters who have more in common with the gothic grotesque than the dashing trickster (Spraggs 2001: 245–7; Parker 2005). Yet despite such fears, and such attempts at a 'realist' rebuttal, the fascination of the outlaw persisted.

The cult of the robber

Of course, writing about crime is not the same as celebrating or exonerating it, but many of the authors of books about smugglers, highwaymen, robbers and so on felt the need to represent their work as a warning and not an example. Like many of the characters we have met in this book so far, it is possible to suggest that what is being explicitly denied is also implicitly being affirmed and desired (Duncan 1996: 67). So the anonymous author of the 1797 *Anecdotes, Bon Mots, Traits, Stratagems and Biographical Sketches of the most remarkable Highway-men, Swindlers, and other daring Adventurers who have flourished from a very early Period, to the present time* worries about a reading of their text which might suggest sympathy with the evil-doers. Instead, they claim that their text has educational purposes and 'that in every work which has hitherto been published on the present subject, the utility of recording examples to offended justice, has been earnestly enforced: and all possible objections to this kind of understanding have been ably answered' (in Sharpe 2005: 62). We can presume that the *Anecdotes* was not primarily intended to be a morality tale but an entertainment, and moreover (as with so many of these texts) it often entertained by contrasting the remarkable adventurers of the road with the greasy cleric or the smug merchant. The authorized reading appears often to be the exact opposite of the more likely one, with the villains having wit and swagger, whilst the powerful are cowardly or arrogant. As Lucy Moore suggests, explaining why people who lived outside society were heroes of their eighteenth-century contemporaries, criminals 'refused to fulfil the roles society had mapped out for them; and common people adored them because they defied the law, throwing off the restrictions of poverty and submission under which they had been born' (1997: 40).

Outsiders are glamorous, and no wonder, then, that the highwayman became a figure used to market a whole range of popular cultural products during the twentieth century: as a staple for children's comics and annuals – the *Dick Turpin Library* had 138 issues between 1922 and 1930 – or in the figure of a Stoke-on-Trent Toby Jug, cigarette card, board game, toys and even pornographic novelty gift (Sharpe 2005: 197). In popular song, poetry, comics and TV shows, the highwayman was a stock figure, along with Robin Hood and the pirate. The first film was the 1906 silent *Dick Turpin's Ride to York*, but the 1925 *Dick Turpin* starring the Western star Tom Mix was the first to define a genre which shared something with the Western in terms of its rural settings, horseplay and fast action sequences. The film historian Jeffrey Richards notes that the highwayman was always a more popular swashbuckler in British films than US ones, 'for she had her own homegrown heroes of the road – the James Brothers, the Youngers, the Daltons' (1977: 228). As we will see in the next chapter, this says more about the dominance of the Western during the first half of the twentieth century, because there were actually rather a lot of highwayman films made by major Hollywood companies. Nonetheless, the highwayman (and the smuggler) have gradually become rather antique characters. They are figures for brass engravings and nostalgic prints and not contemporary Hollywood blockbusters – unlike the pirate or the urban gang. In the end, the many remakes of the generic Dick Turpin story during the twentieth century were capped with the same move into comedy that we also saw happening to the pirates – *Carry On Dick* from 1974. The violent criminal of the 1730s – 'more commonly referred to as Big Dick' – ends up as a figure of pantomime fun, though his escapes from the Bow Street Runners and his romantic entanglements rely on the same basic trickster story. Indeed, when cast as Turpin in the 1951 film *Dick Turpin's Ride*, the actor Louis Hayward described the part as 'Robin Hood in a different hat' (Richards 1977: 217).

Images of banditti, smugglers and highwaymen from the early nineteenth century onwards were certainly all shaped by the currents of romanticism that re-imagined Robin Hood and pirates, too. However, it is also fairly clear that their reception within the seventeenth and eighteenth centuries was often also predicated on a politics that expressed suspicion about those who had wealth and power. Stealing is the simplest form of redistribution, and when the victims are dressed in uniforms or lace, they can afford to lose it. Constant here is also a moral landscape in which the country and sea are associated with purity and generosity, whilst the state, its agents, and the visible worlds of the city connote stiff-backed self-interest. Gillian Spraggs captures the tension well:

At worst, the cult of the robber functions by totally suppressing the rights of the victim, including his or her claim to any sort of imaginative sympathy. It legitimates unprovoked violence and a spirit of hard-hearted rapacity. However, at its best, it becomes associated with a very old myth of resistance and restitution. By going outside the law, which is viewed either as toothless or else as downright corrupt, the outlaw or highwayman takes to himself the power to set right injustices and to punish oppressors who otherwise cannot be touched.

(2001: 263)

Spraggs is not convinced that her 'cult of the robber' in England from the middle ages to the early nineteenth century can be assimilated within Hobsbawm's accounts of 'social bandits' (1965, 1972a) or Seal's version of the 'outlaw hero' (1996, 2009) as if they reflected certain timeless truths about crime and oppression. She is too much of a historian to suggest that knowledge could be de-historicized in such a simple manner (2001: 267, *passim*). I beg to differ, because it does seem to me that the similarities between her accounts and theirs still justify an argument that ties together Robin Hood, pirates, smugglers and highwaymen. They might not mean the same in different times and places, and their meanings have clearly changed over time as their stories have been retold by people with different sensibilities and politics. The influence of romanticism in the early nineteenth century is a clear example, with pre-modern rebels becoming icons of a new form of authenticity – outside the city, outside the work organization and pitted against the wealthy and corrupt. For a Marxist historian like Christopher Hill, writing about popular understandings of crime in the eighteenth century, the message is clear:

This lower class literature reflects a genuine social reaction: sympathy for smugglers and highwaymen, moral support for condemned criminals at Tyburn, all bear witness to popular hatred of the state and its law. It illustrates that hostility to regular and disciplined labour which made free craftsmen resent the factories so much.

(1969: 279)

In the next chapter, we will see what happens when this series of understandings moves across the Atlantic and becomes a story about the freedoms of the Wild West and the corruption of the wicked east.

5

OUTLAWS AND THE FRONTIER

The idea of the frontier is not one that is unique to the USA, but it is fair to say that it is there that it finds its most culturally developed form. The frontier is again a version of one of Scott's nonstate spaces which can include the forest and the sea, but is in this case defined by a relation to the moving boundaries of the state. From the 1850s onwards, 'The West' became a metaphor for the character and destiny of a people, as well as the stage setting for a wide variety of forms of consumption. The most common account of 'the Western' is that it provides an origin story for the United States in which civilization emerges from wilderness. As an explanation, this is rather helpful because it allows many people to understand the killing of Native Americans, the taming of towns and the lynching of outlaws as part of a logic that moved America from colony to world power. Within this broad sweep, there are sub-plots concerning the savage and the civilized, domination and self-sufficiency, simple honesty and talkative greed. These define the Western as a genre[1] and the USA as a nation. Not that these are accurate historical accounts of what might reasonably be called wilderness, or the facts of migration and genocide, or the organization of a capitalist economy. They are myths, in the sense that they tell a story which shapes and is shaped by experience, but is not necessarily an accurate representation of it (Slotkin 1992, Wright 2001).

In this chapter, I will develop a particular reading of this myth, focussing on the idea that elements of it are actually rather subversive in their celebration of that which lies outside, or on the edge, of a developing industrial nation. I want to align elements of the myth with the argument in this book concerning the subversive nature of Robin Hood and his many merry men. I think it is fair to say that most of the academic treatments of the Western that I have read treat it as an ideology for capitalism in the most general sense. That is to say, they tend to assume that this is a genre that tells fables about the rewards and punishments for particular forms of behaviour, and hence assists in socializing people into forms of capitalist individualism (for example, Slotkin 1992, Wright 2001, Kaulingfreks *et al.* 2009). Economic individualism is naturalized and connected to ideas about national destiny, personal character and hard work. Whether this is regarded to be a good thing or a bad thing depends on the politics of the commentator. Whilst I don't disagree with elements of this assessment of what Westerns 'mean', I suggest another trail that might be followed. In a great number of Western texts the problem is industrialization itself. The big organization, the state, the cattle rancher, railroad, Eastern businessman and city slicker are very often the source of the disruption that destroys forms of small-scale community and self-sufficiency. Further, the rebel, outlaw (or even Native American) stands out against 'progress', scale, the city, greed and so on. Slotkin *et al.* note this, too, but my reading of the Western goes further and connects this to a wider set of myths about resistance and redistribution. Once again, these are stories that problematize questions of the economic by celebrating counter cultural actions and lives that lie on the margins of legitimacy. In that sense, the Western contains tensions. Just as it is a story about the making of the Greatest Nation on Earth, so is it also an account of how the local was threatened by industrialization, and of the morality of a people who might resist what others (in suits) would like to call 'progress'.

In the book so far I have been blurring the distinction between 'facts' and 'fictions', in order to argue for the dialectical relationship between action and understanding that Graham Seal characterizes as the 'outlaw hero cycle' (2009). Of course, the dissemination of the myth relies on mass-media technologies, and it is clear that by the time of the 'Wild West' we are in a media-saturated environment. Whilst ballads, songs and broadsheets would gradually spread news of pirates, smugglers and highwaymen, the popular press, telegraph and dime novel broadcasted stories of outlaws much more efficiently. The West develops alongside the beginnings of an industry of mass communication so the idea that there was once a 'real' West, and that it was distorted later in becoming part of popular culture, is actually rather problematic. The West was happening at the same time that it was becoming fictionalized, with key figures actively participating in the making of myths. For example, the story of Billy the Kid was first told by Pat Garrett in his sensational biography *An Authentic Life of Billy the Kid the noted Desperado of the South West*. It was credited to 'Pat F. Garrett, Sheriff of Lincoln County, at whose hands he was killed'. Billy died in July 1881, and the book was out by 1882 (Martin and Shephard 1998: 117). In the same year Jesse James was killed and Frank Triplett wrote the *Life, Times and Treacherous Death of Jesse James*. This wasn't the first book on James either, an earlier one being the 1880 *The Life and Adventures of Frank and Jesse James and the Younger Brothers* by Joseph Dacus (Slotkin 1992: 136–7). Bob Ford, his assassin, re-enacted the murder as part of a travelling variety show, and the James family later invested money in early Jesse James films (Seal 1996: 100). Even John Wesley Hardin, a racist killer, wrote an autobiography which was published in 1896.[2] As I will show below, mythologizing the West was always simultaneous to the action. Selling the story meant making money. In other words, the boundary between the facts and the fictions, between economy and culture, is even less clear than it was in the case of contemporary accounts of pirates or highwaymen.

The chapter begins with an account of the making of the mythic West, particularly in the second half of the nineteenth century. I then consider the economics of this process, and argue that, for most of the twentieth century, the Western was the dominant genre across whole swathes of cultural production. This is followed by a consideration of the place of the outlaw, bandit and related figures that appear to problematize the legitimacy of new forms of social order, particularly in relation to land and ownership. I conclude with some thoughts on what it might mean to propose a radical reading of the Western, particularly with reference to questions of race and gender, and to connect the anti-modern cowboy with other romantic outlaws and social bandits.

The making of the West

> There's a saying that if something is natural and right and fitting, it's 'as American as apple pie'. Not everyone can or wants to bake an apple pie and not everyone can or wants to become a cowboy. But it's fair to say that in the minds of many men, even if only for fleeting moments, there's a hankering to be as free and rugged, as engaging and boisterous, as hardworking, daring and independent, as truly American, as the cowboy.
>
> *(Hassrick 1974: 139)*

As we saw in chapter three, writers of travellers' tales and utopias have often enough used the 'savage' as a means of commenting on the manners and tastes of their own societies. It is sometimes through distance that social criticism or satire can function, and so the authors who wrote extraordinary tales of voyages around the world often chronicled the innocent ways of the savage, at the same time that they recounted stories about huge spiders and trees as high as cathedral spires. Soon enough, in an era influenced by romantic ideas, authors such as Rousseau would assume that savages were naturally wise and childlike, and had not been corrupted by civilization. The myth of America begins like this, as a State of Nature, before the fall which turned Europe into a hell of starvation and intolerance, and provoked mass exodus. But the Promised Land was mostly Eastern, for a century or so, and it took a while for the West to become mythic, rather than just curious.

Just as seventeeth- and eighteenth-century travellers' tales followed the paths of maritime trade, so did tales of the West. Initially these were stories of the 'mountain men' who trapped and traded animals for their fur, but were supplanted by trading companies which became some of the first industrial dynasties of the United States. The mountain man could easily be understood as a version of the Scottish 'highlander', the brave and romantic creature from the far north and popularized in the novels of Walter Scott. Across the Atlantic, James

Fenimore Cooper's reinvention of Scott's frontier romances began with his 1823 *The Pioneers*. Many of his later books told tales of cunning and bravery in the wild involving Leatherstocking, Natty Bumppo and assorted Mohicans. Though not all the savages are bad, nor all the whites good, there is a broad narrative of racial progress at work here, often understood as a necessary historical evolution in which the civilized replace the uncivilized. Around the same time, tales of the Arcadian abundance of the West became increasingly common in the East, with books such as Caroline Kirtland's *A New Home – Who'll Follow?* (1839) nicely capturing a condensation of character and destiny. In 1845, John O'Sullivan, editor of the New York *Morning Post*, wrote an editorial in which he claimed that it was America's 'manifest destiny to overspread and to possess the whole of the continent which Providence has given us for the development of the great experiment of liberty' (in Martin and Shephard 1998: 50). By the second half of the century, the idea of young men going west was being articulated as being part of a national mission. Emanuel Leutze's 1861 painting *Westward the Course of Empire takes its Way* was widely reproduced,[3] and the symmetry between 'westering' and the previous migration across the seas was often noted. The painting, which now hangs in the Capitol building in Washington, is popularly known as *Westward Ho!*, the title of a pirate novel by Charles Kingsley from 1855.[4] 'Prairie Schooners' rumbled settlers across the great deserts and mountains, people who required the character of pirates and highlanders to survive as pioneers.

The natives who had already settled North America were hence understood as savages, even if curious and sometimes noble ones. In 1819 John Heckewelder published *An Account of the History, Manners, and Customs, of the Indian Nations, who once Inhabited Pennsylvania and the Neighbouring States*. A cross between anthropology and the freak show, accounts of 'Indians' were of considerable interest in the first half of the nineteenth century. In the 1830s, the painter George Caitlin showed over 500 paintings of Native American scenes in an exhibition that toured the USA and Europe. In 1841, he published a book, *Manners, Customs and Condition of the North American Indians*.

> From what I have seen of these people I say there is nothing very strange in their character. It is a simple one, and easy to understand if we take the time and care to familarise ourselves with it. The North American Indian in his native state is an honest, faithful, brave, warlike, cruel, revengeful, relentless – yet honourable, thoughtful and religious being. From the very many acts of their hospitality and kindness, I pronounce them, by nature, a kind and hospitable people.
>
> *(Caitlin, in Martin and Shephard 1998: 44)*

In Francis Parkman's *The Oregon Trail* (1849) and Colonel Richard Dodge's *Hunting Grounds of the Great West* (1877), these Native Americans are offered as Rousseau's primitives. Childlike and undeveloped, but capable of expressing

certain truths to civilized man. But as the westering continued in the second half
of the nineteenth century, the Native Americans became more often understood
as simply savages, and as impediments to progress. History justified extermination,
according to the members of the Little Big Horn Association, founded in 1870.
'The destiny of the aborigines is written in characters not to be mistaken. The
same inscrutable Arbiter that decreed the downfall of Rome has pronounced the
doom of extinction upon the red men of America' (in Brown 1991: 189; see also
Davis 2002: 184). Just as there was a historical inevitability to the demise of the
red man, so too did the white man have to follow a path. In 1862, in an essay
titled 'Walking', the American essayist Henry Thoreau wrote, 'Eastward I go only
by force; but westward I go free.' For Thoreau, the East was the site of the city,
of Europe, civilization and constraint, whilst walking towards the setting sun
signified 'wildness and freedom'. Over the next 30 years, this myth became
embedded in popular representations of the people of 'the West', too. From 1861
to 1864, Mark Twain tried to become wealthy by moving around Nevada and
California prospecting for silver, and writing for various local newspapers. His
account of this time, published in 1872 as *Roughing It* (Twain 1985), tells of gold
miners, snow storms, stage coach rides and small towns, all decorated with
Twain's use of slang[5] and a dry irony. He continually contrasts his own effete
Eastern manners with the rowdy confidence of the pioneers, whether in terms of
dress, local knowledge or the ability to swear with wit and enthusiasm. The
inhabitants of his West are both objects of anthropological interest, in the sense of
the traveller's tale, but again also somehow wiser in their innocence than those
who claim civilization. Though Twain ends up being rather sceptical of a promise
of a new Eden, the very idea grows from currents of European romanticism
and its development as American transcendentalism. Both movements were
expressing an anti-modern critique, in their evaluation of nature as necessarily less
corrupted than culture, which manifests itself as a celebration of the wild and the
sublime, and which can be properly understood only by a person of authenticity
and individuality.

From the 1890s onward, the West was becoming history. Though Joseph
Glidden wasn't the only person to invent barbed wire, his 1874 patent was
the one accepted. In the 1880s, reliable and cheap fencing using Glidden's
wire rapidly enclosed the open range, and the industrialization of cattle farming
and expansion of the railroads meant the end of the cattle drive. But by then,
the West had become a time and place which was already a nostalgic touchstone for national character. Before becoming president in 1901, Theodore
Roosevelt's seven-volume *The Winning of the West* (1885–94) and his founding
of the 'Boone and Crockett Club' in 1887 conjoined manly values and
the wilderness life (Slotkin 1992: 30, 37). Perhaps even more significantly,
in 1893, Frederick Jackson Turner, the US historian, gave a talk entitled
'The Significance of the Frontier in American History'. According to Turner,
the fact that the West had now been 'won' augured badly for the future
of the USA. American character was defined by novelty, adaptation and growth,

so without this imaginative geography of a frontier, there was a danger of atrophy.

> Whenever social conditions tended to crystallise in the East, whenever capital tended to press upon labor or political restraints to impede freedom, there was this gate of escape to the free conditions of the frontier. These free lands promoted individualism, economic equality, freedom to rise, democracy ... American democracy is fundamentally the outcome of the experience of the American people in dealing with the West ... the West gave, not only to the American, to the unhappy and oppressed of all lands, a vision of hope.
>
> *(Turner, in Wright 2001: 55)*

The frontier meant a condemnation of Europe, and of the city, but the call to the frontier, to the setting sun, has many other resonances, too – the child leaving the mother, Columbus finding the 'new' world and pilgrims leaving home for a 'Promised Land'. Common to these images is also the idea of escaping from a certain sort of repression – the mummy's boy, claustrophobic routine, those who would stop you from speaking your mind. These are all ways of thinking about constraint, about some agency that prevents you from being what you might be. The West was a place where men, usually, could be who they wanted to be. So by the turn of the century, it was being used as a new version of utopian social criticism, but this time separated by time, and not distance. Painters, illustrators and cartoonists such as Frederic Remington, Charles M. Russell and Frenzeny Tavernier (see Horan and Sann 1954, Hassrick 1974, Durham and Hill 2005) celebrated a dying way of life. For example, Remington's *The Fall of the Cowboy* shows two cowboys, downcast, in the snow, one dismounted to open the gate on a fence which had stopped them from moving freely. Similarly, Owen Wister's celebrated 1902 novel *The Virginian* repeatedly compares the lost West with the talkative, effete East – now overrun with immigrants, blacks, unionists and Wall Street speculators.

Throughout the twentieth century, the historical narrative of westering becomes so embedded as to reshape history and the present. It tells a story about complex social organization becoming simpler as it moved westwards, and then growing in complexity again, but remaining marked by the organization and experience of a sort of primitive democracy. Whatever the historical reality of this 30-year period of emigration, genocide and a certain lawlessness, it is the myth that becomes the truth and eventually gets used to explain history in books. 'Innovation, adaptation and invention – in economics, social organization and government – were characteristics of frontier life', as Billington and Ridge put it in their definitive textbook, now in its sixth edition (2001: 2). The making of the West was the making of a metaphor for time and space, for challenge and responsibility, and for the character and destiny of a people.

The economics of culture

> When the legend becomes fact, print the legend.
>
> *(from* The Man Who Shot Liberty Valence*, 1962)*

This journey from history to myth is also again a story of the inextricability of economy from culture. In other words, the making of the West was simultaneously about the economics of fur and beef, but also about the money that might be made from selling stories about cowboys and lawless towns. In some sense, the beginnings of the story are in the long-standing British and French adventurers' concessions such as the Hudson's Bay Company (1670), and later the North West Company (1779). Like so many of the semi-piratical expeditions of the day, these combined imperial ambitions with a profitable business model based on buying furs from mountain men. These two early companies were in turn challenged by new entrepreneurs in the early nineteenth century. The American Fur Company, the Rocky Mountain Fur Company and many others attempted to 'open up' new territories in order to challenge monopolies and generate profit (Nolan 2003: 16–18). These concentrations of capital and new arrangements for organization, distribution and sales meant that a previous generation of mountain men, trappers and frontiersmen were becoming superfluous at the same time that they were becoming legends. Men like Daniel Boone, Jim Bowie, Davy Crockett and Kit Carson were the precursors to the industrialization of the West, and their mythic character certainly influenced the way that a later group of insecure migrant workers were imagined.

So when publishers of newspapers and dime novels began to write about the cowboy, the heroic individualist outdoorsman frame was hence already in place. Poor pay and dangerous working conditions were transmuted into romantic heroism and folk wisdom. Black, Latino, Asian and Native American workers were written out of an emerging account of rugged white men in a rugged landscape, and so too was any idea that these were workers who were being systematically exploited. There were attempts at organizing labour, such as the 1883 cowboy strike covering five ranches in the Texas panhandle, but the insecurity and mobility of the workforce made any sort of enduring labour successes unlikely (Zeigler 2006). In part, the strike was a protest over wages, but it also reflected the consolidation of ranches into gigantic operations, often owned by Scottish and English capital, and sometimes headquartered abroad, such as the Matador Land and Cattle Company from Dundee (Nolan 2003: 210). In 1882 alone, about $30 million was invested by absentee corporations and syndicates which tightened up on the labour conditions and traditions of smaller ranchers. Though full-time workers were paid well enough, ranching also relied on large numbers of poorly paid seasonal workers, and often enough there was an oversupply of labour desperate to work for any price (Zeigler 2006).

The concentration of ownership and the enclosures of the open range had violent consequences. For a start, it meant that settlers were beginning to get in the way of access to land for cattle, and also in the way of the railways for the distribution of this cattle and for moving more settlers westwards. The technology, workforce and territory required for the mass production and distribution of beef meant conflicts over land, as well as the rapid growth of towns populated by insecure migrant workers. Some of these workers were willing to do other things for money, too, such as Walter Crow, hired by the Southern Pacific Railroad to secure access to land, and who killed five settlers at Mussel Slough, California, a conflict allegedly followed by Karl Marx (Simpson 2006: 6). A long series of local skirmishes, such as the 1876 Lincoln County War or the 1889 Johnson County War, involved some combination of hired hands, wealthy ranchers and groups of settlers.[6] In addition, what Dee Brown has called the 'military-political-reservation complex' (1991: 363) meant that there was big money in feeding the army and provisioning Native American reservations, let alone feeding all the new migrants. This was a tinder box for conflict. It was in the interests of cattle ranchers that 'Indians' were harassed and demonized because this would ensure the presence of a standing army that needed to be fed, and reservation agents who could profiteer from government grants to feed natives now enclosed on land unsuitable for subsistence. The myth of the violent West had economic consequences, as well as economic causes.

Soon enough, representations of the West begin to make money for other people, too. Though journalists and authors had been selling stories about frontiersmen and savage Indians for some time, the mass popularization begins in the 1860s. It was then that the publishers Beadle and Adams began publishing Western dime novels, the US version of the British penny dreadful, with over five million being printed in the first four years (Martin and Shephard 1998: 108) and 2,710 titles published by 1890 (Davis 2002: 286). As the genre developed, titles such as *Buffalo Bill Stories*, *Beadle's Half Dime Library* and *The Five Cent Wide-Awake Library* featured Buffalo Bill, Wild Bill Hickok, the James gang, forty-niners and Billy the Kid, all claiming loudly that they were 'true stories'. Other characters, such as Deadwood Dick, were fictions, but were embedded in a setting by now made up of a tangle of facts and fictions. For example, Nolan (2003: 79–80) claims that by 1869, the dime novel stories of gunslingers were encouraging young guns to test themselves against James Butler Hickok, by now hero of several novels and also Sheriff of Ellis County, Kansas and later Marshal of Abilene. His 1861 fight with David McCanles and others had been covered in an article in *Harper's Magazine* by George Ward Nichols, later to become Hickok's biographer. Martha Jane Cannery, also known as Calamity Jane, then later claimed (or was ascribed) authorship of a 25¢ page pamphlet documenting her life and (almost certainly fictional) romance with Wild Bill (Horan and Sann 1954: 47; Ames 2004: 134). For Hickok, Cannery, Nichols, ghost writers and their various publishers and agents, printing the fictions provided a nice income and encouraged audiences to come to travelling rodeo and stage shows full of 'daring exploits' that would 'thrill' and 'terrify' (Horan and Sann 1954: 129). The idea of the Wild, Wild West also gave newspapers a lot to write about. Mark Twain, in his 1872

Roughing It, parodies the headlines that shout 'FATAL SHOOTING AFFRAY', 'ROBBERY AND DESPARATE AFFRAY' and 'MORE CUTTING AND SHOOTING' (1985: 353, *passim*). Twain, a journalist himself, often enough hints that the stories may not be true, but they are believed, so might as well be.

The West wasn't just being written about in dime novels. James 'Grizzly Bear' Adams was a mountain man who went into the circus business in the 1850s, and by the 1860s was working with the great showman Phineas T. Barnum (Cook 2005: 249). Developing from the circus was the Wild West Show, and in 1873 Wild Bill Hickok toured with Buffalo Bill Cody in the melodrama *Scouts of the Plains*. It was written by Ned Buntline, who had already written 357 dime novels about Buffalo Bill, following a series of stories in *The New York Weekly* in 1869. Cody was combining theatrical and circus appearances with being a cavalry scout, but as time went on, his connections to the 'actual' West seem to have become less important, and in dress and manner he became the first globally known Western star (Slotkin 1992: 69, *passim*; Davis 2002, Durham and Hill 2005). By the late nineteenth century, touring Western shows were big business, with over 50 being active by 1885 – 'The Pickett Brothers Bronco Busters and Rough Riders Association', 'The Miller Brothers' 101 Ranch Wild West Show' and so on (Trolinger 2006: 170). Stars were made – Bill Pickett and Booger Red, rodeo champions; Annie Oakley and Johnny Baker, dead-eye shots; Will Rogers, whose roping skills later got him into silent films. The most famous and elaborate was 'Buffalo Bill's Wild West Exhibition', beginning in 1883, and in 1885 touring for a while with the Sioux chief Sitting Bull. In 1887, the show toured Europe with a replica of the Deadwood coach, 75 defeated Sioux (some sent on the tour as a punishment), 140 cowboys and 250 animals, including buffalo and long-horned cattle. Paris celebrated 'le look cowboy', and the popular culture of the period reflected the West on chocolates, toys, operettas and so on. Later, in 1905, an even larger show, as 'Buffalo Bill's Wild West and Congress of Rough Riders of the World', toured Europe in a series of 67 railroad cars (Rainger 2006: 185). One of the show's early stars, Buck Taylor, was advertised from 1884 as 'King of the Cowboys'. Three years later, he too had a dime novel written about him – *Buck Taylor King of the Cowboys* (Carlson 2006: 17).

A moment that was later to have huge consequences for the Western came in 1894 when Buffalo Bill's troupe were filmed performing a rodeo for Thomas Edison's new Kinetoscope Parlors (Simpson 2006: 21). It was fairly evident that the entrepreneurs of film were going to turn to an established money-making genre for their subject matter, particularly since it involved spectacular action sequences, and indeed the first motion picture to tell a story was a Western. Edwin Porter's *The Great Train Robbery* lasts 12 minutes and was first screened in 1903. It contains horses, a train, outlaws, guns, a posse and the law – all elements that were by then congealed into a mythic narrative, and survive pretty much unchanged over a century later. A few years later, early French silent movies echoed this style, too – *Cowboy* (1907), *Les Aventures de Buffalo Bill* (1909) and many others (Rainger 2006: 184, 190). By now, 'Buffalo Bill's Wild West' was attempting to copy the cinema, with its 1908 tour of 'The Great Train Hold-Up and Bandit Hunters of the Union Pacific' (Slotkin 1992: 86). A few years later, and now in deep financial trouble, Buffalo Bill did make a movie called *The Indian War* (1913), but this wasn't enough to save him. The show finally went bankrupt in 1917, killed by the cinema that was now going to exploit the genre in something like 8,000 films to be released in the rest of the century.[7]

The confusions between fact and fiction continue into early Hollywood. Al Jennings, a real train robber, appears as the star of the 1910 *The Bank Robbery* (Simpson 2006: 22), which was based on a crime that had taken place only three years before. The real Wyatt Earp appeared in Douglas Fairbanks' 1916 film *The Half Breed*, and Jesse James' son, Jesse Edward James, starred in the 1921 *Jesse James Under the Black Flag*. With the growth of Hollywood, the western city of Los Angeles became a gold town for ex-Western lawmen and released criminals to act as advisors and publicists and make a little money, too. Earp, Bat Masterson (OK Corral gunfighter) and Bill Tilghman (pursuer of Jennings) were all friends with William S. Hart, the influential silent movie actor and director (Slotkin 1992: 244). The migrant workers had finally moved to the west coast and were now riding horses and roping as stunt men, and perhaps pretending to die as Indians, too. Sometimes, this blurring often seemed intentional, precisely to create a certain sort of realist warrant. Take the case of John Wayne. In his first six films (1932–33) he is always named John, and in the 1933 *Three Musketeers* he is named Tom Wayne. As Slotkin remarks, at least Buffalo Bill's authenticity claimed some reference to a world outside the star system (1992: 272). By the middle of the twentieth century, John Wayne had become an icon as 'John Wayne', not merely an actor playing parts in cowboy films. The truth and the legend were tightly lassoed together.

For pretty much 80 years, the Western was the genre to measure other genres against. Not just on the silver screen, but newspaper cartoons, comic books, TV and radio series, biographies and novels. Owen Wister's 1902 novel *The Virginian* sold 50 thousand copies in two months. Zane Grey's (1912) *Riders of the Purple Sage* sold over a million hardbacks and the author was a top ten best seller with his other books virtually every year between 1915 and 1924. Later, authors such as Max Brand, Louis L'Amour, Jack Schaefer and non-US authors such as J. T. Edson took the Western novel (itself a clear continuation of the dime novel) into the mid-twentieth century with entire publishing houses specializing in cheap books about gunfighters and pioneers. L'Amour remains the best-selling novelist in US history, with 225 million books printed (Wright 2001: 8). Nonetheless, it was with the moving image that the Western found its widest appeal. For children, there were cowboys with famous horses, such as William Hart and Fritz, Tom Mix[8] and Tony, Gene Autry and Champion, and Roy Rogers and Trigger. Certain characters became brands, appearing in a variety of media, and allowing for a wide variety of opportunities to cross-sell other products. The Lone Ranger appeared in films, a TV series and on the radio; Hopalong Cassidy in some 66 films, many comic books and was the first character to appear on a lunchbox; and

Tex Ritter cross-marketed films and country music. By the late 1950s, eight of the top TV shows in the USA were Westerns, and the genre dominates the 1960s, too – *Gunsmoke* (1955–75), *Have Gun Will Travel* (1957–63), *The Rebel* (1959–61), *Bonanza* (1959–73), *Daniel Boone* (1967–70) and many others. The 1950s were perhaps the peak of the Western, but in pretty much every year between 1926 and 1967 (apart from the 1930s) Westerns usually formed about a quarter of Hollywood's output (Wright 2001: 8).

The West, in its many incarnations, became a narrative written on everything from children's toys to academic texts. It was claimed to define a nation; allowed presidents, intellectuals and astronauts to talk about frontiers and destiny; and constructed a series of icons and settings that most commentators have seen as essentially supportive of capitalist individualism. Yet, as might be supposed, the problem with 'reading' a genre like the Western in this way is partly its sheer scale, but also its own internal tensions and heterogeneity. Not every representation of the West in every media over the past 150 years can line up as evidence for a nationalist pro-capitalist myth. There are too many outlaws for that, too much money stolen from trains and banks, and too many villains with sparkling eyes. If the Western is a story about the beginnings of modern industrial society, it is also a story about what it means to oppose industrialization, and live free, outside the law.

Out law

> The law, the honest ones carry it hard and clean all their lives. Behind their backs the others buy it, sell it, dirty it, tie it into knots.
>
> *(from* Lawman*, 1971)*

In contemporary English, calling someone a cowboy suggests they are self-interested and not bound by the rules of civil commerce. The origin of the term is not so different from this. It appears to refer to Tories or Loyalists who fought with the British during the American Revolution. Cow-boys, usually hyphenated, stole other people's cattle (Wagner 2006: 22). Indeed, the meaning of cowboy until the mid-1880s was primarily derogatory in a general sense – meaning drunk, cattle thief and so on. Terms such as horseman, cowhand, ranchhand, buckaroo and cowpuncher were preferred (Carlson 2006: 15–16). So a cowboy was a cultural problem, someone who stood (at least sometimes) outside the law, and was often a casual worker and a migrant. In other words, the cowboy was not an employee who stayed in the same job, in the same place. George Orwell, in his short essay on Mark Twain, suggests that Twain's books have the central theme: 'This is how human beings behave when they are not afraid of the sack.' Though Orwell is disappointed in Twain's continued refusal to move from satire to social criticism, this idea of the West is a radical one – 'If you disliked your job you simply hit your boss in the eye and moved further west' (1968: 325).

So though it is certainly true to suggest that the cowboy myth is strongly shaped by individualism, the corollary of this is that it is equally strongly articulated against the claustrophobic alienation of the city and the work organization. We have Western songs that told how hard the work was, about the loneliness and suffering of the job, but also which celebrated the beauty of nature and the freedom to roam, away from civilization and 'where the churches grow':

> I thank you Lord that I am placed so well,
> That you have made my freedom so complete;
> That I am no slave of whistle, clock, or bell …
>
> *('The Cowboy's Prayer', in Weiner 2006: 162)*

There are also songs that bemoan the changes that have happened with the end of open grazing, and the 'wire fence a-closin' up the range' (op. cit., 165). Freedom from constraint also suggested that these were workers who were not overly concerned with loyalty to their employers. After the enclosures, a cowboy who was loyal might be referred to as a 'pliers man', on the basis that he spent most of his time mending the wire that rustlers were continually cutting (Hassrick 1974: 55).

But the loyal cowboy might also have been a masked rustler at night, because the Western contains an inverted sense of legitimate and illegitimate employments. One of the few consistently negative stereotypes is the bad businessman. Most often railroad tycoon, big rancher, town mayor or shop owner,[9] such characters provoke the ordinary citizen into crime and violence. In the first third of the twentieth century, these ideas were part of US popular culture anyway, with the huge power and wealth of the 'robber barons' buying politicians and crushing organized labour. The reforming outlaw from William S. Hart's silent films was an early example of populist politics, but the casting of Tyrone Power as James in the 1939 version of *Jesse James* sees populism writ large, with Jesse fighting the 'ever growing ogre' of the railroad. This was a film influenced by the Robin Hood plots of some early gangster films, and in the same year we also see Jimmy Cagney driven to violence by injustice in the 1939 *The Oklahoma Kid* (Simpson 2006: 212). There were quite a few 'outlaw as hero' Westerns in the early 1940s, but this sort of theme really begins to dominate from the late 1960s, with classic examples being *Once Upon a Time in the West* (1968), *The Wild Bunch* (1969), *Pat Garrett and Billy the Kid* (1973) and *The Long Riders* (1980).

The attraction of the outlaw goes back further than this though, with a very substantial interest in lawlessness from the 1850s onwards. Sometimes this was the result of a productive confusion between Civil War guerrilla forces and gangs who simply robbed for profit. Southern sympathies were clear enough, and those who robbed from the rich were often assumed to be redistributing from the rich North to the poor South. After the war, at the beginning of the period of the golden West, groups such as the Kansas Jay Hawkers appear to have been folk heroes, mercenaries and outlaws all in one. The various groups now referred to as the James Younger gang grew out of Civil War skirmishers such as Quantrill's Raiders. Often enough already involved in bank and stagecoach robberies, they mutated easily enough into criminal gangs with ready justifications. An 1872 editorial in the Kansas City *Times* compared the James gang to the Knights of the Round Table, men who 'live out of their time'.

> It was done here, not because the law is weaker but because the men were bolder, not because the protectors of person and property were less efficient but because the bandits were more dashing and skilful; not because honest Missourians have less nerve but because freebooting Missourians have more.
>
> *(cited in Barry 2000: 228)*

Another example would be the Dalton Gang, originally from an extended family that made money by being both marshals and Indian police, but later diversifying into protection for whisky bootleggers and train robbery (Nolan 2003: 155, *passim*). There were also Mexican or Central American bandits such as Joaquin Murrieta – the inspiration for Zorro[10] – whose legitimacy depended on Latino hostility towards the USA. Most importantly perhaps, outlaw activities were being covered by a press avid for sensational stories.

The first reported train robbery happened on 22nd May 1866 in Indiana, when the Reno brothers stole $15,000 from the Ohio and Mississippi Railroad, a classic example of robbing from the rich. 'Road agents' and gangs were now being written up in a way that combined outrage with fascination. Take the case of someone like Henry Plummer, Sheriff of Bannack, Montana, and also the leader of a band of outlaws allegedly called 'The Innocents'. Thomas J. Dimsdale's *Correct and Impartial Narrative of the Chase, Trial, Capture and Execution of Henry Plummer's Road Agent Band* was published as a series of articles in 1865, and relied on accounts from those involved, plus a considerable amount of authorial licence (Nolan 2003: 120, *passim*). What Slotkin calls 'dime novel populism' (Slotkin 1992: 51) portrayed the gang as Rob Roy's clansmen, or Robin Hood's merry men, with an emphasis on the honour that might exist among thieves in a corrupt world (op. cit., 132). One of the James gang wrote to the *Kansas City Times* in 1872, claiming to rob the rich to feed the poor, and signing the letter 'Jack Shepherd, Dick Turpin, Claude Duval'. Or at least the editor claimed to have received such a letter which, given their sympathies, was rather convenient (Seal 1996: 96).

Stories about Jesse James, Billy the Kid and the James Younger gang had a very wide circulation, as did the ever-more creative accounts of the various gangs of the period – most with names simply made up by the press anyway – the Hole-in-the-Wall Gang, the Train Robbers Syndicate, the Kid Curry Gang, the Powder Springs Gang, the Robbers' Roost Gang, the Butch Cassidy Gang and so on.[11] Accounts of 'bad men, desperadoes, rustlers and outlaws' have sold well since (see Horan and Sann 1954 for many examples). Just like the controversies over the 'Newgate novels' I mentioned in the previous chapter, dime novels about the James Boys in particular caused a moral panic about imitation and led to their banning from 1883–89 (Slotkin 1992: 128). This didn't prevent the ambiguity of these characters continuing to be exploited by a press which needed to fill newspapers with stories, and which could always use Robin Hood and Dick Turpin as mythological models. Little quirks were always helpful, too, such as Marion Hedgepeth, a hired gun who dressed like a banker in Derby hat, or Black Bart, the outlaw poet who signed himself 'Po8' and never fired a shot, but would leave justificatory poems with his victims:

> I've laboured long and hard for bread
> For honor and for riches
> But on my corns too long you've tread
> You fine-haired sons of bitches
>
> *(Nolan 2003: 131; Horan and Sann 1954: 83, 149)*

Black Bart was a familiar name already, it being attached a century before to a famous pirate, a Robin Hood of the seas, and the subject of many legends about his tea-drinking, audacity and violence (Burl 2006).

As Ames notes, often the tolerance of 'criminals' is related to the extent that they could be re-imagined as folk heroes. This was true of pirates and smugglers in the eighteenth century, and it was certainly true in the Old West. Butch Cassidy was widely known as the 'Robin Hood of the West', Jesse James as 'America's Robin Hood' and Joaquin Murrieta as the 'Mexican (or Chilean) Robin Hood', or (in the 1936 film) *The Robin Hood of El Dorado* (Ames 2004: 50, 100; Horan and Sann 1954: 30; Simpson 2006: 6). Sam Bass, who robbed stages and trains in the 1870s, was 'Robin Hood on a fast horse' or 'Texas' beloved bandit'. He had a song written about him – 'The Ballad of Sam Bass' – and even a waxwork in Madame Tussaud's in London. Simultaneously, those in power were often seen as corrupt, stupid, violent and so on. So in 1875, when the men from the Pinkerton detective agency blew an arm off Jesse James' mother in a botched attack on the family home, this simply contributed to the idea that the James Younger gang were the heroes of freedom, against the evil railroad men and bankers. Allan Pinkerton himself then started to write novels which made the cowboy into an anti-union detective, perhaps partly as an antidote to the populism which even Theodore Roosevelt identified when he complained that the Robin Hood legend had a lot to answer for (Ames 2004: 109; Slotkin 1992: 141).

The romanticization of the gunman and the robber is not really surprising in the context of the post-Civil War West. The routine abuses perpetrated by large employers, the corruption of local politicians, the displacement of natives and settlers, and the massive violence of the law and army all added up to a culture in which power was easily (and often correctly) equated with self-interest:

> The East is always associated with weakness, cowardice, selfishness, or arrogance. The Western hero is felt to be good and strong because he is

involved with the pure and noble wilderness, not with the contaminating civilization of the East.

(Wright 1975: 57)

Good guys don't wear suits, don't talk too much and don't know much about education and culture. Even when not an 'outlaw' in obvious terms, the Western hero has resistance to the East written all over his body. Robert Mitchum, a typical granite-faced Western actor, once claimed he had two acting styles 'with and without a horse' (Simpson 2006: 174). The cowboy is a silent hero, who watches carefully and talks little. In the novel, *Shane,*[12] a man known only by that one name, has a 'quiet power'. As he tells the boy Bob, 'A man who watches what's going on around him will make his mark' (Schaefer 2003: 2, 6). Real men don't talk too much. They speak plainly, and take their time to trust people. For example, Wister condemns a travelling salesman, in the face of his taciturn Virginian, as having

> a hateful taint of his profession; the being too soon with everybody, the celluloid good-fellowship that passes for ivory with nine in ten of the city crowd. But not so with the sons of the sagebrush. They live nearer nature, and they know better.
>
> *(1998: 24)*[13]

There is more than an echo of the Byronic hero here, too, in which brooding silence and solitude becomes the guarantee of a certain authenticity. Shane again: 'He was battling something within him, that old hidden desperation and his eyes were dark and tormented against the paleness of his face. He seemed unable to look at us' (Schaefer 2003: 115).

This is someone tormented by history, and many Western heroes are clearly aware of their history, of their place. Unlike the fly by night Easterners, who bring a shallow modernity with them, the Westerner is grounded and honest. They also understand that honest violence might be needed in order to defend a way of life against change, perhaps against the threat from the East. Crucial here is the idea of legitimate violence. Shane puts the matter well again:

> Listen Bob. A gun is just a tool. No better or worse than any other tool, a shovel — or an axe or a saddle or a stove or anything. Think of it always that way. A gun is as good — and as bad — as the man who carries it. Remember that.
>
> *(Schaefer 2003: 55)*

The question, then, is how we decide who is good, and who is bad, and here the matter will usually be settled in favour of smallness against bigness, of the West against the East, or tradition against modernization. However, even honest violence presents a problem to any community. As one of the villagers in

The Magnificent Seven (1960) says, 'We know how to plant and grow, we don't how to kill!' That is why they hire the gunslingers, most of whom die on their behalf. Will Wright's structural analysis of the 'classical' Western[14] suggests that the violent beginnings of law must always be outside the law.[15] The hero, nameless and unknown, enters the community, solves the problem through an act of violence, and is then expelled, in order that civil society can begin again (1975: 48). Wright's paradox is that 'if the values of society are accepted, they cannot be defended; and if they are defended, they cannot be practiced' (op. cit., 162). To put it another way, selfish individualism and the collective market are in considerable tension. You need to be an individual to trade and benefit in the market, but the market needs social regulation if it is not to collapse into a war of all against all.

So much about the Western seems to coalesce around this question of law and legitimacy. There are lawless towns that grow and die with the railhead, or the gold rush, and that only leave cemeteries behind them. Abilene's first jail was torn down by vigilantes before it was completed, and like Dodge, Tombstone, Deadwood, Wichita and others, the idea of the hell town that needs taming is a central part of the myth.[16] The sheriffs and marshals function as bouncers, hard men who can enforce the law, but who suffer because either their consciences, or the reactions of the townsfolk, result in them leaving town or getting shot. In that sense, the good lawman often gets to look rather like the outlaw. Both make law, in a moral sense. In Wayne's last film, *The Shootist* (1976), his gunslinger has a clear code: 'I won't be wronged, I won't be insulted, and I won't be laid a hand on. I don't do these things to other people and I require the same from them.' Whether shootist or sheriff, these are characters who are brave enough to stand out against the times, against power, in order to inaugurate the possibility of a more just social order. The Western hero is always an outlaw of sorts, because he (and it is almost always a he) understands that power makes the law, and that power and justice don't always stand in the same place. Perhaps most importantly, they know right and wrong, and don't twist this simple difference with fancy words. As Davy Crockett says in *The Alamo* (1960), 'There's right and there's wrong. You gotta do one or the other. You do one and you're living. You do the other and you may be walking around, but you're dead as a beaver hat.'

Cowboys now

The December 2008 issue of *Cowboys and Indians* (vol. 16, no. 8, subtitled 'The Premier Magazine of the West') has 314 pages, of which about 250 are adverts. In these pages, 'Western' is an aesthetic term that applies to watches, jewellery, furniture, clothing, belts, boots and so on. It is also a vaguely defined geographical area, a lifestyle (with certain sorts of cars and houses) and a set of recreations (rodeo, skiing, riding, camping, hunting). As ever, money is being made from selling the West. Country and Western music, cartoon characters, lunchboxes, cheap tin stars and toy pistols from the East form part of a family of commodities which are defined through this dense fusion of history, myth, and finally, cliché. The 'Old West tourist hell' of Deadwood, Dodge City and Tombstone relies on the cliché nowadays, with tours selling stagecoach rides and gunfights happening every hour, on the hour (Nolan 2003: 225). Yet one of the oddities of the present is that it isn't the age of the West. It can be argued that from the 1860s to the 1960s, this was the single most popular setting, character and genre across wide terrains of popular culture across the world.[17] But urban crime, superhero and science fiction films now far exceed the numbers of Westerns being made by Hollywood; Western novels no longer dominate the best-seller lists, and there are no new cowboy series on TV. It was often asserted in the 1960s that the space race was the new frontier, which meant that 'Western' became rather an old fashioned idea in comparison with the shining rockets of the future (Parker 2009).

This unfashionability may well have something to do with the contemporary problem with the West and the 'Indian'. Over the past century, Native Americans have moved from being 'devils in human shape' (Brown 1991: 59) back to being noble and authentic characters and repositories of ancient and quotable wisdom.[18] Chief Joseph of the Nez Percé was claimed to have said, 'The country was made without lines of demarcation, and it is no man's business to divide it' (op. cit., 316). The massacres of men, women and children, the mutilation of bodies, forced marches, concentration camps, show trials and broken treaties that happened in the century or so between early misty romanticism and later guilty romanticization are well documented. So too is the deliberate slaughter of food sources to ensure that the natives hung around the trading post. That way, profits could be made in the name of security, whilst a racist ideology justified the expropriation of land. The Western is far too complicit in an account of civilization as the imperial dominance of whites to be an easy genre for the twenty-first century. Its anti-modernism is often of the most redneck kind, whether directed at natives or migrants. In an 1895 essay, Owen Wister wrote of the West as an escape from the 'debased and mongrel with its hordes of encroaching alien vermin, that turn our cities to Babels and our citizenship to a hybrid farce, who degrade our commonwealth from a nation into something half pawn shop, half broker's office' (1998: 331). The Black, Latino, Asian and Native American workers in the West seem to have been invisible to him, so concerned was he to establish a Walter Scott-type lineage that includes the Arthurian legends and takes in Saxon pirate adventurers like Drake and Raleigh.

In the same year as Wister's essay, a black American, probably called 'Stag' Lee Shelton, killed a white man in a St Louis bar. The stories and songs of Stagolee, Stack O'Lee and Stagger Lee that grew from this incident might not fit into these very white accounts of the West, but they became outlaw myths for a generation who were descended from slaves. Indeed, the huddled masses, as well as the natives who were there already, don't fit easily into a contemporary understanding of the significance of the West. But neither does another rather important group – women. As with the pirates, there are examples of women in the Wild West myth – Calamity Jane, Annie Oakley, Cattle Annie McDougall,

Little Britches Metcalfe, Pearl Hart – but they are largely anomalies. They are interesting, and might be celebrated as examples of a feminist politics, but this is because they are examples of the very few women in the myth who don't fit some clear categories. Belle Star may have been 'a swaggerer with a six gun on either ample hip' (Ames 2004: 131) and many Western books have sections on 'the gentler sex' (Nolan 2003: 165, *passim*; Horan and Sann 1954: 129, *passim*), but most women are portrayed in much more predictable ways – the suffering housewife, the raped hostage, the accomplice in love, the golden-hearted prostitute and so on. Women usually only make sense in relation to men, and are found in homes, towns and gardens, looking after men, yearning for men, being wounded by men. The Western director Budd Boetticher put it neatly (though without any obvious irony) when he suggested that a woman's job in a Western film is to react. 'In herself she has no significance whatsoever' (in Simpson 2006: 217). The Western woman who falls in love with the Western man might be a self-confident individualist sometimes, but she is not so independent that she wants to manage without a man at all (Wright 2001: 152). She always has a soft heart, particularly when she looks out of the window, wistfully.

So there are clear problems with the imperial and patriarchal myth of the West that make it rather difficult to rehabilitate for contemporary sensibilities.[19] For those on the left, the problem is even more acute. The politics which conjoins John Wayne and George W. Bush also appears to embrace union-busting, trickle-down economics, family values and perhaps even the ruthless individualism of Ayn Rand (Kaulingfreks *et al.* 2009: 162, *passim*). This reading is certainly credible, yet I think that it underplays the radical possibilities of the West that begin with a critique of capital from the point of view of those being displaced in time and in space. Crucial here is land, because it is land (visually and politically) which functions as the condition of possibility of the Western, and very often the control of land is the fulcrum for a Western plot. Will Wright makes the important point that Jefferson and the founding fathers imagined an agrarian democracy of small-property owners. They could never have believed that the land would be exhausted, but the logic of the myth is that when there is no more free land, the purest sense of freedom must also disappear. In its place, employment relations (and hence class relations) will inevitably develop as people are forced to work for others in order to feed themselves. As Wright puts it – 'the market can only be civil if the wilderness is endless' (2001: 5, 19).

The Western moving image continually plays with pans across endless space, into different sorts of contained space, and then perhaps out again. People ride into town, or gallop out of town. They swing into saloons, or are seen from windows and doors as they ride past fences, or along streets. And almost always, at some point, they are figures in a landscape that reduces them to straggling points, whilst the grasslands spread to eternity and the ancient mesas reflect the setting sun. It always seems that there is more space, more justice and less law, outside and nearer the land. The inside only makes sense with reference to the outside, because very often these are stories of settling, of the putting down of roots which in some way bind and bound the land, or of a fence post that Shane helped the family to put up, and even after he has gone, at the end of the novel, it can't be moved. As the only woman in the novel says to her husband – 'See, Joe. See what I mean. We have roots here now that we can never tear loose' (Schaefer 2003: 149). The paradox is simply the multiplication of fence posts, or barbed wire, and the industrialization of space. Once everyone puts down roots, and the open range is enclosed, dotted with towns and connected by railroads, there is no space left for the Western, or for someone else to grow roots.

We could easily view the twentieth-century Western as a requiem for a relation to land and freedom, as a long mediation on this paradox of the West. The land, the wilderness, is authentic because it heals and regenerates (Wright 1975: 189). Those closest to the land are the nomadic romantic heroes, but they cannot settle, and are doomed to continue wandering. Robin Hood, pirates, banditti, smugglers and highwaymen all have this problem, too. They are interesting when they are on the move, and they usually end up dead because they are on the move. In the Western, those who settle, as farmers or shopkeepers in the town, can find roots, but open the land to a colonization that necessarily destroys its potential for generating authenticity. The idea of a natural law – 'a man's word is his bond' – is in tension with capitalist law – the idea of wanting to 'own all the land in the valley' (Wright 2001: 32). The way of life described by the Western is always dying, fighting against the very civilization it inaugurates. Westerns are almost always tragic for the main characters, allowing the small people and the women to continue living their lives whilst those who understand justice die or ride out of town. At the end of *The Searchers* (1956), John Wayne's character looks in at us through a doorway, and then turns away. He can never finally come in and settle. The Western hero does not occupy the same time as us. Butch and Sundance, before they fade to sepia after robbing trains and banks, are told by a friend, in no uncertain terms, 'It's over! Don't you get that? Your time is over!'[20] The long, elevated opening and closing landscape shots show us space stretched out like time, and place us in the geological indifference of the mountains, or reflected in the cool eyes of the man with no name.

In 1897, Frank James claimed that his gang were engaged in a war 'between capital and labour, greed and manhood' (Simpson 2006: 6). Whatever James meant, the Marxist revolutionary hero and the individualist Western hero are actually rather similar in the end, particularly in their diagnosis of that to which they oppose themselves (Wright 2001: 102). One attempts to resist the encroachments of big business individually in the name of the small-property owner, the other collectively in the name of the working class, but both oppose the concentration of ownership, the ethics of the greatest good of the greatest number, and are willing to use violence against violence. Embedded in these icons, whether Che or Jesse, is a certain distance from convention, which again takes us back to the Byronic hero, and an understanding of charisma and tradition as forms of legitimacy which are fundamentally different to state rationality. That is to say that the mythical Western hero is also at heart an anti-bureaucrat, an anti-organization man, who breaks rules and exceeds limits (Wright 2001: 192).[21] They, like their pirate or Mafia cousins, will not be found selling their lives to an employer or following orders, however powerful the person who issues them. Neither will they necessarily be hidebound by tradition. Simply because something has always been done in a particular way doesn't mean that a single individual cannot bravely resist complacency in the name of justice (op. cit., 118). The Western hero is produced by history but forced to struggle against it, whether personally, in terms of their ghosts, or publicly, in taking on the powerful in the name of honour, or the powerless. It seems evident to Slotkin that there is more than a little of Hobsbawm's social bandit in the outlaw (1992: 153). I would take this further, too, and say that there are central elements of the Western that are explicitly critical of the modern work organization, the employment relationship, and of the forms of 'organization man' encouraged by industrialization and modernity.

It is common enough to suggest that the Western, and its heroes and villains, simply provide a pro-capitalist mythology. After all, it is in the USA – the very home of twentieth-century industrial capitalism – that the Western is primarily located and it would be surprising if it were not marked by these origins.[22] Its making and selling also reflect the various ways in which culture can make money, indeed the inseparability of practice and representation, and 150 years later Western imagery still provides a brand to sell everything from hats to houses. It is also important to note that the 'reality' of the cowboy was insecure wage labour on behalf of capital, just as the pirate often worked for the state. Yet, as this chapter has shown, other politics can be found here, too, particularly in terms of the resistances to Eastern industrialization – the railroad, the city slicker, the banker and the big businessman. Bill Cody puts it rather well: 'men, women and children have conquered the wilderness by going to the frontier and staying there – not by crowding into cities and living as do worms, by crawling through each other and devouring the leavings' (in Davis 2002: 186).

I think that the Western can be understood as anti-modern, not just pre-modern, and I think this is a distinction that makes quite a big difference. It does not long for capitalism, but resists its encroachments, and the forms of character that it produces. Now this might be dismissed as nostalgia, rather than politics, as Billington and Ridge do:

> Western politics, mistakenly called radical, was most often really a protest against change; and its fundamental program was to maintain the locally democratic, agrarian, small-business oriented social order of the frontier era in the increasingly industrialised world of the late nineteenth and twentieth centuries.
>
> *(2001: 388)*

But in what sense is a protest against change not radical? Particularly now, in an era of global organization, when the commons are enclosed and the frontier displaced to outer space or virtual reality. Localization, sustainability and smallness are concepts which seem increasingly radical, and perhaps even necessary to deal with the dangers that capitalism presents to people and to the land. Perhaps this is something that the Western social bandit knew, but we may be in danger of forgetting, or easily dismissing as a form of nationalist ideology. Perhaps in a post-Western age, we can finally begin to learn from the myth of the West.

In the next chapter, we will be staying in the USA, but moving to the city. The idea of the 'urban jungle' can certainly be found in London in the 1750s, but it became a very well-developed metaphor in twentieth-century New York and Chicago. It is there that we find the gangsters who bring the economic outlaw into the heart of civilization, and the wilderness into the labyrinths of the metropolis.

6

THE MAFIA

Behind every great fortune, there is a crime – Balzac
(Epigraph from Mario Puzo's novel The Godfather *(1969))*

In the late seventeenth and early eighteenth centuries, New York harbour was an excellent place for smugglers and pirates. There were merchants on shore, hiding places off shore and a weak government that did little to interfere (Ellms 2006: 134). For most of the eighteenth century, Ellis and Bedloe's Islands were not the site of the building that welcomed the westering masses from Europe, or the site of the Statue of Liberty, but a place for the gibbets that hung pirates. As New York gradually made the transition from Tortuga to Gotham, many urban gangs began as 'river pirates' who stole and smuggled along the Hudson and East rivers (Sante 1998: 204; Asbury 2002: 57). By the nineteenth and twentieth centuries, the outlaw has come to inhabit the city, and this involves an odd involution, in which the nonstate spaces of the outside come inside. In part, this is a question of visibility, because the Mafia and their associates are hidden in plain sight. They don't need mountains or forests, but secrete themselves within the labyrinths of the town, in the 'under' world, in the dangerous areas where the immigrants live, behind locked doors in strip joints and gambling dens. This proximity to power, rather than geographical distance, has meant that the comparison between the Mafia and legitimate business has been a very common one. If the nineteenth century tended to suggest that the romantic robber was elevated above ordinary life in many respects, then understandings of organized crime in the twentieth century are often predicated on an older idea that they show just how bad the forces of law and the market actually are. Nonetheless, when the Mafia are compared to a business organization, it is often with a certain amount of hesitancy. The commentator makes the 'analogy' but then withdraws into moralizing, usually trying to leave 'real' business and the evil Mafia clearly separated.[1]

Perhaps it would be simpler to say that the Mafia are a business organization, but that they are a romanticized organization that articulates a version of labour that appears to be widely admired. Unlike virtually every other private sector organization, the US Mafia has been mythologized in popular culture, particularly since the 1970s.[2] It is common enough to argue that the gangster seemed to replace the outlaw as the counter cultural anti-hero of choice for Hollywood. Perhaps this should not surprise us, because the combination of work and leisure, a varied set of engaging tasks, intense belonging, charismatic leadership, great food, high pay and violence has much to commend it, and also connects the Mafiosi with outlaw gangs and pirate ships as powerful examples of imagined alternative communities. In that sense, they inherit from Robin Hood the idea of the twinkling-eyed villain and his merry men, but prefer concrete boots to castrating clerics. In order to understand something about the nature of the imaginary that the Mafia operates in, I will also need to make some claims about its major competitor, the state. The Mafia is an organization that trades in violence. This presents a problem, because as we have seen so far it is the state that normally claims a legitimate monopoly on violence to further its interests, many of which are commercial, too. Finally, I want to comment on the romance of the Mafia in the context of contemporary managerialism. There have been many attempts to enchant versions of alternative economies, and I will suggest that the Mafia is one, even though its contemporary manifestations are often more like the 9 to 5 than the galloping outsider.

As with previous chapters, cultural representations and economic practices are blurred in some typical ways. The distinction between representations of gangsters, and gangsters themselves, has never been very clear. Stories of 'black hand' gangs were common on the west coast of the USA from the late nineteenth century onwards, and they seem to have gradually become accounts of an organization called the Mafia from about 1916 onwards (Sante 1998: 233). John McCarty's compendious book on gangsters in film (2004) documents well over a thousand films made between 1915 and 2003, a huge list of images of wise guys on mean streets, and sharp dressers with unpredictable tempers. Even then, we can go back earlier, perhaps to D. W. Griffiths's (1912) *The Musketeers of Pig Alley*, in which the underworld of New York was visualized in the colourful terms later popularized by Herbert Asbury in his urban chronicle *The Gangs of New York* (1927) and his many later 'true crime' books, including *The Barbary Coast* (1933), *The French Quarter* (1936) and *Gem of the Prairie* (1940) about the San Francisco, New Orleans and Chicago underworlds respectively.

Shadowing this cultural parade are endless stories about the ways in which gangsters would imitate the models of urban masculinity they saw on the screen, and screen actors would 'research' what the gangs did in order to provide realism to their acting (Adler 2007, Gambetta 2009: 251, *passim*). For example, Joe Browne, who starred in several silent films, was a gangster and friend of Capone.

'Crazy Joe' Gallo, a member of the Profaci family in the 1950s, 'grew up wanting to be like movie gangster George Raft. He would stand on streetcorners flipping a half dollar and talk without moving his lips. He also affected the black shirt and white tie of Richard Widmark in the film *Kiss of Death*' (Balsamo and Carpozi 1997: 371). Indeed, Raft (himself an ex-hood) claimed that gangster movies taught gangsters how to speak. These boys were often infatuated by stardom, it being another version of respect that a man of honour might understand. 'Lucky' Luciano always felt his story was destined for the movies, and his point-man in Hollywood, 'Bugsy' Siegal, used to hang around with George Raft, Gary Cooper, Cary Grant and others. Bugsy even had a screen test at one point, but then dropped the idea and had glossy signed photographs made up instead (McCarty 2004: 242).

So when Mario Puzo's book *The Godfather* came out in 1969, it was building on a long tradition of well-researched fictional representations that had a habit of becoming facts. Some Mafiosi resented, or claimed to resent, these slurs on ordinary hard-working, law-abiding Italian Americans. Joe Colombo, then the leader of the Profaci family, began the 'Italian-American Civil Rights League'. He allegedly got the words 'Mafia' and 'Cosa Nostra' dropped from the script of the *Godfather*, but this did not stop the film and its sequels from being massively influential. As Balsamo and Carpozi put it, from the 1970s onwards 'if your name ended in a vowel, you were in the Mafia' (1997: 393). Henry Hill, an ex-mafiosio turned celebrity, wrote that the wiseguys loved it because 'it made them feel big-time … It just gave them a sense of empowerment' (2004: 40) and that they quickly started to use the words and phrases from the film. For example, shooting someone through the eye (as happened with Bugsy Siegal) became a 'Moe Greene special', after the incident of the same name in the film. Sammy 'The Bull' Gravano, an underboss for John Gotti (himself a media star), said that the book and film 'influenced the life, absolutely … I would use lines in real life like "I'm gonna make you an offer you can't refuse"' (Gambetta 2009: 269).

But it isn't simply a question of life (and death) imitating art, because, as with Western outlaws, the boundaries between life and art are simply unclear. For example, Joe Pistone (who spent five years undercover in the mob) thinks that most of the wiseguys read his book when it came out, and most of them quite liked it (Pistone 1987: 410). The film *Donnie Brasco* (1997) was written around the book, just as *Goodfellas* was written around Nicholas Pileggi's account of Henry Hill's life in the Mafia, *Wiseguy* (1985). Amazingly, *Wiseguy* was making Hill tens of thousands of dollars in royalties whilst he was still in the witness-protection programme. Hill also alleges that Nora Ephron wrote *My Blue Heaven* (1990, with Steve Martin as a New Yorker in the witness-protection programme) after talking to Hill because her husband happened to be Nick Pileggi. In such a context, historical truth is a difficult category to deploy, simply because the cultural so rapidly becomes the economic, and vice-versa. Real-life Mafia stoolies write 'treatments' of real-life incidents for Hollywood projects – such as Henry Hill and Sal Polici's *Getting Gotti* (Hill 2004: 100). Actual incidents, such as blowing up restaurants, digging up buried bodies and so on, are rewritten for the screen. Wiretapped conversations comment on the latest episode of *The Sopranos*; the actor who plays Tony Soprano's son is arrested for robbery on the Upper East Side; and the actor who plays Paulie Walnuts in *The Sopranos* was arrested 28 times and nearly became a made man before becoming an actor (Gabbard 2002: 14). Even more bizarrely, Louis Eppolito, an ex-policeman turned bit-part actor in *Goodfellas*, writes an autobiography called *Mob Cop* that ends up many years later as evidence in his imprisonment on charges of murder, bribery, money laundering and drug dealing on behalf of the Gambino family. Eppolito himself had tried to become a movie producer after leaving the NYPD, but even after his imprisonment, a screenplay of his life was being planned (Winter 2006, Adler 2007: 246–7).

This inter-textuality is beautifully played out in *The Sopranos* itself, where Silvio is often doing speeches from the *Godfather* films, to the general applause of the other mobsters. In one instance, he even corrects another character when they get the dialogue wrong. This character is Christopher Moltisanti, a wiseguy who desperately wants his life to have some significance and so he attempts to write a gangster script and unsuccessfully pitches it to a Hollywood executive. The culture industry and Mafia business operations seem to be very difficult to disentangle. Both will sell pretty much anything for money, but the latter is slightly more modest about its activities. Mafia members who forget *omertà* and sell their stories find themselves outside the organization, and possibly end up with a bullet in the eye. In this regard, it is remarkable that the boundary between legitimate entertainment capitalism and organized crime still manages to hold at all. Perhaps, as Rawlinson suggests, it is the very spectacle of the Mafia that gets in the way of the analogy becoming a serious comparison (1998). If the Mafia was more ordinary we would be able to see it as a form of economics, and organization, which happens to be defined as illegal. As we have seen in the book so far, being illegal certainly doesn't prevent something from being glamorous, and also encourages us to again ask questions about what marks the boundary between the outlaws and the capitalists.

Mafia business

TONY: I wanna know why there's zero growth in this family's receipts. You're supposed to be earners. That's why you got the top-tier positions. So each one a you go out to your people on the street, crack some fuckin' heads … create some fuckin' earners out there. My uncle … the boss of this family, is on trial for his life. And what you people are kickin' up there is a fuckin' disgrace. You know how much lawyers cost? A major RICO[3] like his? I'm the only one supportin' him. This thing is a pyramid, since time immemorial. Shit runs downhill, money goes up. It's that simple. I should not have to be comin' here, hat in my hand, remindin' you about your duty to that man. And I don't want to hear about the fuckin' economy

either. I don't wanna hear it. Sil, break it down for 'em. What two busi-
nesses have traditionally been recession proof since time immemorial?
SILVIO: Certain aspects of show business, and our thing.
TONY: Now that's it. That's all I gotta say.

(The Sopranos, 'For All Debts Public and Private')

Our thing, *cosa nostra*, is both show business and street business. To treat it as
either one or the other would be misleading. HBO make money by selling *The
Sopranos*; there are long-standing connections between Hollywood and gangsters
(Adler 2007); and both industries have a business model that makes money by
selling anything that will sell. Tony Soprano's motivational speech could, with a
few small modifications, refer to a company that does anything. Something comes
down, and money goes up. But despite the timelessness of the model, there is
something very modern in Tony's speech, too. He speaks of loyalty and extraordinary effort, of a form of commitment that (according to some) is a new thing
in business (Parker 2000). Before, so the story goes, businesses were slow, grey
places populated by slow, grey people. Now, as we allegedly hurtle into the new
age of the turbo-global, we need passionate organizations populated by innovative
and autonomous intrapreneurs. So in Anthony Schneider's pop management
book, *Tony Soprano on Management*:[4]

> In an age of economic uncertainty, corporate turmoil, anxiety and down-
> sizing, leaders are being forced to work at warp speed with different
> methods, new systems and shifting teams. … Leaders must step up and steer
> new courses to get companies back on track and regain public confidence.
> They must adapt to meet the challenges of today's business environments.
> And Tony Soprano is the surprising role model for this new breed of leader.
> His methods may appear unconventional, but we can all learn strategies and
> tactics from the way that he manages people, resolves conflict, negotiates
> and leads.
>
> *(2004: xii)*

Schneider's book might do little more than re-brand the self-righteous certainties
of the upwardly mobile, but he has hit on an interesting issue. What can the
Mafia tell us about organizing? In 1986, according to the President's Commission
on Organized Crime, the US Mafia was turning over $65.7 billion, tax free. This
made it second only to the oil industry in terms of size (Durden Smith 2003: 202).
In Italy in 2009, excluding drugs and arms, the Mafia was estimated to have a
revenue of about $107 billion, roughly 7 per cent of GDP.[5] This is, by conven-
tional measures, a real success story – whether in terms of profitability, number of
employees, historical durability, geographical spread, product and service diversification and so on. Balsamo and Carpozi claim that 'today's underworld take
refuge in the self-respecting guise of legitimate entrepreneurs; they have ably
organized themselves in much the same manner as giant corporations' (1997: vii).

This is a corporation which, as Arlacchi puts it, has a three-pronged business strategy – discourage competition, hold down wages and ensure that you have liquid capital (1988: 89, *passim*). The Mafia deals, or has dealt, in lemons, security services, trade-union arbitration, gambling, entertainment, alcohol, cigarettes, drugs, construction, fuel, laundry services, trucking, restaurant supplies, waste disposal, soft drinks, garment manufacturing, fast food, banking, religious relics, candles and holy objects. Legitimate companies also trade in all of these products and services (perhaps with the exception of certain drugs). Hill suggests that the relationship between the Gambino and the Lucchese families was like a competitive partnership – 'like General Motors and Ford' (2004: 100; see also Gambetta 1993: 100, *passim*). The profits that were made would then find their way back into the pockets of US businesses and consumers through legitimate US banks.

My point here is that much Mafia business is just ordinary business, and that the dividing line between Mafia business and some other 'uncorrupted' business is actually rather difficult to see. 'Business' (whatever it is) must include Enron, Shell in Nigeria, Union Carbide in Bhopal, Firestone in Liberia, Ford's decision about the Pinto, the Exxon Valdez oil spill, the Zeebrugge ferry-sinking, the Piper Alpha oil rig fire, the Banco Ambrosiano and so on (Sutherland 1983, Punch 1996, Minkes and Minkes 2008). When Balsamo and Carpozi describe the Mafia as a 'conspiracy which, for the most part, is run like many diversified industries or businesses' (1997: vi), the reversibility of that metaphor is actually rather helpful. Some of the old Mafiosi have become the new robber barons, pillars of the community, with pasts that can be laughed away, and connections to power that are as invisible as social class. In Martin Scorsese's *Casino* (1995), the gangsters have become gambling and entertainment corporations, and the locations of the graves in the desert are simply forgotten.

So how is the Mafia organized? No one really knows, and even the origin of the word itself is a mystery, with many competing etymologies[6] and a first appearance in an official Sicilian document dating from 1865 (Gambetta 2009: 209). Since the 1860s, there seems to have been a generic organizational form, though (like many other businesses) there have been different periods of centralization and decentralization, different terminology, and different structures within (and relationships between) Sicily and the USA. In the broadest of terms, each Mafia family is led by a boss (*capo*), perhaps assisted by an underboss (*sotto capo*) or advised by a counsellor (*consigliere*). Reporting to, and paying for, this strategic apex will be several mid-ranking Mafia members (sometimes termed *capodecina*, or head of ten), and beneath them the soldiers (*soldato*). Each soldier, or 'made man', will also have a network of 'connected' guys who aren't actually Mafia members, but who might be involved in Mafia business. However, each family is often also represented at some sort of higher organizing body, governed by the boss of bosses (*Capo di tutti capi*), and variously referred to as the commission, syndicate, combination, outfit or organization. According to many Mafia histories, in the early 1930s Lucky Luciano divided New York into the 'five families', then centralized the US Mafia on New York. This brought the warring families under the governance of his commission. However, there is also evidence that, both in the USA and Sicily, there were already long-standing arrangements that existed to resolve collective disputes, agree on territories or competing products, and issue contracts on problematic members.[7] Nonetheless, there is a certain managerial mythology around Luciano. Claire Sterling describes him as 'a clear-sighted corporate executive with a rare gift for rational organization, the Lee Iacocca of organized crime' (1991: 100). As he put it himself, 'All us younger guys hated the old mustaches and what they was doin'. We was tryin' to build a business that'd move with the times and they was still livin' a hundred years ago' (in Sterling 1991: 63).

In order to modernize the Mafia, Luciano and Meyer Lansky also established a contract-killing agency – later called 'Murder Incorporated' by the press. As a contemporary associate put it, 'If they had been President and Vice-President of the United States, they would have run the place far better than the idiot politicians' (in Durden Smith 2003: 71). Murder Inc. was credited with 1,000 killings between 1935 and 1945, and was managed by a board of directors who had to vote on contracts. The managers of Murder Inc. would then allocate one of their staff to carry out the contract, but they in turn often sub-contracted these operations to freelancers. As McCarty describes it, 'Gang murder was put on an organized, assembly line basis. Operating like a modern big-business enterprise … ', or using a different metaphor, like the 'gunslingers' hired by the land barons of the Old Wild West (2004: 210).

So successful was the US Mafia in the 1930s that their interests began to move west, particularly into Las Vegas, with the opening of Bugsy Siegal's casino, The Flamingo, in 1947. In the film *Casino*, we are told that 'Las Vegas was just like the Wild West.' Deserts which had been wilderness landscapes for noble outlaws were now to become neon-lit versions of Dodge and Tombstone. The newly wealthy Mafia also had increasing influence back in Sicily, assisting to establish a commission there in the 1950s, and along the way bringing 'new management techniques' to the island (Durden Smith 2003: 114). The Sicilian Mafia had tended to be territorially based, not functionally organized with different families concentrating on different products as it was (partially) in the USA. The US Mafia also encouraged diversification into areas such as drugs and prostitution that would have been unthinkable to the old men of respect (Lewis 1984: 96). So well did the Sicilians learn their lessons that, by the 1970s and 80s, the Sicilian Mafia were no longer the country cousins. Instead, thanks to their control over the heroin and cocaine supply lines, they were now using the US Mafia as distributors for an operation that was bringing huge profits back to Palermo (Sterling 1991). Imported Sicilians, or 'Zips', without social-security numbers, fingerprints on file or the desire to write a book, were now replacing the increasingly flabby US Mafia at the cutting edge of a business, which was still moving with the times.

So just why have the Mafia been so successful? In part because this multinational business has operated a paperless office for nearly 150 years, and has hence avoided the relative certainties of bureaucracy. Communication is 'by voice. Nothing is written in the Mafia' (Balsamo and Carpozi 1997: 436). This is an organization that thrives on interpersonal relationships, and refuses the vulgar simplicities of clarity. Business conversations often involve oblique references of the 'you know that thing we talked about' variety, just in case someone else is listening (Gambetta 2009). In order that an instruction is communicated, each link in the chain must have a private conversation with each other link in the chain. Joe Pistone, the cop who went undercover as Donnie Brasco, remarks that he had to remember everything that had been talked about until he could call in a report to his FBI contact agent (1987: 104). Like the cowboy, talking too much is sometimes regarded with suspicion. The Sicilian word *omertà* conveys this sense of a manly silence and, perhaps because of its similarity with the Sicilian for 'humility' (*umirtà*), a certain self-righteous piety, too (Lewis 1984: 33). Unlike brash attempts at corporate branding, this is an organization that attempts not to leave any traces, and that covers its tracks. As Henry Hill noted, 'we paid cash for everything. This way, there were no records or credit card receipts' (2004: 35). More recently, after the arrest of Bernardo 'Tractor' Provenzano in 2006, many tiny scraps of paper – 'pizzini' – were discovered which referred to his various business associates by number. He was number one, and the numbering went up to 163. According to Longrigg and McMahon (2006), 'the ghost of Corleone' never used mobile phones, and 'believed in keeping the organization out of sight, the better to do business'.

The Mafia attempts to leave no footprints, no noises, and to occupy non-state spaces within the city. Its history is vague, its present is undocumented, and its fact and fiction are deeply intertwined. Unlike the noisy PR of Ford and Disney, members deny that the organization exists at all, and often refuse to use the word (Gambetta 2009: 218). Don Calò Vizzini, a Sicilian Mafia Don, being interviewed by a newspaper journalist in the 1950s:

> Don Calò: 'The fact is that every society needs a category of person whose task it is to sort out situations when they get complicated. Generally these people are representatives of the state. But in places where the state doesn't exist, or is not strong enough, there are private individuals who … '
> Interviewer: 'Mafia?'
> Don Calò: 'The Mafia? Does the Mafia really exist?'
>
> *(Dickie 2004: 253)*

Let us take that at face value. Perhaps Don Calò was inadvertently asking a rather interesting ontological question about organizations in general. We imagine they exist, because they constantly tell us that they do, but what is an organization but a moving network of people and things? This certainly seems to fit with contemporary ideas about the death of bureaucracy, and the growth of a network society. Indeed, from the 1980s onwards, much of the literature on post-Fordism and the third Italy stressed that the success of industrial districts was about semi-visible informality, not the gigantic apparatus of the contemporary corporation.[8] The sort of words and phrases that attempted to capture this rotated around the idea of a network of family-run firms, hence 'cohesion', 'inter-firm linkages', 'trust', 'co-operation' and so on. In this post-bureaucratic world, written contracts were rare, but senses of loyalty and inter-dependence with other organizations were high. Sterling notes that the Mafia also entered into partnership arrangements with the Camorra from Naples, the Calabrian 'Ndrangheta, the Hell's Angels, various US-based Latino gangs, the Chinese Triads, Caribbean gangs and so on (Sterling 1991: 386). This seems a sensible business model for all concerned, reflecting as it does the globalization of international business (Enderwick 2009).

Perhaps Don Calò was right. The Mafia does not really exist, any more than any organization really exists. There is a network of people doing business, money is going up and shit is coming down, but the distinctions between culture and economy, informal and formal, legitimate and illegitimate, makes little sense.[9] So, the line that divides the Mafia from real business might be less about some sort of description of what a business organization looks like, or what the Mafia looks like, and more about its methods of doing business.

Business ethics

> He showed with his words and deeds that his Mafia was not criminal. It stood for respect for the law, defence of all rights, greatness of character: it was love.
>
> *(in Dickie 2004: 122)*

> Wise, dynamic, tireless, he was the benefactor of the workers on the land and in the sulphur mines. Constantly doing good, he won himself a wide reputation in Italy and abroad. Great in the face of persecution, greater still in adversity, he remained unfailingly cheerful.
>
> – from the funeral notices of Don Calò Vizzini, who died in 1954
> *(in Lewis 1984: 21)*

Setting aside the cartoon maniac, this book is testament to the idea that bad guys have moral accounts to justify what they do. In fact, they are often the same sort of reasons that 'good' people use to justify what they do (Matza 1964, Ruggerio 2000a). For the Mafia, this appears to be organized as an account that makes business rather central. Indeed, looking after your own, and looking after business, are condensed into pretty much the same things. Of course, sometimes this involves violence, but not always, because there is no business reason for too much violence. As Virgil 'the Turk' Sollozzo put it in the original *Godfather* novel, 'I don't like bloodshed. I'm a businessman and blood costs too much money' (Puzo 1969: 91; Gambetta 2009). Even his competitor agrees with this. Sonny Corleone, despite wanting revenge on Solozzo, understands that 'his knocking off the old man is purely business, nothing personal' (op. cit., 96). And business, in this context, means looking after your interests, and the interests of those who are close to you. Don Calò and Don Corleone's power come from their reason-ableness, their capacity to listen carefully, and then 'make you an offer you can't refuse'. This might involve threatened or actual violence, but it might not. Such business-like behaviour brings understanding, even among those who end up losing the game. In *The Godfather Part II*, after attempting to betray Michael Corleone, Sal Tessio is being gently but firmly taken away to be killed by Michael's soldiers. After asking if there is anything that he can do, Sal says to Michael's *consigliere* Tom Hagen, 'Tell Mike it's only business. I always liked him.' We never see Sal again.

It is important to get this clear. The Mafia is an ethical business, if by ethics we mean that it is run according to certain widely shared moral codes. The participants understand that other people might not share these codes, but that fact doesn't make them any the less binding on the people who play the game. Indeed, this can be seen as something like a duty, with certain associated rights and responsibilities.

> TONY: We're soldiers, you know. Soldiers don't go to hell. It's war. Sol-diers, they kill other soldiers. We're in a situation where everybody involved knows the stakes, and if you're gonna accept those stakes … you gotta do certain things. It's business. We're soldiers. We follow codes. Orders.
>
> (The Sopranos, 'From Where to Eternity')

But this duty can extend more widely, too. There is a demonstrable market amongst many consumers for Mafia products and services (Rawlinson 2002). People want drugs, prostitution, gambling and protection, and it is quite possible to argue that supplying these items at reasonable prices and with a certain pre-dictability is in itself a public service. That's certainly what eighteenth-century smugglers tried to claim, so when Frank Falcone, the fictional Don of Los Angeles in Mario Puzo's *The Godfather*, is debating whether the families should get involved in the drug trade, he argues that:

> At least if we control it we can cover it better, organize it better, make sure it causes less trouble. Being in it is not so bad, there has to be control, there has to be protection, there has to be organization, we can't have everybody running around doing just what they please like a bunch of anarchists.
>
> (1969: 292)

To which Don Corleone replies, 'We have to be cunning like the business people, there's more money in it and it's better for our children and our grand-children' (op. cit., 295).

Of course, if one were to be symmetrical, this could in itself become a wider moral judgement about legitimate business organizations, too (Gond *et al.* 2009).

The Mafia do not have a corporate social responsibility statement, but does this mean that they are an irresponsible organization? More irresponsible than organizations that trade in alcohol, cigarettes, semi-automatic weapons or burgers that give people heart disease? In John Huston's *The Asphalt Jungle* (1950), the financier of the heist suggests that 'Crime is nothing more than a left-handed form of human endeavour'. It was only a few years previously, in the wake of the 'robber barons', that Edwin Sutherland coined the term 'white collar crime' in a 1939 address to the American Sociological Association. His now classic 1949 book contained a sustained comparison between organized crime and 'respectable' crime. For Sutherland, the underworld and the business world appeared to share a similar attitude to ethics and law amongst legitimate and illegitimate entrepreneurs. Business people, he says, are hostile to the law: 'In this respect, also, they are akin to professional thieves, who feel and express contempt for police, prosecutors and judges. Both professional thieves and corporations feel contempt for government because government interferes with their behaviour' (1983: 95; see Rawlinson 2002). This is obviously a conclusion that might outrage most contemporary business ethicists but, to be fair, we should simply say that all business people have their 'ethics'. As Al Capone allegedly said, 'All I do is supply a demand, capitalism is the legitimate racket of the ruling classes' (in Southwell 2006: 7).

Dealing with the state

> Michael Corleone: 'My father is no different than any other powerful man, any man who is responsible for other people. Like a senator or a president.'
> Kay: 'You know how naive you sound?'
> Michael: 'Why?'
> Kay: 'Senators and presidents don't have men killed.'
> Michael: 'Who's being naive Kay?'
>
> *(from* The Godfather, *1972)*

The biggest business problem that the Mafia has to face is not other Mafia families, or popular outrage, but the power of the state. In that sense, too, they share much with the resistance of social bandits from Robin Hood onwards, with the sheriff in his castle being replaced by cops and politicians. As a few writers have noted, the more the state regulates a particular market and hence restricts the agency of legitimate business, the more attractive these markets become for organized crime. Or, to put it the opposite way, if the state deregulates, legitimate firms make money (though often in illegitimate ways) and there are fewer angles for Mafia groups (Enderwick 2009: 174; Gond *et al.* 2009). The ideal situation for Michael Corleone (or any pirate and smuggler) is high levels of regulation and taxation but ineffective enforcement, much like the years of prohibition in the USA. Many writers describe the Mafia like an octopus, or a cancer, that has somehow infiltrated into the state, but these metaphors bring with them the assumption that the ideal type state is an impartial bureaucracy which is then corrupted by organized crime. If we adopt a different image from Weber, that of the state having a monopoly of legitimate violence within a particular area, then it becomes possible to think about the state and the Mafia as competitors. As Weber put it, 'today, the use of force is regarded as legitimate only so far as it is either permitted by the state or prescribed by it … The claim of the modern state to monopolize the use of force is as essential to it as its character of compulsory jurisdiction and of continuous operation' (1978: 56; Tilly 1985). So the question is not violence or no violence, but who can use violence – in order to enforce the functions of policing, judging, administering, taxing and so on – and in what contexts.[10]

One of the earliest reports on the Mafia, Leopoldo Franchetti's 1877 *Political and Administrative Conditions in Sicily* (in Dickie 2004: 47, *passim*), argued that the Mafia emerged as a result of the 'democratization' of violence. Not only could anyone legitimately use violence, but the boundaries between politics, economics and crime no longer made any sense. Violence was a key form of capital, but since the state was illegitimate, and often effectively non-existent, it wasn't owned by anyone in particular. In the violence industry that consequently emerged, the Mafioso

> acts as a capitalist, impresario and manager. He unifies the management of the crimes committed … he regulates the way labour and duties are divided out, and controls discipline amongst the workers. (Discipline is indispensable in this as in any other industry if abundant and constant profits are to be obtained.) It is the Mafia boss's job to judge from circumstances whether the acts of violence should be suspended for a while, or multiplied and made fiercer. He has to adapt to market conditions to choose which operations to carry out, which people to exploit, which form of violence to use.
>
> *(Dickie 2004: 53; see also Gambetta 1993)*

In *The Godfather Part II*, a business meeting takes place in Cuba. With one long camera shot we pan down a meeting table, attended by men from General Foods, ITT, the Panamanian Mining Corporation, South American Sugar, Michael Corleone, representing tourism and leisure interests, and representatives of the pre-revolutionary Cuban state. Hyman Roth, the smiling and ruthless financier who has organized the meeting comments, 'We now have what we have always needed – real partnership with the state.' Roth goes on to say that we are 'now free to make our profits', and that 'we're bigger than US Steel'. The point here is that the word partnership must be taken quite literally. In order to deal with the state, the Mafia must infiltrate it, must co-opt parts of it in order to ensure that the state's interests do not contradict its own. In 1987, one of the prosecutors in Palermo's 'maxitrial' concluded by suggesting that the Sicilian Mafia was 'a state within a state, an antistate, with its own government, army, territory, rituals, moral code and juridicial order' (in Sterling 1991: 344).

In the US context, it was prohibitition that allowed the Mafia to buy parts of the state. The Volstead Act, which lasted from 1920 to 1933, was partly an expression of bourgeois fears about the cultural impact of the beer and wine drinking masses. However, as an expression of the popular will, it was a huge failure that resulted in millions of ordinary Americans being criminalized for doing things that they enjoyed at the same time that the state appeared to be a front for the robber barons who controlled capitalism. So the smuggler mythology was easy enough to reinvent, with rum-runners importing alcohol from Canada and the Caribbean whilst bootleggers manufactured hooch and moonshine in illegal stills. As a result, the figure of the ruthless urban gangster mutated into a Robin Hood-type moonraker who brought simple pleasures to the people whilst the Keystone Cops bumbled around and fell over. This history fits into the structural features of Seal's (2009) outlaw hero cycle very neatly, and also established a context in which it was much easier for the Mafia to buy favours from the police, politicians, administrators, legislators and so on. Under Warren Harding's presidency there were regular reports of drinking and other speak-easy leisure pursuits in the White House. As we will see in the next chapter, the mythology of John Dillinger's lonesome 'gentleman bandit' versus J. Edgar Hoover's massive but inept Federal Bureau of Investigations must have seemed attractive when the morality and effectiveness of the state was so questionable.

In Italy, the weakness and corruption of the state has been endemic since the Risorgimento, most particularly in the poor south. As Lewis puts it, 'The vendetta was the weapon ready to hand of the poor and otherwise defenceless in a society where law did not exist and justice meant the baron's court and the baron's torture chamber' (Lewis 1984: 29). Secret societies, or alternative forms of social order, were common in a land that was continually invaded, and where ordinary people were endlessly oppressed. However, by the late nineteenth century, the Mafia was being used as a security force in an alliance between feudal landowners, the church, local administrators and vote-hungry politicians. At various points, all of them felt they needed strong-arm men to further their interests. Despite suppression under the fascists, the US Army effectively handed Sicily back to the Mafia in 1943 as they looked for strong local leadership that was demonstrably anti-fascist (Lewis 1984). This economic power, combined with a state recovering from destruction and occupation, established the conditions that pertained in Italy for the next half century. The Mafia's stranglehold over the Christian Democratic Party (in the person of Gulio Andreotti) was the most visible element of a conspiracy that articulated the interests of just about every key section of Italian society – from the Vatican Bank to the P2 Masonic Lodge. For example, the Ucciardone prison in Palermo became a rest home for 'retired' Mafia who ran their businesses from jail, and had their meals sent in from the best restaurants in Palermo. This was 'a Mafia university' where poisonings and slips on the stairs were common (Lewis 1984: 204). Since the Mafia's politics are mobile, being largely concerned with business, more recently they have allegedly swung behind Silvio Berlusconi and his Forza Italia. When the power moves, so will interests.

Calvin Coolidge (another prohibition president) asserted that 'the business of America is business'. He would have approved, then, that, after prohibition ended, the big bootleggers used their expertise to set up legitimate businesses – Seagrams, Capitol Wines and Spirits, Alliance Distributors and so on. Joseph Kennedy, father of Jack and Bobby, had a licence to import gin and Scotch for medicinal purposes, and financed rum-running from the Caribbean. His profits allowed him to buy into Hollywood studios, and brought him into contact with Frank Costello, 'the prime minister of the underworld' (Southwell 2006: 192). Tony Montana, the sociopathic gangster in Brian De Palma's remake of *Scarface* (1983), puts this sort of entanglement rather more graphically – 'You know what capitalism is? Getting fucked. The fucking bankers? The politicians? They're the bad guys. They'll fuck anything and anyone for a fucking buck.' De Palma claims (in his commentary on the film's DVD) that it represents 'the capitalist dream gone bizarre and beserk', but the evidence seems to suggest that the bizarre and the beserk are a fairly normal part of the dream. Whether dealing with organized crime, or organized business, representatives of the state often take their percentage – whether as taxes or bribes. Balsamo and Carpozi, in another moralizing moment, suggest that innocent US citizens are the unknowing victims of organized crime, 'made a helpless sucker by the common denominator of greed and avarice upon which this invisible government gorges itself' (1997: vi). They might well add that the visible government often does the same thing, to which needs to be added the activities of organized business.

All economic outlaws confuse easy distinctions between inside and out, asking where does the straight end and the crooked begin? In the case of the Mafia, this question is asked with more intensity, because of the business model, and also because of their spatial and temporal proximity to power. The outlaw is usually outside and far away, whilst the gangster is hidden in plain sight. In many areas of the economy, some of the money being generated by both 'legitimate' and 'illegitimate' business operations is being reinvested to buy off the state, and ensure that business goes on as usual. Whether we call them gifts, campaign contributions, lobbying, bribes, taxes or the World Trade Organization, the point of these exchanges is to ensure that businesses can do business without too much conflict with the powerful groups that operate on behalf of the state (Dickie 2004: 2). Business groups like the Confederation of British Industry or the Mafia's Commission look after the collective interests of their members by conspiring against the suckers who pay the bills. As Hyman Roth understands, it sounds better if you call a cartel a 'partnership'. That way, everyone seems to be winning.

Identifications

Many organizations like to claim that they are held together by a common culture, a shared sense of identity and so on (Parker 2000). Not only might these sort of claims bond members more closely to the collective, as they imagine the warmth and emotional intensity that is being invoked, but they also might guarantee displays of dedication and sacrifice that are strategically valuable to those in power. In Sicily, one of the ways that *vendettas* were avoided or resolved was by joining families through the practice of co-fathering, sometimes translated as becoming a godfather. Once men had become *compari* at a Christening, they were supposed to respond to each other's requests. This was a sort of social glue, one based on conceptions of inside and outside, honour and disgrace, family and enemy. In the relative absence of the state, and in a place with little social or geographical mobility, the extended family (based on common residence and economic interests, as well as blood and marriage) was the emotional centre. This isn't a modern workplace that insistently claims to care in order to avoid labour turnover and gain extraordinary effort, or a corporation owned by a distant dynasty, it is a family that does business. But, importantly, you cannot leave a family without fearing the possibility of never being able to return, because the emotional damage goes far beyond contract.

Families are not based on a series of calculations about career, but a single decision that can (almost) never be reversed. Either you are in, or you are out. As Lewis puts it, the Mafia is 'a form of primitive human society … its cruel laws are those of tribesmen exposed to continual danger who can only hope to survive by submitting to the discipline of terrible chieftains' (1984: 26). The stakes are high, the loyalty is unquestionable, but the rewards could be huge. As Tony Soprano asserts − 'This family comes before everything else … *everything*. Before your wife and your children and your mother and your father. It's a thing of honour' (*The Sopranos*, 'Fortunate Son'). This speech is made as Tony is performing the ritual (involving a card with the image of a saint, a pricked finger and fire) which will make Christopher Moltisanti into a 'made' man, a 'wiseguy', 'straightened out'.[11] According to many Mafia accounts, the ritual is the end point of a selection process that takes years, and makes even the most demanding recruitment and selection processes seem rather casual by comparison. Joe Pistone, an FBI agent who infiltrated the US Mafia, tells us that after a long period of hanging around as a 'connected guy', and having 'made your bones' (killed someone), you then have to be vouched for by two made men. If you finally make it, 'you are elevated to a status above the outside world of "citizens". You are like royalty' (Pistone 1987: 77). For example, in 1924, Frank Capone (Al's brother) was shot by a policeman in the Cicero area of Chicago. Frank was laid out in a $20,000 bronze casket, and followed by 100 shiny black limousines. Aldermen, police officials, judges, state legislators and congressmen mourned, and fellow mobster Dion O'Bannion sent 3,000 rosebuds (Balsamo and Carpozi 1997: 269). This is a family that wants everybody to know that death produces solidarity, and a very public display of alliances.

In *The Godfather*, one scene has us with the *capodecina* Pete Clemenza in the kitchen of the Corleone's house. In the foreground, Clemenza is lecturing

Michael Corleone on how to make a good meat sauce, whilst in the background his men are eating, drinking and laughing.

> Come over here kid. Learn somethin'. You never know, you might have to cook for twenty guys someday. You see, you start up with a little water, then you fry some garlic. Then you throw in some tomatoes, tomato paste. You fry it. You make sure it doesn't stick. You get it to a boil. You shove in all your sausage and your meatballs. Add a little bit wine, and, a little bit of sugar. And that's my trick.

This image of a boss cooking for his subordinates is highly unusual. Senior managers (of either gender) might pay other people to cook for their team, or they might dutifully stand at a barbecue handing out burnt burgers to embarrassed employees, but the white heterosexual male Pete Clemenza is really cooking. What is more, he seems to enjoy cooking, and his soldiers seem to see nothing unusual in the idea of their boss cooking for 20 of them. This is 'commensality', the bond that comes from a common table, and (for Mennell *et al.* 1992) the most enduring issue in studies of food. Clemenza is reproducing the original moment when food enters the social, as something that requires the collective organization of time, space and materials. As Barthes (1977) suggested, the sort of food Clemenza is cooking connotes something, too – a certain 'Italianicity', with wholesome reds, yellows and greens. We might go further and suggest that it also connotes an unpretentious peasant experience,[12] an authentic companionship around simple hearty pleasures. This seems less like a work organization, and more like what we would usually recognize as a 'family'.

Directly before Pete Clemenza gives Michael Corleone his recipe for meat sauce, Michael has been talking on the telephone to Kay, his girlfriend (and later his wife). She asks him if everything is alright, he is non-committal. She asks him to tell her that he loves her. He says nothing. She asks him again, and he looks embarrassed and tells her that he can't talk right now. When he hangs up, Clemenza mimics a romantic Italian man telling a woman that he loves her in a silly, sing-song voice. In a recognizably predictable manner, a woman has been put in her place. There is a broad structural relation between food, home and leisure. Though food can certainly be located in the liminal spaces and times of the conventional work organization, even then it has something of the character of non-work to it. As is obvious, this brings food close to another broad relation, the association of women with the domestic and private sphere, and men with work and the public sphere. Much of the time, women cook, and men sit and eat. But this is not merely a sexist or patriarchal organization like any other, it is an organization that makes a lot of money from pornography, strip clubs and prostitution, and that has traditionally excluded women almost entirely from any formal membership or decision-making power. Though there is an increasing amount of evidence that women have played a supportive role for many years, and that they are increasingly moving into prominent positions as key men are imprisoned (Siebert 1996, Longrigg 2005), the convention has been that women are not included in Mafia business.

Whilst there is a common sentimentality concerning the mother and the wife, they are largely absent, though present at the family dining table or social occasions. The women actually present in the organization are mistresses, strippers and whores, but they would certainly not be regarded to be part of the 'family', and would be very unlikely to appear at the dining table. This double exclusion no doubt helps to construct a masculine group identity at work and functions on two fronts, since women are both elevated and demeaned, protected and abused. Structurally, it makes little difference, since both result in the same 'othering' – the feminine being placed firmly outside the organization. For example, according to Gambetta, in Sicily before the 1980s it used to be forbidden by oath to 'touch the women of other men of honour', and also even 'to speak to women about things concerning the Cosa Nostra' (1993: 147, 121). Perhaps it was precisely these attempts at exclusion that meant that a domain of objects and activities associated with the feminine were displaced into the masculine, such as food and its preparation. That way, the divide could be maintained and men could act as family to other men.

There are some interesting psycho-dynamic consequences which follow from this, particularly in terms of the idea of representations of the Mafia as providing a gang identification, perhaps like merry men and pirates. Since the archetype of the family is that the mother is associated with the food, in an organization with no women but with a strong image of itself as a family, a man might take on this role. Gabbard (2003: 157, *passim*) explores this in terms of the idea of *Peter Pan*'s 'Lost Boys' who have to construct their own family because their mothers are no longer there. Hence the strong sense of tribalism that seems to appeal both to actual Mafiosi, and all those (often male) viewers of Mafia films who have wanted to be part of the gang, too.[13] But in order to be part of a gang of boys, women must be kept at arm's length, so men must do some of the cooking. A community of men who make little distinction between work and play, for whom belonging is no longer a choice but the pay is good and the food is great. As I noted earlier in the book, the term 'goodfellows' is a much older English word, originally found in Robin Hood texts and often applied to highwaymen, and connoting a trustworthy friend and drinking partner (Spraggs 2001: 71). Unlike the individual highwayman, but very like the pirate gang, identifying with the twentieth-century Mafia allows you to be inside and outside at the same time.

Noble gangs

> TONY: When America opened the flood gates, and let all us Italians in …
> what do you think they were doing it for? Because they were tryin' to save
> us from poverty? No, they did it because they needed us. They needed us
> to build their cities and dig their subways and to make 'em richer. The
> Carnegies, and the Rockefellers, they needed worker bees, and there

we were. But some of us didn't want to swarm around their hive and lose who we were. We wanted to stay Italian and preserve the things that meant somethin' to us. Honour, and family and loyalty. And some of us wanted a piece of the action. Now, we weren't educated like the Americans. But we had the balls to take what we wanted. And those other fucks, those other, the G. P. Morgans, they were crooks and killers, too. But that was their business, right? The American Way.

(The Sopranos, 'From Where to Eternity')

Don Calò Vizzini would probably not have approved of the American Way. Tony Soprano is far too noisy for that old Sicilian man of respect. Like his earlier Italian ancestor, Cosimo de Medici, Don Calò was a sphinx-like man, a man of few words who shaped the destinies of those around him through a Machiavellian indecipherability (Padgett and Ansell 1993).[14] Albert DeMeo, the son of Roy DeMeo of the 'Murder Machine' crew, was given a copy of Machiavelli's *The Prince* by his father on his 11th birthday (DeMeo 2003: 95). For Machiavelli, grandiose displays of power and wealth were not really necessary. Roy DeMeo was unimpressed by Paul Castellano's huge white mansion on Staten Island. 'Big Paul wanted people to think of him as an executive, a white-collar corporate leader. If you really had power, my father told me, you didn't need to show off' (DeMeo 2003: 97). Roy compared Castellano unfavourably to Aniello Della-croce, a Gambino underboss. 'That old man can do more with a wink or a nod than Big Paul ever did' (DeMeo 2003: 97). But his taciturn manner hid the fact that Dellacroce was a tired old man. He was taped in 1985 saying:

Things change now because there's too much conflict. People do whatever they feel like. They don't train their people no more. There's no more … there's no more respect. If you can't be sincere, you can't be honest with your friends, then forget about it. Ya got nothin.

(Balsamo and Carpozi 1997: 459)

This nostalgia, this weariness, also helps to dissolve another boundary between the romanticism of organized crime and the dull world of conventional business organizations. 'The old Mafia bosses who've survived the dramatic changes over the years are today very much tired corporate executives' (Balsamo and Carpozi 1997: 269). Pino Arlacchi (1988: 126) and Claire Sterling (1991: 76) both note that every generation of the Mafia complains that there were rules and respect in the old days. Now, as Pistone (1987) puts it, 'our thing' is becoming 'my thing', or as Tony Soprano opines, 'Lately, I get the feeling that I came in too late, that the best is over' (Adler 2007: 234). Watery-eyed mobsters lament the passing of the good-old days. Honour is a thing of the past, and everyone uses drugs. Henry Hill, now off the witness protection programme, now the gall to complain that everyone is an informant nowadays (2004: 35). Even the businesses that the Mafia is involved in seem to be becoming dull and grubby.

According to Kemp, the Mafia are behind toxic waste dumping on the Somali coast, which destroyed Somalia's fishing industry, and are contributing to high levels of piracy in the gulf (2009: 75). Or, in Roberto Saviano's startling account of the Comorra in Naples, 'the system' works to smuggle containers full of counterfeit sportswear from factories in China to be sold in markets in Saint-Étienne and Stoke-on-Trent (2008).

Of course, if the Mafia is now just another job, just another way of earning a living, then perhaps the intense and intimate world of homosocial banter no longer exists either. Or perhaps, even worse, it never existed. Perhaps everyday life for a gangster was always more boring than that. 'Unlike the images we got in movies like *The Godfather*, the Mafia in real life is repetitive. Conversations are mind numbing. "What are we gonna steal today? How are we gonna steal it?"' (Pistone 1987: 408). I suspect that for the audience, and for Mafia members (clearly over-lapping categories), the fantasy of the gangster is inevitably damaged by contact with everyday life. The boredom of hanging around with some fairly boring people in poorly decorated social clubs seems exciting because it can be imagined as an escape from 'real' work. Indeed, it is the articulation of everyday organizational lives as dull that helps us believe that being a wiseguy must be exciting, witty, sexy and just a little dangerous. As an economic outlaw, the Mafiosi is someone who is no longer shackled to the 9 to 5, and lives a life that evades power and celebrates freedom. But, take it from the son of someone who knows:

> On screen, the life of the Mafioso is glamorous and exciting, filled with danger and intense, dark-eyed women. In the real world, the gangster is an exhausted middle aged man who comes home at dawn to a disillusioned wife and a dog dish that needs cleaning.
>
> *(DeMeo 2003: 239)*

The wife, the child and the dog dish. They are the other that has now (at least partly) been included in the post-*Godfather* world, most particularly the world of *The Sopranos*. Now molls, guns and banter have been supplemented by wives, sisters and children. This is very often funny, and frightening, and sad, but it does mean that the world of the lost boys is becoming more like *Death of a Salesman*. When the Mafia becomes everyday life, the magic must disappear. Tony puts it beautifully – 'cunnilingus and psychiatry brought us to this' ('I Dream of Jeannie Cusamano'). He is a hard man gangster with bad dreams and rebellious teenagers, who sees a therapist for his panic attacks, and self-righteously justifies 'our thing' as the American Way. Tony Soprano is merely 'an all American everyman, the prototypical struggling businessman' (Gabbard 2002: 28).[15]

Hobsbawm, writing before the post-1970s glamorization of the Mafia, was clear that the proto-revolutionary tendencies of such organizations were highly limited. He was prepared to allow them into the Robin Hood category only in certain circumstances because, 'As we have seen, the chief tendency of *Mafia's* development is away from a social movement and towards at best a political pressure-group and at worst a complex of extortion rackets' (Hobsbawm 1965: 52). Once again, the 'fact' and the 'fiction' collide, but what Hobsbawm doesn't consider (probably because he is a historian) is what the popularity of representations of alternative business might be telling us about fantasy and imagination. Robin Hood, Jack Sparrow, Dick Turpin, Billy the Kid and Tony Soprano are characters that draw together history and the selling of tales about history. Crucially, they are also all figures who are defined by their struggle with authority, and who seek a way of life which is not overlooked and supervised by power.

In the next chapter, I will bring this catalogue of noble outlaws up to the present day, as well as thinking about the differences between heroes and gangs, and insiders and outsiders. It has been clear enough, over the past five chapters, that not all outlaws are the same, even if they share common features. What is the difference between jewel thieves and gangsters, bushrangers and bank robbers?

7

MODERN BANDITS

The film opens with a bizarre twin-cannoned motor vehicle resembling a cross between a tank and a submarine speeding though country lanes. The vehicle arrives at a farm, opens up, and draws in a number of ducks and hens (using reverse-action cinematography), at which point a gun battle ensues between the motor pirates and farm workers. Leaving the latter for dead, the vehicle speeds off, only to draw alongside a motor car, robbing the occupants whilst in motion. Meanwhile, the police have been alerted and give chase. The viewing copy ends abruptly as the vehicle careers into a pond.

(Doel and Clarke 2002: 148)

This is the English director Arthur Melbourne-Cooper's *Motor Pirates* from 1906. The new technology of the motor car is being understood in terms of the crimes it might allow. If robbers became mobile, how could they be stopped?[1] But at the same time, another novel technology, that of film, is being developed and sold. The people who paid to see *Motor Pirates* were often going to see images of law breaking, speed and violence. In films like Edwin Porter's 1903 *The Great Train Robbery*, the 1906 silent *Dick Turpin's Ride to York*, *Robin Hood and His Merry Men* from 1908, D. W. Griffiths's 1912 *The Musketeers of Pig Alley*, or the early 'heist' film *Alias Jimmy Valentine* (1915), the outlaw and criminal is inscribed into twentieth-century film from its beginnings. A fascination with outsiders who threaten the social order, and particularly its economic foundations, has been good business, and as ever it was also accompanied by moralizing voices who saw in the early moving pictures 'a direct incentive to crime, demonstrating, for instance, how a theft could be perpetrated' (from *The Times* in 1913, cited in Pearson 1983: 63).

The book so far, from Robin Hood to the Mafia, is broadly presented as a chronology, but it is a history of the present, too. Outlaw bands, pirates, smugglers, highwaymen, bandits, cowboys and organized criminals of various ethnicities form a fair chunk of twenty-first century popular culture. They may have their roots in history, but they easily made the jump into film, TV, comics, the internet and poseable action figures. In a sense, the consumer culture of the twentieth century onwards reproduced all these characters simultaneously, making their chronology a mere matter of variable *mise en scène*. In 1905, the Aldine Publishing Company had Buffalo Bill, Dick Turpin, Rob Roy, Jack Sheppard and Robin Hood libraries of penny dreadfuls. They constituted a parade of more or less noble robbers and, as each chapter has shown, all sorts of inter-textualities now became possible. It seems to me that Seal's (2009) 'outlaw hero cycle' both broadens and solidifies by the late nineteenth century. The similarities between a wide range of figures allow for comparisons and borrowings which provide a kind of 'grammar' for the outlaw, a set of combinatorial possibilities involving clothing, motive, weaponry, setting and so on. As a result, many newer examples of outlaws are then almost inevitably understood through a frame which is already well established.

This chapter brings the story up to date and tries to place some preliminary order on these disordered characters. Whilst recognizing the porosity and imprecision of all boundaries, I believe that we can think about the outlaw in at least two dimensions. The first is whether we are seeing a presentation of heroic individualism or some sort of collective. Sometimes, as with the highwaymen, the emphasis is on the character of the single individual, alone with their bravery and romantic intensity. Other traditions spend more time on the idea of the group – mob, gang, band[2] – which provides an alternative form of sociality and economic life for its members. The notable individuals within the group might sometimes withdraw into melancholic musing, like Schiller's Karl Moor, Byron's Conrad or Michael Corleone, but more often they are the jolly and smart goodfellows who inspire the merry men. Setting aside the outlaws with an earlier ancestry covered in the first half of this book, the twentieth century seems to produce more representations of groups than individuals. As we will see in this chapter, a major form is the development of corporate versions of organized crime as an alternative form of economic life bound by different codes and symbols – the Mafia, the Yakuza, the Hell's Angels and so on.

The second dimension is one that relates to the urbanization that shapes the idea of the criminal from the eighteenth century onwards. The earliest outlaws inhabited the far-away places – mountains, seas and forests – but the urban outlaw comes to live in our midst, hidden right in front of us. The idea of disguise, a common enough trope for many tricksters, becomes even more relevant as the jewel thief rejoins the party after the crime or the gang slips away into the alley. As we have already seen, the involution of the outside then produces some complex spaces – prisons, slums and clubhouses, for example – in which the enclosure can be understood as a kind of escape, a freedom from interference. Apart from the endless reproduction of the 'classical' outlaws – merry men, pirates and so on – the twentieth century seems to produce more insiders than outsiders.

Perhaps the underworlds of the city become more convincing backdrops than wild places for a population who only see the country from the windows of their motor car. As we will see below, if threatened, the outlaw might flee from the city, but they are just as likely to flee to another city using the planes, trains and automobiles that also allow for them to be mobile within and between states.

So it seems to me that the dominant form of outlaw from the late nineteenth century onwards is the organized criminal as a member of a group that hides on the mean streets of the city. Despite this, we can still see echoes of the romantic outsider and the individual noble robbers, and it is with these that we will begin.

Noble individuals

As we saw with the trajectory of Robin Hood, to make an outlaw noble, it helps to make him a noble. So a castrating outlaw becomes the Earl of Huntingdon, and his motives both patriotic and redistributive. The idea of the gentleman robber, ever ready with a winning smile, a witty quip and courtly generosity can be found in many different guises, but a particularly clear one is the idea of the upper-class burglar. In E. W. Hornung's 25 late nineteenth-century 'Raffles' short stories, the English class system is clearly used in order to impute non-financial motives to a gentleman and his old school chum Harry 'Bunny' Manders as his initially unwilling accomplice. Arthur J. Raffles is charming, funny and clever, has played cricket as a spin bowler for England, and turns these cultural assets to robbing the rich, almost always in order to serve some higher purpose, vaguely defined. In the first story 'The Ides of March' from 1898, when Bunny realizes what he is involved in, he wants to be disgusted by Raffles but can't manage it:

> My blood froze. My heart sickened. My brain whirled. How I had liked this villain! How I had admired him! Now my liking and admiration must turn to loathing and disgust. I waited for the change. I longed to feel it in my heart. But − I longed and waited in vain!
>
> *(Hornung 1898)*

Raffles deploys his justification for stealing pocketfuls of diamonds in describing his first burglary.

> I never meant it for anything more, but I'd tasted blood, and it was all over with me. Why should I work when I could steal? Why settle down to some humdrum uncongenial billet, when excitement, romance, danger, and a decent living were all going begging together? Of course, it's very wrong, but we can't all be moralists, and the distribution of wealth is very wrong to begin with.
>
> *(Hornung 1898)*

Despite such acute economic analysis, the stories are not usually exercises in swashbuckling redistribution. As George Orwell notes in his 1944 essay, 'Raffles and Miss Blandish', Raffles is only interesting because of the seeming contradiction between his elevated social status and his criminal behaviour, not because he is a 'good' character. Raffles and Bunny do steal from the rich, rarely engage in violence and would never steal from their hosts at a weekend party at some splendid country mansion – though believe it is perfectly reasonable to steal from the other guests. They charm us because they dress well, understand that certain things are 'not done', and get into some splendid scrapes which set the blood rushing. They steal because it is exciting, and the people and places they steal from (museums, the wealthy on a cruise, dowagers with too much jewellery, as well as assorted cads and rotters) won't really miss it. This is the English highwayman in a spiffing dinner jacket using any number of cunning disguises and accents to engage in sportsman-like japes. Importantly, in the early stories, Raffles is the 'Amateur Cracksman', as opposed to the working-class 'professors' who are in it for the money. It is his lack of economic need which sets him apart from the common professional thief, as well as an occasional brooding darkness in his character. The later stories change focus, with Bunny returning from a prison sentence to find Raffles in disguise and in hiding. They both then have to earn a living from theft and continually evade the law, closer to the professors than they might like.

The Raffles character first appeared in film in 1905, and since then there have been five more films, two TV movies and a TV series. He also became a character in pulp novels by Philip Atkey, writing under the pseudonym Barry Perowne, from the 1930s onwards, but more importantly, has become a recognizable character type in many films as the charming rogue who steals in order to punish the greedy and demonstrate his cunning and bravery. Raffles also found another, much longer life under the pseudonym Lord Lister, a master thief in German pulp magazines which initially ran for 110 weekly issues from 1908–10. Its popularity was such that there were Lord Lister stories – both original and in translation – published in Danish, Dutch, Italian and French, as well as in Malaysia, Indonesia, Argentina, Brazil, Russia and Turkey over the next 60 years. In some of the stories, initially the French ones, Lord Lister's real name changes from Raffles to John C. Sinclair (with a pseudonym of Lord William Aberdeen), but the idea of a charming aristocrat is central to all the versions. Lister is a master of disguise, a doctor who can cure the sick and speak many languages. He uses theft to punish the bad, reward the good and protect the poor, and is ably assisted by a variety of jolly loyal friends and skilled man servants.

In French, a character with very similar features was Arsène Lupin. In the 20 volumes written by Maurice Leblanc from 1905–39, this gentleman thief defeats many villains (including the Germans) and outwits the law (sometimes personified as an English detective called Herlock Sholmes). At least 20 French, English, Spanish and Japanese films have been made, as well as five TV shows, four stage adaptations and several comics and animations. After Leblanc's death in

1941, the character regularly re-appeared in new stories, sometimes as himself, sometimes with a slightly different name. So typified had this character become by then that a version of the gentleman thief could feature in any number of contexts, as a charismatic and charming confidence man in a heist movie such as *The Thomas Crown Affair* (1968 and 1999), for example, but it is always their class position and charm which sets them apart from the common outlaw. In the 1966 film *How to Steal a Million*, the burglar is the young and very beautiful Peter O'Toole:

> Audrey Hepburn: 'For a burglar, you're not very brave are you?'
> Peter O'Toole: 'I'm a society burglar. I don't expect people to rush around shooting me.'

Class becomes an expression of chivalric values, such as those of the well-dressed pirate captain or dancing highwayman. In older European societies, the idea of an upper-class outlaw was somehow more possible, as the examples of Raffles, Lister and Lupin illustrate. In frontier societies, such as the Wild West, aspects of such behaviour were both less likely and more suspicious. As we saw in chapter five, the English gentleman was unlikely to be a figure that carried with him any virtues in Tombstone, being rather too well dressed and talkative, but courtly manners could still matter in distinguishing the noble robber from the ignoble one. As Peter Carey makes Ned Kelly say to his daughter in his novel *The True History of the Kelly Gang*:

> In the heat of the furnace metals change their nature in olden days they could make gold from lead. Wait to see what more there is to hear my daughter for in the end we poor uneducated people will all be made noble in the fire.
>
> *(2001: 305)*

Bill Miner, for example, 'the gentleman robber', served several prison sentences in Canada and the USA in the early twentieth century for stagecoach and train robberies. He was said to be unfailingly polite to his victims and the police. Despite the fact that he was a US citizen, his celebrity status in British Columbia was such that the train tracks were thronged with his supporters as he was being taken to jail in 1904. Since then, a restaurant chain has decorated its walls with his picture and named a pie after him,[3] and a film, *The Grey Fox*, was made in 1983. In a sense, manners then become a piece of evidence about character. Like Major Stede Bonnet, Captain Roberts, Claude Du Vall, James MacLaine and Black Bart the Po8, Miner becomes a figure who was doing his best to be good in some difficult circumstances. So the fact that 'a gentleman bandit' never shot anyone, or never robbed his hosts, or only stole from those who could afford it, then becomes comprehensible in terms of the immorality of others – both 'real' robbers and the wealthy. This is a relative judgement, but a powerful one nonetheless.

Another way of achieving a similar effect is to have a back-story of upbringing or circumstances which show us how an innocent was driven to extreme measures. This would usually be to paint the powerful as somehow the cause of the suffering or death of friends and relatives, or the architects of an unjust social order. There are plenty of examples of such figures in the Wild West, particularly relating to the injustices of the post-Civil War period and the incursions of Eastern industrialism, but a contemporaneous example would be Australian bushrangers such as Captain Thunderbolt. Frederick 'Thunderbolt' Ward was supposed never to have shot at anyone, even the police, during a career as a horse thief and highwayman in New South Wales from the mid-1850s to 1870 when he was shot dead during a robbery. He would never rob from women, and would return money to those who needed it more than he did. A couplet said to have been composed and used by Ward went:

> My name is Frederick Ward, I am a native of this isle;
> I rob the rich to feed the poor and make the children smile.
>
> *(Seal 1996: 143)*

Three hundred people viewed his dead body, but in typical trickster fashion, some accounts suggest that it was an uncle of his who was killed, and that he actually emigrated to the USA, even turning up at the funeral disguised as a woman to see his uncle buried. His justified criminality began when another uncle was drowned whilst crossing a river in flood on instructions from the management of the Tocal Cattle Station. Thunderbolt, allegedly wanting retribution, was arrested stealing cattle from Tocal 18 months later. In 1863, he escaped from the Cockatoo Island prison and commenced on seven years of bush ranging during which he committed over 200 robberies on his trusty horse 'Combo', stashing his earnings in caves where (some say) the money is to this day.

Thunderbolt is one amongst many similar stories of Australian outlaws at a time when British colonial rule was widely regarded to be cruel and unjust. Bushrangers such as Ben Hall, Jack Donohoe, Frank Gardiner and, most famously, Ned Kelly, have very similar myths associated with them (Seal 1996: 119, *passim*). The 1860s ballad 'The Wild Colonial Boy' captures this collective sense of a defiant opposition to the landed classes, and an eventual death at the hands of the authorities. In Kelly's case, his hanging in 1880 was preceded by a story of a poor Irish-Australian background shaped by oppression by the British.[4] His father was transported for unknown crimes and, after imprisonment on charges of cattle stealing, died when Ned was 11 years old. The Kelly family were then subject to continual harassment by the law, often with dubious cause, with various members of the family (including Ned) spending time in jail. Ned was legally declared an outlaw (as Hall had been) after killing three policemen who had been sent to hunt him down, and set to robbing banks. During one bank robbery, Ned was supposed to have commented that the banks were crushing the poor working man, and went on to burn the mortgages and ledgers that he found (Seal 1996: 157). He also wrote a long letter explaining why he had been driven to crime and cementing an account of heroic resistance, corrupt police and a punitive legal system, all against the back drop of ethnic, religious and class oppression. As Carey makes Ned say, 'you must also remember your ancestors would not kowtow to no one and this were a fine rare thing in a colony made specifically to have poor men bow down to their gaolers' (2001: 181). Kelly, whose favourite book was supposed to be *Lorna Doone*, is always courteous to those he robs, and more sinned against than sinning. The final battle, with Kelly's gang famously armoured, ended up with the rest of the gang killed by the police, and Kelly himself tried for murder by Sir Redmond Barry, a hanging judge who died of a carbuncle on his neck 12 days after Kelly was hung. In pronouncing the sentence, the judge said:

> An offence of the kind that you stand accused of is not of an ordinary character … A party of men took up arms against society, organized as it was for mutual protection and regard for the law. … Unfortunately, in a new community, where society was not bound together as closely as it should be, there was a class which looked upon the perpetrators of those crimes as heroes. … There seemed to be a spell cast over the people of this particular district, which I can only attribute either to sympathy with crime or dread of the consequences of doing their duty.
>
> *(in Seal 1996: 161)*

Kelly, like all good outlaws, refused to bow his head and apologize. He was defiant all the way through and tried to argue his case, refusing the judgement of authority to the very last. There was great press interest in the trial, photographs were taken and a petition to spare Kelly's life gathered 30,000 signatures. A century later, the armour, a skull, a revolver and a death mask provide relics for contemporary displays and controversy. The first film dates from 1906, the 60-minute *The Story of the Kelly Gang*,[5] with at least nine more films and a TV series made since. Kelly has also become Australia's Robin Hood, easily reproducible in songs, pot-boiling novels, plays and boys' comics, cartoons, paintings, stamps and so on as variously a republican, a man who knew the land, a brave leader of brave men, an honest and down-to-earth Australian, and a champion of the underdog – even the aboriginal (Seal 1996: 167, *passim*).

In some sense, Kelly, as well as Raffles, Lupin, Miner, Ward and others, inherit an image of the noble robber in which the individual is pitted against an unjust social order. Their chivalry comes from a certain idea of manners and fair treatment, but also from a context of inequality, whether that be the jewels of the wealthy dowager, or the privileges of the colonial elite. However, as I suggested earlier, the figure of the individual is comparatively rare in the modern period. Kelly was, after all, sometimes a member of a small gang, too, even though his individual fame far exceeds that of the idea of the collective. In the next section, we will look at the outlaw who is more clearly part of a gang – a hero who is part of a group.

Gang heroes

The distinction here is whether the individual or the gang are the dominant terms, yet this is not always clear. Robin Hood is an individual, but clearly associated with a gang made up of other individuals who could be referred to collectively as the merry men. Other gangs – the Mafia, Yakuza, Triads, Tong, Yardies and so on – are comprehensible without referring to particular individuals, even though there are plenty of examples of such people who can act as exemplars of their way of life. So perhaps we can refer to some forms of crime as an alternative organization, whilst others appear to be examples of organizations led by charismatic outlaw heroes. If the criminal gang appears to represent an alternative collective way of life within the city – as we saw with the Mafia in the previous chapter – then the gang led by a charismatic individual seems to inherit traces of the romantic individual, struggling against circumstances and possessed of an acuity that most of us lack.

The US crime wave of the 1930s falls fairly neatly into a Western outlaw model of gangs with leaders and hideouts, though the hideouts are often in the city, too. This is in part related to their mobility, because whilst the FBI and Eliot Ness[6] had fought against Capone in the city, 'automobile bandits' such as John Dillinger, Pretty Boy Floyd and Bonnie and Clyde were highly mobile. Powerful new cars with V8 engines and the 800 bullet per minute Thompson submachine gun meant that they could outrun and outgun the authorities (Burrough 2005: 17). The idea of a clear division of labour for robbing banks, combined with a language for 'casing' the 'jug', setting explosives, organizing the 'git' and so on provided fantastic copy for newspapers, as it had since the earliest versions of the cant of the London underworld. This was particularly true in a context when the banks were hardly loved, being the representatives of robber-baron capital throughout the depression. Banks foreclosed on mortgages and threw good people into poverty and dustbowl starvation. The final couplets of Woodie Guthrie's (1939) song 'Pretty Boy Floyd' captures this nicely:

> Well, as through the world I've rambled, I've seen lots of funny men.
> Some rob you with a six gun, some with a fountain pen.
> As through this world you ramble, as through this world you roam
> You'll never see an outlaw drive a family from its home.

During 1933 and 1934, newspapers were full of tales of bandits and gangs. Charles Arthur Floyd, an Oklahoma boy shaped by the depression and victimized by the police, became a celebrity in early 1932 with tales of killing policemen and robbing banks. The *Muskogee Daily Phoenix* compared him to Billy the Kid, and the legend rapidly spread. Papers were full of sightings and speculation, even publishing a letter he wrote to the governor of Oklahoma pleading for the reward for his capture to be withdrawn because 'I have robbed no one but the monied men' (Burrough 2005: 20–1). Also in the news were Clyde Barrow and Bonnie Parker,[7] a star-crossed couple with a back story of poverty and aspiration, who drove around robbing gas stations and drugstores; 'Baby Face' Nelson, a laughing maniac who appeared to be playing a character from James Cagney's 1931 film *Public Enemy*; the joking 'Machine Gun' Kelly; and Ma Barker, the supposed leader of the Barker-Karpis gang. According to most accounts, Ma Barker was barely capable of organizing dinner, let alone the kidnapping of wealthy bankers, but the press did not let the facts get in the way of a good story, and all the principals in the drama were provided with names and motivations which would ensure that readers kept buying. This was certainly true of the most famous robber of all – Dillinger.

John Dillinger was usually described as a gentleman criminal. He came from a solid middle-class family, and stories about him stressed that he dressed well and quipped with those that he robbed. Tales of his courtesy to women, telling gang members not to swear in front of them, for example, were common, and read by Dillinger himself. He was well aware of the importance of a good press, and often got it. Letters of support were printed in Indiana newspapers, one correspondent writing:

> Why should the law have wanted John Dillinger for bank robbery? He wasn't any worse than bankers or politicians who took the poor people's money. Dillinger did not rob poor people. He robbed those who became rich by robbing the poor. I am for Johnnie.
>
> *(in Burrough 2005: 165)*

When arrested in 1934, he told reporters that, as 'an expert in my business', he could 'play tag' with the police as much as he liked because they were 'like fox hounds that don't know what's going on. … Right now none of those smart-aleck coppers have got a bit of evidence that I killed anybody or robbed any bank' (op. cit., 204). Crowds thronged to where he was being held and tried, and the press scribbled down stories of his chivalry and wit. His lawyers (defence and prosecution) played to the gallery, too, perhaps sensing that their reputations could be made in the media spotlight. After escaping from prison by using a wooden gun, he was then sighted everywhere, crossing state lines before the cops got there, and associated with every crime, whether he was there or not. He was the well-groomed underdog, and popular support was so great that even President Roosevelt felt minded to complain about the romanticization of crime (op. cit., 345), just as his cousin had 40 years earlier when he claimed that the Robin Hood legend had a lot to answer for when it came to outlaws.

Apart from Kelly, all of the key figures of the post-depression crime wave were dead by the end of 1934, clothing and locks of hair cut off their dead bodies, huge crowds wanting to see the corpses, and front-page newspaper stories describing their bullet-ridden cars and bodies. Dillinger died in front of a cinema showing *Manhattan Melodrama*, starring Clark Gable as a gangster who comes good in the end, and passers-by dipped handkerchiefs in his blood. The film was immediately marketed by MGM using Dillinger's death and there were five thousand people at his funeral. Their stories had been shaped by a press eager to sell newspapers, and a public keen for melodramatic breakfast reading about ordinary people stealing from the rich and evading the sheriff's men. J. Edgar Hoover's 'comic opera cops' appeared to always be missing the outlaws, and ending up killing innocent bystanders, just as the Pinkertons had with the James Younger gang in the previous century. There is even evidence that the actions of the principal characters was shaped by precisely this sort of interaction between story and action. Burrough observes that a story about Clyde handing money back to an old man during a bank robbery saying, 'We don't want your money. We just want the bank's', suggested that Clyde had read an account of Dillinger saying and doing exactly the same thing during a robbery six weeks earlier (2005: 225).

On the other side of the law, and echoing Allan Pinkerton half a century previously, in 1933 Hoover brought in Courtney Ryley Cooper, a specialist in pulp crime stories, to write articles portraying the FBI director as a master detective. These may well have helped stimulate the rash of FBI-themed movies in the following year, the best known being Jimmy Cagney in *G-Men*, in which the forces of law and order overcome various public enemies (op. cit., 317). The *G-Men* movies have faded into history, but the films starring the gangsters have continued, with three featuring Bonnie and Clyde – including a star-studded 1967 one with Faye Dunaway and Warren Beatty – and several films each for all the major characters of the 1930s crimewave. Most recently, *Public Enemies* (2009) reprised the Dillinger story with Johnny Depp in the lead role for a contemporary audience by now familiar with a long list of 'heist' or 'caper' films in which a group of charming misfits rob someone who doesn't really deserve to have the money. The remakes of the 1960 *Oceans 11* in 2001 (with two sequels) and of the 1969 *Italian Job* in 2003 testify to the continuing popularity of the gang with heroes genre. Whilst some versions can be noir (such as the 1956 *The Killing*), comedy (*Quick Change* from 1990) or thriller (*The Score*, 2001), contemporary versions tend to be extraordinarily stylish vehicles for an all-star cast and a saleable soundtrack. Typically they will feature some interesting new technology, cunning disguises, precise timing and a broad sympathy with the sparkling-eyed rogues. Sometimes they get away with it and are sitting on an aeroplane drinking champagne at the end. Sometimes they don't, but there is usually a pile of cash waiting for them in a safety deposit box for when they come out of prison.

These are usually gang films, in the sense that the job needs a group of people to pull it off, but they are as much about the principal characters as well. Like the merry men or the pirate band, they are given cohesion and direction by someone with charm and a different understanding of conventional morality.

It may not be as glamorous as Danny Ocean robbing Las Vegas casinos, but in the British context, an obvious parallel is with Ronald and Reginald Kray, two London gang leaders from the 1960s who dressed well, gave money to the families of associates in prison, and courted journalists, politicians and show business and sporting celebrities with much skill. The press gleefully recounted a combination of playboy manners, charitable events, working-class family values and a string of West End nightclubs and country houses where celebrities mixed with 'characters' from the East End. Gangsters in residence for swinging London, they loved their mother Violet and were always kind to their friends. Just as well known was the fact that they were brutal enforcers with anyone who crossed them, earning money for 'The Firm' through protection rackets, extortion and fraud. The entanglements between the media and the Krays are endless. The 1963 film *Sparrows Can't Sing* was filmed in the East End, some of it at the Krays' 'Kentucky Club', and according to the Assistant Director Peter Medak, the production company paid protection money to the brothers. The coverage of Reggie's wedding in 1965 highlighted the famous boxers in the congregation, the gleaming Rolls-Royces outside and the images were captured by David Bailey – photographer to the stars. As part of the construction of their identity, it also seems fairly evident that Ronnie and Reggie were attempting to dress and talk like Capone, muttering just like screen gangsters, driving big American cars and wearing well-made suits with expensive accessories (Pearson 1995: 77). John Pearson's book on the Krays was originally commissioned by the publisher McGraw-Hill in 1967 at a request of the brothers via 'Mafia interests' in New York (op. cit., 7). Reggie and his new wife even met George Raft, ex-gangster and Hollywood star, when he was visiting London.

The romantic myth of the outsider clearly continues in their presentation of themselves. As one of them says to Pearson, in an interview quote which could have been scripted for *The Sopranos* or *The Italian Job*,

> Ordinary straight life's just not for the likes of us. That's why we're in a separate world. You see, we get bored with most of the stupid things straight people seem to enjoy, when they could be out drinking or doing a spot of villainy. What's the best thing in life? Getting money. And after that? Spending it.
>
> *(in Pearson 1995: 52)*

This self-presentation of villains as different, and probably better, than ordinary people is mirrored by another similarity – the slightly contradictory claim that organized crime and the organized economy are morally equivalent anyway, whatever the official line might be:

> What is straight business anyhow? Be honest. It's just a bloody racket, same as our way of life. All of that keeping in with the right people, going to the proper school, an' knowing how much you can fiddle an' get away with.

> All of those lawyers and accountants to squeeze you round the law. What's all of it except one great big bloody racket?
>
> *(op. cit., 87)*

Perhaps becoming somebody is better than being nobody, and all somebodies have to engage in behaviour which ordinary people might condemn. Byron's Conrad would agree with that, even if Ronnie and Reggie might translate that into the price of 'respect' and 'reputation'.

In prison after 1969, the Kray twins continued to benefit from their celebrity, though the money was supposed to be held in trust by others. The idea that they looked after the poor – as what Pearson calls 'an East End Benevolent Society' – and kept the streets clear of nastier forms of crime has become standard stories about these two lovely but misunderstood boys (op.cit., 324). And these accounts sell well, with four ghost-written joint or single autobiographies – *Our Story*, *A Way of Life*, *Born Fighter* and *My Story* – a film, *The Krays*, made in 1990 (and directed by Peter Medak), and endless books about them and stories about their marriages and divorces in the press. They continued to benefit financially from many of these projects, even though the money had to be held in trust. Ronnie died in 1995, and Reggie in 2000, but towards the end of the 2000s Kray memorabilia was regularly going on sale, including suits and cufflinks, paintings and letters.

In the film, Ronnie Kray – played by the Spandau Ballet member Gary Kemp – muses that 'glamour is fear', in order to explain why everyone admired him. His sparkle derived from the fact that he was capable of generating terror, and this equation has worked nicely for many modern criminals who have written about their hard childhoods and bloody pasts in criminal gangs. Whilst the Krays were painting away in jail, John McVicar, a violent English armed robber who escaped from prison many times, published his *McVicar by Himself* (1974), which became a film in 1980 with The Who's Roger Daltrey starring as McVicar. Jimmy Boyle, a Scottish gangland murderer, wrote *A Sense of Freedom* in 1977, which became a film two years later. Mark Brandon 'Chopper' Read's 1991 *Chopper: From the Inside* was turned into the film *Chopper* in 2000, a story of a murderous Australian gang member. In all these cases, one account is that these are morality tales about what happens if you wander away from the straight and narrow, yet the books and films are also celebrations of the gritty authenticity of salt-of-the-earth characters. These are men who will take no shit, who are witty and honest, and who end up using their celebrity to develop writing careers as a journalist, poet and novelist respectively. Others, like 'Mad' Frankie Fraser, Ronnie Biggs and Dave Courtney, have become C-list media commentators and chat show guests. At the same time as they refuse to condone the violence of their youths, they show that crime can pay, as long as you stick to tough working-class and masculine values.

Dillinger and the Krays have gangs, but they aren't gangs. The collective is a condition of their possibility, but their characteristics are pretty much the same as that of the romantic outlaw. However, the gang itself has become more than merely a context for crime. As the chapter on the Mafia showed, the idea of a group of organized criminals who live a life in the shadows of the city has become an account which has continuities beyond any particular individual. We first met this story in stories about sixteenth-century London, and as it moves across the Atlantic it provides the precursors of the 'organized' criminal gangs of the twentieth century. Just as capitalism was becoming organized into corporations and cartels, so were alternative economies based on violence becoming told and sold as structured and strange.

The organized gang

The mythologization of the gang in general terms needs to be placed in a long tradition of interest in strange ways of life and secret societies, and though it is related to the myth of the outlaw, it is not quite the same. In an 1850 report on New York written by Police Chief George W. Matsell, he listed a series of gangs with exotically dangerous names – the Daybreak Boys, the Buckaroos, the Hookers, the Swamp Angels, the Slaughter Housers, the Patsy Conroys and the Border Gang (Sante 1998: 204). These gangs were unified and divided by ethnicity, occupation or territory, and then further defined themselves by the clothes that they wore, the weapons they used or the language they spoke. So the Plug Uglies wore big plug hats stuffed with leather and wool, whilst the Shirt Tails left their shirt tails out. According to contemporary accounts, battles would last for days, deaths were frequent and the police or army would have a difficult job to get the city back under control. Often enough, the gangs would also engage in specific economic activities, as river pirates, robbing sailors or new immigrants, providing security services for certain establishments (the speciality of the Dead Rabbits) or turning out votes on election day (as did the Bowery Boys). The Tong, a US version of the Triads, began in the California goldfields in the 1860s and provided splendid material for a newspaper 'horrors of Chinatown' piece to add to all the other accounts of the depraved activities of various ethnic groups (Sante 1998: 143, *passim*). Herbert Asbury's *Gangs of New York* from 1927 was building on a long tradition, one that painted the city as a wild place of 'rookeries', 'warrens' and 'ghettos', full of fears but entirely seductive, too.

London gangs had been described in similar ways for centuries. John Gay's play *The Mohocks* (1712) had satirized an early version of this terror, with accounts of organized criminal gangs – the Dead Boys, Scowrers, Hawcubites and so on. Pierce Egan, who wrote *Robin Hood and Little John* penny dreadfuls in the 1830s, also wrote *Life in London* sketches with descriptions of 'b'hoys' and 'g'hals' dressed to impress and engaged in low-level crime. Half a century later, as Geoffrey Pearson shows, the 'hooligan'[8] moral panic of the 1890s was written up in similar terms, with stories of boys with big boots, caps and scarves fighting each other in the streets, or setting on old ladies and any passers-by they didn't like the look of (1983: 75, *passim*). The 'Lion Boys', the 'Pistol Gang', the 'Velvet Cap Gang' and even the 'Dick Turpin Gang' were featured in newspapers regularly during the summer of 1898. In Australia, a parallel term was the 'Larrikin', a type who also seemed to wear scarves, heavy boots, belts with big buckles and stylish hats. Gangs were also often associated with particular forms of illegal activity, such as the female 'Forty Elephants' or 'Forty Thieves' gang mentioned in London newspapers from 1873. It allegedly concentrated on shoplifting, with a sideline in blackmail after seduction, with women dressing in specially tailored clothes and being organized by 'queen' Diamond Annie. Their lavish parties and decadent living echoed that of the 1920s aristocrats, and the gang was supposed to have lasted until the 1950s (McDonald 2010).

The naming of gangs and people appeared to be a tremendous way to sell newspapers. Back in New York, the Leslie gang, led by Western George, often referred to in the press as 'King of the Bank Robbers' was comprised of veterans of previous gangs with predictably criminal names – Red Leary, Shang Draper (the panel-house king), Worcester Sam Perris and Banjo Pete Emerson (Sante 1998: 208). Allegedly, they were held in high esteem and estimates of their profits varied between $7 and $12 million in the 1860s and 1870s. Other gangs appear to have focussed on particular economic specialisms, such as the Bliss Bank Ring, the forgers of Chester McLaughlin's Valentine Ring, 'General' Abe Greenthal's pickpocket ring, or the violence for cash practiced by the Whyos. Sante reproduces 'a take-out menu of Whyo services' (op. cit., 215):

Punching	$2
Both eyes blacked	$4
Nose and jaw broke	$10
Jacked out	$15
Ear chawed off	$15
Leg or arm broke	$19
Shot in leg	$25
Stab	$25
Doing the big job	$100 and up

Important for accounts of these gangs, whether then or for Asbury writing in the 1920s or Sante in the 1990s, are baroque and exotic stories about what they did and wore – Humpty Jackson who used to carry copies of Voltaire, Spencer, Darwin and Huxley; Spanish Louie who carried two colts and two eight-inch knives, and wore all black, topped off with a black sombrero; or the phenomenally ugly Monk Easterman, who had a collection of 500 pigeons and 100 cats (Sante 1998: 218–20).

Sante concludes that accounts of New York gang culture show how violence and business gradually become intertwined: how Jews and Italians replace the Irish, but blacks and Germans are barely mentioned; how the stories move from being about a faceless mob to being a series of legends about individuals; and how 'whimsical' their self-presentation often seemed to be.

One conclusion might be that the gangs were permitted to thrive, to kill each other and to drink themselves to death, by authorities who were mostly concerned with containing their activities and would gladly allow the gangs to act as the agents of natural selection in the slums. The gangs repaid this courtesy by demonstrating their mingled respect and derision for the world outside their turf through parody: parody of order, parody of law, parody of commerce, parody of progress.

(Sante 1998: 235)

During the twentieth century the parodies continued, with all the irony which that implied, but the economics seems to have ceased to be a parody on the basis of sheer scale and entanglement with globalizing commerce. At this point, the gang becomes called organized crime, as if its previous manifestations were somehow not organized enough to deserve such a serious label.

In 1971, the criminologist Mary McIntosh suggested that urbanization and industrialization produces structural changes in the organization of crime. The 'craft' thieving which develops with the growth of the urban required anonymity in theft and disposal, and an individual or small gang could earn enough to live by robbing people and dwellings with relatively little likelihood of capture. However, the 'project' theft which develops from the nineteenth century onwards involves hardened targets – banks, lorries, trains, safes and so on. Larger numbers of people, including specialists, are required, and a more complex division of labour and language is produced by the loose groupings that are needed to arrange such crimes. Of course, this sort of 'heist' crime is only one aspect of the economics of organized criminals, with the trading of alcohol, cigarettes, drugs, sex and so on being a lucrative and largely predictable business model which requires a complex and global procurement, storage and distribution network. Hobbs, 30 years later, concludes that the organizational structure of crime is most like the family business, despite 'the enduring myth of the London underworld' (1997, 2001). But whether business or counter culture, and whatever the relation between fact and fiction, these myths can be sold for money.

Accounts of the culture and economics of organized crime have been ubiquitous since the early twentieth century. As we saw in the previous chapter, the most celebrated in the global north are probably the Mafia, but there are plenty of others worldwide. Just to take one example, the Yakuza of Japan, according to Southwell (2006: 58), have 150,000 members in 2,000 gangs. With origin stories dating back to the seventeenth century, the Yakuza were (like the Mafia) given considerable inadvertent assistance in the black market and anti-communist aftermath of the Second World War. Accounts of their patriarchal hierarchy, strict rules of deference in behaviour, the severing of fingers as punishments for disloyalty, and full body tattoos all stress the idea that they are a society within a society (Saga 1995). They recruit from social groups who would normally be regarded as low status – motorcycle gangs such as the Bozozoku, Korean migrants, orphans, bastards, those rejected by their families and the *burakumin* underclass

(Glenny 2009: 344). The economics are also impressive, with the largest Yakuza clan, the Yamaguchi-Gumi, estimated at a turnover of $50 billion a year (Southwell 2006: 61). A great deal of money was also being made selling Yakuza films, for 30 years from the 1960s to 1990s, the Japanese equivalent of the Western. About 100 a year were being produced in the 1970s, and the story line mainly saw the weak and oppressed being helped by a group of outlaws with a highly ritualized code of honour. *Shura no Mure* (*A Band of Daredevils*, 1984) is the Yakuza equivalent of *The Godfather*, being the story of Kakuji Inagawa, the founder of the Inagawa-Kai clan. Needless to say, the clans were heavily involved in the financing and production of these films, and also provided an enthusiastic audience for flattering descriptions of their activities. A film that was less flattering, Juzo Itami's 1992 *Minbo no Onna* (*Mob Woman*) about Yakuza extortion, resulted in a punishment beating and the director's eventual suicide (Gambetta 2009: 252).

The list of other gangs and organized criminal societies who have been variously celebrated and excoriated in just about every form of media imaginable is huge, so I will restrict myself to mentioning some of the better-known examples (Southwell 2006, Glenny 2009). The Chinese Triads (called the Tong in North America) have for over a century been the archetype for Oriental inscrutability, selling opium to the stupid Westerners whilst smiling and pretending incomprehension. In fiction, they were famously presented as Sax Rohmer's 'Celestial Order of the Si-Fan', a fiendish and secretive organization led by the cerebral Dr Fu Manchu. More recently, the wealthy and violent Russian Organizatsiya, or Mafiya, are now supposedly connected to the 'vory-v-zakone' code of prisoners' honour which involves a complex tattoo code like that of the Yakuza. Iconic in 1960s popular culture are the US and Scandinavian biker gangs such as the Hell's Angels, Bandidos and the Outlaws. In New Zealand, some of these groups have now been appropriated by Maori, such as the Mongrel Mob and Black Power. Self-consciously Hispanic groups such as La Eme and Nuestra Familia are similarly important in the southern USA and Mexico. In central America, drug cartels such as the Cali and the Medellin have become famous, the latter led by Pablo Escobar, at one time the richest criminal in history, owner of a private zoo, and generous benefactor to poor Columbians (Bowden 2001). The 'rude boy' culture of Kingston Jamaica provides a Stagolee mythology for Yardies and Possies. In Brazil, 'The Commands' deal drugs, act as an unofficial police force and provide social welfare in some of the poorest parts of urban slums. In India, Dawood Ibrahim's Mumbai-based D-Company (which he runs from Dubai) has gained massive profits and notoriety, in part because of complicity in radical Islamic terrorism, but just as importantly through its connections to Bollywood, with several films made about its activities and often celebrating the *dacoit*-like characteristics of its leader.

The list could easily go on, but the point is clear enough. The transformation of the urban gang member into the global networks of organized crime has not diminished their allure, either for those who write books and make films, or those who are attracted to a life lived by another law. The blurring of fact and fiction is again evident, with Vory tattoos becoming markers of criminality in popular film, gang leaders such as Christopher 'Dudas' Coke and his Shower Posse becoming local celebrities in Kingston, Jamaica,[9] and a Camorra boss naming his child Ivanhoe (Saviano 2008: 257). In all these examples, the content is more than just business – whether it involves forms of symbolism, a defence of a particular ethnicity or kin relation, the protection of the poor or a code of honour amongst thieves with distinctive forms of retribution. Whether these are justifiable and evidenced claims is not the point – they are told and sold by members and cultural intermediaries and certainly borrow from the outlaw hero cycle. In economic terms we might well conclude that they are simply ways of doing business on the other side of the law, but their mythology suggests more than that and adds some sort of moral-political justification to their activities. As a piece of Red Command graffiti in São Paulo said, 'the State is the biggest criminal for making us poor' (in Southwell 2006: 143).

Bandits now

Modern bandits inherit much from their older cousins, including a wide variety of justifications for alternative business. Some are very similar to the rural outlaw, with the Australian bushranger being the obvious example, whilst others reverse the class and context to become the 'gentleman burglar'. In both cases, some sense of non-economic motive is crucial to distinguishing such noble robbers from common ones. Kelly and Raffles are a little like two aspects of the post-seventeenth-century Robin Hood – a patriot resisting foreign occupation and a noble with a chivalric understanding of manners. Whilst these understandings do not disappear in the twentieth century, they do become more collective, and more urban. It is rarer to see heroic individuals and more common to see individuals as part of a group, or even to see them as representatives of a group. Tales of an urban underworld populated by wild gangs coalesce into tales of organized crime – a whispered network of guns, drugs and shipping containers that threaten our way of life, but which are traded in a counter culture of endless books, magazines, films, cartoons and books such as this.

The attractions of secret societies, both economic and cultural, are of interest here, but so too is the way in which conspiracy theories so often posit the state, big business and organized crime as symmetrical (Parish and Parker 2001). Indeed, it could be suggested that if conspiracy theory tells us something about popular fears, then organized crime is no worse than any other form of organization – whether that be global capitalism or the self-protecting labyrinth of state bureaucracy. At least, as Tony Soprano might say, the organized criminal is honest about what he does, just as Raffles, Ned Kelly and Dillinger are brave and honest enough to seek a life less ordinary and try to set the world to rights.

In the next chapter, I will bring together these accounts of 800 years of economic outlaws and alternative business in order to make a claim about their importance for an understanding of contemporary culture, economy and resistance. It is clear enough that all these characters have mattered to a lot of people for rather a long time. Their representations have been bought and sold since Robin, but perhaps this is now a matter of yellowing history, and tells us nothing about the political concerns of the present age. Does Captain Jack Sparrow have anything to say to the world of email and offices, Big Macs and cheap flights to the sun?

8

THE COUNTER CULTURE AND ORGANIZATION

Thought for the day ...
Life at work is like a tree full of monkeys, all on different limbs and at different
levels. Some monkeys are climbing up, some down. The monkeys on top look
down and see a tree full of smiling faces. The monkeys on the bottom look up and
see nothing but assholes.

(spam email from 2005)

In this chapter, I want to situate the contemporary outlaw within an understanding of a 'counter culture' to organization and economy that I think we
find in popular culture more generally. I'm going to suggest that outlaw myths
are important places to find the counter culture, but they are not the only
place, hence this chapter. In what follows, I will try to make an argument
which broadly situates the popular as opposed to power. In some ways this
is an uncontentious argument because, as I suggested in chapter one, many
people writing about culture would take that as given. My problem is that
most of the time they ignore organization and economy, and assume that
resistance is a cultural matter. But Robin Hood and his Merry Men are commenting on organization and economy, at the same time that their many representations have been traded for cash. It is simply not possible to pull culture and
economy apart, because actual examples already show them to be entangled in
complex ways.

Consider, for example, a little book titled *The Little Book of Management Bollocks*
(Beaton 2001). Priced at £2.99, it is a contemporary chapbook, designed to
be displayed next to the till in a book or gift shop and bought as an impulse
purchase. It contains 100 or so satires of management nostrums, and is presumably
the sort of thing that you might imagine giving to one of your colleagues at work
in order to laugh at the antics of your managers. For example,

MOTIVATION #1
It is often assumed that money is the only motivational factor.
Wrong.
Fear is also important.
Save money. Use fear.

You might also give them a coffee cup with 'Thank God It's Friday', rear view mirrors for their PC, a '52 ways to have fun at work' pack of cards, a postcard that suggests, 'You Don't Have to be Mad to Work Here, but It Helps', office voodoo kit, or David Brent screensaver. Telling the boss to stick it, in a wide variety of ways, is the small act of revolution which makes all these artefacts interesting. So in this chapter I will argue that the assumption that work is boring and degrading, and that escaping from it can be fun, reflects a wider culture that simultaneously celebrates and denigrates work and organizations, and endlessly attempts to prick the pomposities of the powerful. Or, to put it another way, the 'culture of organization' is continually being contested by the 'counter culture of organization' (see also Ackroyd and Thompson 1999: 99). As with the general argument about outlaws, I will argue that both elements call their other into being, like a kind of shadow, or perhaps the return of that which has been repressed. In order to make this argument, I will look at the sort of artefacts that decorate offices and relate these things to a wide variety of popular representations of work organizations which are often found in advertising, TV programmes, websites and so on. All are meant to provoke a little ironic laugh, perhaps a shared smile. I will characterize all of these representations as being elements of this counter culture, an enduring and sustained cynicism concerning the organized worlds that organized people inhabit. I think that my outlaws are another part of this counter culture, and perhaps a more enduring one, and that they need to be understood in a similar way – as cultural texts that comment on organization and economy.

Culture of organization

In a tradition of representation that we inherit from what might be called organizational gothic (Parker 2005), since the industrial revolution, workplaces have been very often imagined as places of repetitive violence – bored bodies serving machines; lowering mills and office blocks; rows of heads bent in sullen silence. Whether in Marx, Dickens, Weber or Kafka, the image is one of repeated acts of indignity, leaving hidden injuries that last a lifetime. The monotonous rhythms of crashing metal, or clicking keys, gradually stamp the souls of people into the shape of workers. These sorts of images can be seen as a form of representational criticism, a way of re-describing the turgid familiarity of work in shades that highlight its horror. This is, perhaps, one of the things that social science can do, too – take the everyday and denaturalize it. Much critical work on management and organizations elevates this estrangement into a political virtue, as if showing people their reflections in a different mirror would be enough to make them realize that the work worlds that they inhabited were damaging both themselves and others. Yet the 'realist' stories of misery, intrigue and megalomania told by those who write empirical versions of critical work on management and organization often risk a certain sort of superiority, perhaps assuming that the oppressed don't understand their oppression.[1] 'Look how limited your lives are', they might say. 'You don't see the bars of the cage that traps you.' But somehow the author knows, because they have peeped behind the curtain and have seen that the booming voice of the Wizard of Oz is a trick.

In this chapter, I intend to perform a related, but slightly different trick. For reasons I will explain below, I want to begin with the idea of a 'culture of organization', which is a condensed way of thinking about a culture in which a wide variety of representations of work and organizations are traded as routine symbols and understandings. Some of these representations are very positive indeed, and as I mentioned in chapter one, it is these that have often been the focus of critical work – airport management books, recruitment advertising, popular management magazines, MBA texts, B-School PR, careers guidance, management-skills training, government propaganda and the majority of management science in academic journals. These are precisely the sort of texts with which critical academics have (rightly in my opinion) attempted to engage in their theory and practice. But let's try to find a little balance here, because the good publicity that management gets seems to be much less than half of the story, and there is a real danger of overstating its effects and reach. I am going to argue that, in a wide variety of other domains, the positive representations are being endlessly re-framed, and often actively contested. In previous work, I have suggested that business ethics, critical management studies and anti-corporate protest constitute different elements of this contest (Parker 2002). To that list might be added trade-union activism, sabotage, absenteeism and many forms of organizational misbehaviour. Those manifestations of the industrial counter culture have provided fertile ground for a generation of researchers in organizational sociology and industrial relations, and much of this work nicely demonstrates the limits of management control and ideology (Ackroyd and Thompson 1999).

But here I want to concentrate on some more mundane aspects of the counter culture of organization that often seem to be missed by industrial sociologists. Rather than presenting work organizations as gothic places, all straight lines and mysterious looks in true German expressionist style, here I wish to re-present them as underworlds which conceal subversive post-it notes and email spam. The Jack Sparrow poster, teddy bear-covered computer, *Office Kama Sutra* and the 'ihatemyboss' websites surfed at work – all these things speak against the dehumanization of work, or even against work itself, though they are clearly also parasitic on the culture of organization. They need their 'other' in order to make sense. My intention is not to ironize these things, to merely be clever about them, but instead to explore their sarcastic insistence and satirical power. I want to take materials like the subversive coffee mug, and make them central, rather than ignoring them or claiming that they are merely a safety valve for the machineries of power.

The hidden transcript

Motivational posters should be striking, simple, and effective. For example:

Failure is only a staging point on the road to success, or
Take charge of your job, Take charge of your life, or
Good is good, but excellent is better, or
Work harder, you fat arsed bastards.

(The Little Book of Management Bollocks)

The pastiches of management language that we find in *The Little Book of Management Bollocks* only make their sense if we counterpose them to the positive representations that we also find within the culture of organization. For example, a McDonald's recruitment poster. Imagine this text on the screen of a Nokia 3310:

no 9 2 5 job 4 me.
I've mde frnds as well as ...

And then, underneath that image, the golden arches logo and the strapline 'everyone tells a story'. This is a nice condensation of an organized world. Communication, technology, work, money and happiness all blended into a smooth and tasty milkshake. The marketing of happy flexible employees for transnational capital never tasted so good. And, if one were working in a business school, surrounded by pious and evangelical versions of market managerialism, this brand of ideology would pass as a certain common sense, so common is it.

I don't want to dwell too much on what the counter culture articulates itself against, but it's important for my argument to continually recognize that, in a structuralist manner, the cultural formations that I collect in this book only really make sense in the context of what they oppose themselves to, that which they counter. You need a law to be an outlaw, organized economy to produce organized crime, and a culture of organizing to make the counter culture make sense. Indeed, negative representations of the world of organizations are actually very common indeed, even if we usually overlook them. Setting the world of outlaws aside for a while, in film blockbusters such as *Bridget Jones' Diary*, *American Beauty* and *Fight Club* we have plots that are organized around the idea of authenticity outside work. In countless other films, the organization is the problem, populated by heartless bureaucrats or hungry careerists (or even organized criminals or vampires). Redemption is to be found in telling your boss to stick it, or placing a stake through his heart, and then walking out of the door to freedom, the beloved, the child, or the dog. Even the dog's friendship is better than the countless hypocrisies and humiliations of work. In much of the media, this is now no more than the deployment of a very common stereotype. If you want a bad guy, whether in *Spiderman* or the latest James Bond film, then make him a millionaire tycoon.[2] Even in science fiction, which we might imagine to be most divorced from such questions, many now classic films have shadowy evil corporations as the ultimate source of the problem that needs to be overcome – The Tyrell Corporation in *Bladerunner*, Omnicorp in *Robocop*, Skynet in *Terminator* and The Weyland-Yutani Corporation in the *Alien* films.

I think we can add to this a whole series of small ways in which the same generalized scepticism is routinely deployed in endless acts of production and consumption. For example, there is something chasteningly illustrative about the selling of a 'Fuck Work' sticker ($1.49, plus postage and packing, and an extra 99¢ if you want it magnetized). This is an impossible object (or at least, a hypocritical one), since it in some sense attempts to deny the very labour that went into its production. Its very existence blurs the relation between economy and culture, at the same time that it appears to separate them. Someone imagined it, and then other people designed it and chose a typeface that someone else had designed, marketed it, optimized the production schedule, pressed the button that made the machines run, packed it, designed a website, distributed it, sold it and collected the profit, or even the interest from their investment. Someone else bought it with money that they earned from working, but can probably never stick it up at work for fear of the consequences.[3]

Whilst the 'Fuck Work' example is rather extreme, a lot of money is clearly made through selling other examples of the counter culture of organization. *The Little Book of Management Bollocks* is one example of a long line of work-related satirical books. C. Northcote Parkinson's *Parkinson's Law* (1958), *Up the Organisation* by Robert Townsend (1970), *Managers and Magic* (Cleverley 1971) and Martin Page's *Company Savage* (1972) are all book-length articulations of a view of organizations as inept bureaucracies populated by pompous and stupid executives. (And all sold enough to be reprinted and republished several times.) More recent examples are *Bureaucrats: How to Annoy Them* (Fishall 1981); *The Official Rules at Work* (Dickson 1996); *The Bluffer's Guide to Management* (Courtis 2000); *The Little Book of Office Bollocks* (Gelfer 2002, not the same as the other bollocks book); and *How to be a Sincere Phoney* by Jim Boren (2003).[4] Found in a similar place in the book or gift shop might be *The Tiny Book of Boss Jokes* (Philips 2002), or *250 Dumb Dares for the Workplace*, which is 'guaranteed to keep the office entertained'. The *Office Kama Sutra* (Balmain 2001) contains instructions for the 'dance of a thousand sticky notes' and suggests many ways in which offices can become sites of libidinous excess. Rather deliciously, it also has a reversible book jacket which will allow you to pretend that you are actually reading a book called *Getting What You Want at Work: Ten Steps from Fantasy to Reality*. Or you might choose Voodoo Lou's Office Voodoo Kit containing a corporate doll (with male and female sides), pins and Executive Spellbook. The book explains what is wrong with bosses (playing golf, eating big lunches, driving a Lexus), their assistants, the computer nerd and so on. It then proposes various voodoo remedies that will deal with them, and provide the owner with 'your ticket to the corporate high life'. The same is probably not true of the Office Profanity Kit, containing a mini talking punchbag which swears at you when you hit it, and three stamps with the mottos, 'This is F★★CKING

URGENT', 'Complete and Utter BULLSHIT' and 'I haven't got time to read this CRAP'.

Television is another place to find examples of similar sentiments. In 2003, Princess Productions managed to convince the British ITV network to buy a series of their show 'Office Monkey'. Each half an hour show was a reality TV version of giving the boss the finger.

> Offices are dull dreary places where nothing ever happens. That's why we bribed two members of offices around the country to disrupt their work places in the funniest ways possible. The winner gets a holiday, and the right to call themselves: Office Monkey.
>
> *(http://www.princess.uk.com/programmes/individual/recent/office.htm#)*[5]

The sniggering, squirming embarrassment that accompanied victory was painful to watch, but tapped into some deeply rooted assumptions about what work is, and what work does to people. Office humour is generally spiteful, a form of vengeance that generalizes the hypocrisy and pomposity found in so many workplaces. This has been exploited by many British situation comedies in their portrayal of figures of authority.[6] *On The Buses* (1969–73), *Are You Being Served?* (1972–83) and the remarkable *Reginald Perrin* shows (1976–79) all contain various supervisory or management characters whose vacuous vanity is regularly exposed (Hancock 2008). Perhaps iconically, in the latter we have the pompous CJ (the CEO of Sunshine Desserts) pronouncing pearls of managerial wisdom – 'I didn't get to where I am today by ... '[7] Often, these dramas were also post-war satires of social class in an era of accelerated social mobility, particularly of the 'jobsworth' who is acting up in terms of status and authority. So, Captain Mainwaring, the bank manager in *Dad's Army* (1968–77) or the leisure centre manager Gordon Brittas in *The Brittas Empire* (1991–97) are both claiming airs and graces which they clearly do not possess. Nowhere was this better satirized recently than in the mock reality TV show *The Office* which ran for two series on the BBC between 2001 and 2003, and then was remade for US TV in 2005 with seven series made at the time of writing. The banal self-delusion of David Brent and his ordinary organization made the show a cult hit, and a substantial amount of merchandising (DVDs, books, scripts, notepad, pen and pencil, sticker, mug, badge, ruler, mouse mat, calendar) was rapidly spun off from the series, as well as an official *Office* website which encouraged the submission of pictures and stories about work.

The other iconic anti-work satire of the last few decades has been the Dilbert cartoons by Scott Adams. Co-opted by an entire generation of management academics and trainers, Adams's syndicated strip explores the incredible stupidities of office life through the eyes of a naïve junior (Ackroyd and Thompson 1999: 116–18). Many episodes of *The Simpsons* picked up on similar themes concerning Homer's work at Mr Burns' power plant (Rhodes 2001, Turner 2004: 164, *passim*; Ellis 2008), and these themselves had been prefigured in Matt Groening's 1980s cartoons such as the *Work is Hell* collection (2004). Senior managers read articles titled 'How to Make the Veins in Your Forehead Throb Alarmingly' in a magazine called *Lonely Tyrant*. An even more surreal portrayal of work is the collection *My New Filing Technique Is Unstoppable* (Rees 2004) which contains assorted employees abusing each other about their filing systems, computers that insult you in the most profane fashion, and a character called Dr Niles Fanderbiles from the Quality Perfection Department who delivers self-righteous homilies in a Chinese accent. These satirical portrayals of work can also be found in plenty of underground comics and zines. Celebrations of sabotage and slacking, and descriptions of alienation and boss hatred are a powerful theme, as Stephen Duncombe catalogues (1997: 79, *passim*).[8]

Given its easy access at most workplaces and relative anonymity, it is hardly surprising that the internet has become the spiritual home for a great deal of anti-work expression, as well as many ways to avoid working. As my epigraph to this chapter suggests, the circulation of various anti-management spam mails is now a routine part of office culture. Surfing during work time is a problem for organizations in itself, and various snooping technologies have been developed to prevent it, just as other counter technologies have been developed to allow rapid movement between illicit web trivia and 'real' work on the computer. After all, if you were playing 'Hate Boss', you would almost certainly not want your superiors to know. This is a downloadable game that lets you execute hateful photos of 'your boss or somebody who makes you crazy' (http://www.downlinx.com/proghtml/303/30334.htm). Bored with this, you might go and have a look at websites and weblogs like mybossisatosser.co.uk, ihatemyboss.ca, fthisjob.com, or even ihatemydamnjob.com, which contains the following categories for you to insert your own stories:

- General Workplace Stories and Crap. Come here to bitch about all the above.
- My Boss, The Idiot. Do you have one of THOSE bosses?
- Who has the Crappiest Job? You think your job has what it takes to have the crappiest job?
- What I Hate the Most … What's the one thing you can't stand at work?
- Tales from the Cubical Farm.

The website workorspoon.com has a particularly delightful origin. SpoonMan was 'preparing to grind another thin shard of his life away at "that place"', and on the way to the shower, picked up a spoon from the kitchen. He then proceeded to stare in the mirror, deciding whether to go to work or gouge one of his eyes out with the spoon, unsure which was worse. 'This site is your chance to bitch and complain to the whole world about how fucking stupid your company really is.' Or, in case you prefer to sing your satire, on another site we have 'The All-Occasion I Hate My Mind-Numbing Corporate Job Song':

> I hate this job
> It's a dead-end job in a horrible place
> You know how I despise it

> My heart is filled with loathing and antipathy
> 'Til I cannot disguise it
> It's disgusting, it's demeaning, it's degrading,
> It's like eating from a trough, ooh
> Have I mentioned how I absolutely hate it?
> But please don't lay me off, no
> Don't you lay me off.
>
> *(www.fjordstone.com/zongoftheweek/z0509.html)*

All these examples work precisely because the counter culture of organization is embedded into so many assumptions about what work is and what it is not. For example, an advert for cheap flights suggested that you could 'Tell the boss to stick it … where the sun don't shine' because holidays are articulated as a way of escaping from work. A promotion for Christmas parties is called 'P45' (the UK tax form you get when leaving, or being sacked from, work), 'because you never liked your boss anyway'; or even the advertising for Kit Kat chocolate bars ('Have a break. Have a Kit Kat'), because even having a break from work is part of the routine of work itself. Indeed, such minor acts of hedonism can even be productive – 'Archimedes was in the bath, not the office' as Kit Kat's advertising also helpfully reminded us. Almost any leisure-related product can make a useful reference to the repressive structure of the working week, such as the restaurant chain 'TGI Friday' (Thank God It's …), the TV show 'TFI Friday', or the hundred and one pop songs that have Friday on their mind and celebrate that the weekend is here. A particularly odd example was the English theme park Alton Towers, which put up a website 'ihatework.co.uk' encouraging employees of other organizations to 'escape the workplace rat-race' by printing off a coupon for a cheap day out. The clear implication of the site was that you might pretend to be ill that day, and this provoked a small media storm in May 2004 with the Confederation of British Industries claiming that Alton Towers was acting irresponsibly in encouraging unauthorized absences. The PR people from the theme park of course denied this was the case, but one might wonder how tolerant the park management might be if other organizations encouraged their own employees to go shopping when they should be pushing people onto rides.

I suspect that most of the examples in this section have not surprised you. They are mundane and common elements of a shared set of cultural assumptions, and do not need to be tortured with much semiotic labour in order for them to make sense. I think that the question that then arises is how we might think about these artefacts in a more general sense, and ask what they tell us about the contested culture of organization and economy.

Culture in organizations, and of organization

Images of smart knowledge workers on laptops contrast sharply with the idea of a bored cubicle drone surfing for porn. Whilst a great deal of attention has been paid to the former set of images from within critical studies of work, there has been relatively little attention paid to the latter. This is rather odd, given the very substantial increase of interest in organizational culture over the past two decades, but perhaps that tells us something rather interesting about the temporally and spatially restricted ways in which culture has been conceptualized within the business school. If culture, following Raymond Williams (1976), is the *whole* way of life of a people, then it seems that studying the culture of organization should not stop at 5.30, or end in the reception area. Ackroyd and Thompson's excellent study of 'organizational misbehaviour' (1999) illustrates this nicely, concentrating as it does on behaviour *in* organizations. Though the authors mention Dilbert (dismissively), and also use the term 'counter culture', they seem to be primarily working within the long sociological tradition of work on oppositional 'subcultures' from within the workplace. This is not a problem in itself, but it begins to explain why the wider sense of culture argued for here sits uneasily with their approach.[9]

As I noted in chapter one, a discipline that has not suffered from these restrictions is cultural studies, which finds its origins in the blurring of definitions of culture offered by Williams. In principal, cultural studies offered the possibility that *Spiderman* and Dilbert could be just as important as Dickens and Zola. Yet, despite the canonical beginnings offered by Willis (1977), attempting to understand the specific relation between lived culture and lived economy seemed to become less and less important as cultural studies developed. As has been commonly observed, contemporary cultural studies has been more at home studying representations of leisure rather than work, consumption rather than production. It has all too often ended at 9.00, and began again at 5.30, or missed the structure of the working week altogether in order to celebrate the oppositional agency of the weekend (for example, Hall and Jefferson 1976, Dyer 1993, Newitz 2006). But, as Willis's work demonstrates, there is nothing intrinsic to a cultural studies approach that would make it ignore work organizations. So what might a cultural studies of the counter culture of organization look like? A good place for such an engagement to begin might be with Smircich's (1983) dismissal of the idea that organizations *have* cultures, and her sponsoring the idea that organizations *are* cultures. Not a new move in itself, given the century-long interest in atmosphere, informal structure, personality, climate and so on, but an articulation that licensed a resurgence of interest in participant observation and ethnographic work within the business schools (Parker 2000). Studies of symbolism, photocopier stories, resistance, narratives, rituals and ceremonies became common enough, and quasi-anthropological terminology was used to bring back tales from these strange organizational tribes.[10] Much of this work was fascinating and valuable, but the idea of the organization as a container still tended to be the dominant one. So, what was being studied was culture *in* organizations, with all the boundaries which that implied. But very little of the material covered in this chapter so far could reasonably be included in such a temporally and spatially restricted definition of culture. Indeed, I would argue that that is precisely why the counter culture has so often been left out. It is too much like leisure for theorists of work, and too much like work for theorists of leisure.

Studying the counter culture would necessarily involve a more general shift to thinking about the culture *of* organization, which then also includes the cultural representations of market managerialism. The distinctions between 'serious' business and the frivolities of culture necessarily become blurred if we consider the culture of organization as including the child's 'My First Business Day Playset', an episode of the TV show *The Apprentice* or *Dragon's Den*, or even the ACME company in the Looney Toons cartoons (Rehn 2004, 2008). This move is one that would require a certain symmetry between different cultural domains, whether that be photographs of office life displayed in London galleries (Cohen and Tyler 2004), a management guru book such as *In Search of Excellence*, or a spam satirical email about the 'Special High Intensity Training (SHIT)' course your managers want you to take. The key question would be a simple but general one – 'what does it mean to live in an organized society?' And that question, in this chapter, takes a rather more specific form – 'how are dissent and resistance to capitalist economics and work organization culturally articulated?'

One of the interesting things about such a question is that its empirical materials cut neatly through at least two of the dualisms which have been manifested across the human sciences – culture and economy, and dissent and co-optation. Firstly, as I have already mentioned, most of these TV shows, books and novelties are meant to make money. Even the 'Fuck Work' sticker is being sold for profit, and the whackaboss internet sites are paid for by advertising. So the production of culture through vicious parodies of organizations and management is clearly one element of the economy, and something that could be understood as at least in part reflective of interests and markets. Secondly, counter-cultural artefacts and practices all comment on the constraints that work constructs, whether temporal, emotional, financial or whatever. In some sense, the materials gathered above exemplify the supposed tragedy of mass culture, of selling dope to the dupes who are enslaved by the iron cage (Horkheimer and Adorno 2002). On the surface, there is little heroic agency in these portrayals of microserfs, McJobs and netslaves, but a great deal of disgust and self-pity. Yet this very acknowledgement is itself an indication that the people who produced and consume these materials are (at the very least) reflexive agents who can satirize the bars of the cage that traps them. As is pretty obvious, the meanings that particular objects can provide do not reside only in the objects themselves, or only in the people who make them, but both. The 'Fuck Work' sticker needs work to make it, and work to make it mean something. So would a poster of a swaggering pirate, or a wild-eyed gangster. Even the personalization of office space can itself be a subversive act, even if it is merely to place teddy bears on the computer monitor. So, depending on the context, a 'Thank God It's Friday' mug could be a deeply felt condemnation, a barely noticed cliché, an artefact that intensifies work by allowing for 'refuelling' at the desk, or a piece of junk in a car-boot sale. The ambiguity of people and things is nicely exposed by this material. Savage satire and dull powerlessness are co-constituted, as are cash and culture, because 'Fuck Work' is still a sort of work. But what kind of work is it, and who benefits?

Selling subversion and subverting selling

> The purpose of your social life is to enhance your career. Regard every drinks gathering as a chance to market yourself. Think of every office outing as a career enhancement opportunity. See every dinner party as a self-branding exercise. Treat every sexual experience as preparation for when you get fucked by your employer.
>
> *(The Little Book of Management Bollocks)*

As I suggested above, I think that the culture of organization is co-constituted by (at least) two powerful and dialectically related currents. One is market managerialism, and all the marketing that goes along with it. A Bill Gates world of self-actualized self-managers in a dynamic global economy is one that is told and sold from the minarets of corporate skyscrapers the world over. But it is not unchallenged. The other current is a multitude of critical representations of this ideology – whether in business ethics, trade unionism, anti-corporate protest, film sub-texts, satirical books, fucktheboss websites and so on. It seems to me helpful to think of these cultural currents as engaged in a contest for a form of representational hegemony. This is a cultural political struggle that is being carried out on many different levels. The organized pressure groups who wish to encourage ethical investing for pension funds might be at one extreme, whilst the 'Fuck Work' sticker is at the other. Representations of economic outlaws are yet another – more oblique than the explicit strategies of pressure groups, but much more widespread than the sticker. I am not going to make any claims about the relative importance or relevance of one particular example of representational politics, but simply note that this is a tactical question, a question about likely and desired outcomes. It seems clear enough that there is a danger of co-optation at one extreme, whilst irrelevance is the obvious accusation at the other.

After all, it would be easy enough to dismiss many of the materials in this chapter as trivia, as ephemera with little enduring significance. This is certainly the thrust of Ackroyd and Thompson's (1999) review of the long tradition of industrial sociology in this area. Rather like Hobsbawm's assumption that the party is more important than the social bandit, Ackroyd and Thompson see strikes and sabotage as more important than a Dilbert cartoon, and I suspect most people would agree with them. This is partly because sociologists of work have tended to look at the things that people *do* in workplaces, and research on resistance and misbehaviour is no different. For example, Halford (2004) and Warren (2006) have both studied the resistance to hot-desking by personalizing office space, whilst Lupton and Noble (2002) looked at the appropriation and decoration of office PCs and Anand (2006) surveyed the demographics of cartoon displays on office doors. Whilst this sort of research is certainly relevant, it explores only a small part of the counter culture, and again I think this is largely because so much of it falls between academic disciplines. The supposed gap between culture and economy, consumption and production, hence represents a problem created by boundaries, and has little to do with the objects themselves. As I noted in chapter one, even the 'cultural economy' work now beginning to be developed in sociology and geography has tended to follow these demarcations, laudably stressing the work of cultural production, but not engaging much with the consumption of images of economy and organization. My point is not that either approach is wrong, but that they are both partial. The counter culture of organization seems to require an analysis that would consider both an anthropological and a humanities sense of 'culture'. Hence documenting elements of the counter culture of organization is to make us notice them in the way that James Scott wishes us to notice the hidden transcript (1990). Disguised in plain sight, these practices and materials are central to constituting a sense of an oppositional or dissenting identity both in the workplace and beyond.

Leaving disciplinary divides to one side, re-presenting elements of the counter culture involves a certain interest in their oppositionality, and an important reminder that much critical work already happens outside the academy. Ordinary people are not that ordinary, and critical academics not that observant. Academic hubris, whether intellectually elitist or politically vanguardist, can be nicely tempered with a recognition that *The Little Book of Management Bollocks* has probably sold many more copies than any critical text ever has. This is something that might lead some people to feel optimism about resistance to market managerialism. Yet there also is a clear danger of romanticizing all this as 'resistance', just as there is of fetishizing something called power. The culture of organization and the counter culture of organization are co-produced, dialectically related, and I think that it would be a mistake to see either one as prior to the other. Another way of putting this, and an argument that can also be turned on critical studies of consumption and production in general, is to insist that what counts as dissent or compliance depends entirely on context. There is no metric by which the oppositionality of the 'Fuck Work' sticker (or the computer teddy, or pirate film) could be measured outside the contexts within which they are deployed. If, for example, you were a creative in an advertising agency, the display of the sticker might mean no more than a nod towards the 'rebel sell' (Heath and Potter 2004). If you worked in a bank, you would almost certainly be inviting a stern word with your manager, and probably displaying an attitude that is unlikely to result in promotion.

So it is the very ambivalence of these counter-cultural representations that I think is so important to keep in mind, but this is not only a matter of their 'meaning' for people in particular situations. It also becomes an issue for the researcher, in terms of the morality of the tales they tell. I was told about the colleague of a friend, a lecturer in a further education college, who keeps a clock on his wall stopped permanently at five to five. Or, a workplace ethnographer who told me about designers who had parodied their organizational logo by re-designing it in 'inappropriate' ways. Or a poster on the back of an office door – 'Everyone Brings Joy to this Office. Some when they enter. Some when they leave.' Or, a distant senior manager in the National Health Service who forwarded fake PowerPoint slides which parodied a lesson in corporate strategy. Or, rubbed into the dirt on the back of a lorry, an unhappy face with MON underneath it and a happy face with FRI underneath it.[11] In all these cases, the juggernaut of the organization is still there, and the humour can just as easily be understood as resignation rather than revolution. Like the scratches on a prison wall, they confirm the existence of the wall. But also like the scratches on the prison wall, they demonstrate that the wall is not all that there is. I don't know whether this is a tragic gesture or a heroic one, and I think the answer must be that it is both. Always both, because to reduce it to either one is to simplify a complex play of resignation, possibility, humour and anger to no more than a sign of what the researcher wanted to see in the first place.

All of the materials that I have gathered together in this chapter are subversive, whether the subversion is badmouthing the boss, taking a holiday or laughing knowingly at the stupidities of organizations. Some of them are also often almost invisible, like the faded and endlessly copied satirical notice next to the photocopier. The counter culture of the early twenty-first century is not a source for *either* optimism or pessimism, but both. It reflects a culture in which big organizations have now become the status quo, and they mark the diverse people and materials that do their work within them in a wide variety of ways. There is no simple and single response to the counter culture because it, like work, is contested terrain. That is why so many of these materials make us laugh, and why the laugh so often catches in our throat. The rent still needs paying, the alternatives are hard to see, and the familiar faces and routines of work have their own comforts. But outside work, in the forest, on the highways and seas and in the underworld of the city, are the outlaws. They have been there for hundreds of years, and I think that they connect Robin Hood to David Brent, and *Pirates of the Caribbean* with *The Little Book of Management Bollocks*. We might daydream about pirates at our desks, or put a 'Fuck Work' sticker up in a corner of the factory, but this sort of resistance to power and imagination of something different is not new.

In the final chapter, I'm going to pull these threads together, and show how the outlaw is an impossible object, too. Like the counter culture of work, Robin Hood makes boundaries and confuses them at the same time. Insides and outsides, facts and fictions, economy and culture, incorporation and resistance, all are made by the outlaw, as a figure who marks where things end and something else begins.

9

POPULAR POLITICAL ECONOMY

Justice being taken away, then, what are kingdoms but great robberies? For what are robberies themselves, but little kingdoms? The band itself is made up of men; it is ruled by the authority of a prince, it is knit together by the pact of the confederacy; the booty is divided by the law agreed on. If, by the admittance of abandoned men, this evil increases to such a degree that it holds places, fixes abodes, takes possession of cities, and subdues peoples, it assumes the more plainly the name of a kingdom, because the reality is now manifestly conferred on it, not by the removal of covetousness, but by the addition of impunity. Indeed, that was an apt and true reply which was given to Alexander the Great by a pirate who had been seized. For when that king had asked the man what he meant by keeping hostile possession of the sea, he answered with bold pride, 'What thou meanest by seizing the whole earth; but because I do it with a petty ship, I am called a robber, whilst thou who dost it with a great fleet art styled emperor.'

(The City of God against the Pagans, *Saint Augustine, Book IV, chapter IV*)

Translations of Saint Augustine's early fifth-century text vary, with 'robberies' (*latrocinia*) sometimes translated as bandit bands. His argument in the text as a whole is that legitimate power on earth is granted by the one true God, not by polytheistic gods or mere mortals, but in making the argument he necessarily equalizes the claims of different kinds of men and the institutions they make. In other words, kings and pirates do the same sort of things. Charles Tilly makes the same argument in more analytic terms. States are involved in war-making to control territory, eliminating opposition within that territory, protecting clients and extracting the value needed to carry out these activities. This he describes as organized crime – 'quintessential protection rackets with the advantage of legitimacy' (1985: 169).

This is the central equivalence in so many stories about alternative business and economic outlaws. It reverses assumptions about economic and political legitimacy by claiming that pirates and kings are either the same, in terms of their activities, or that pirates are better, because they do not lie about what they do, or that they even redistribute the wealth which has been hoarded by the powerful. This is the logic that turns the reviled criminal into a heroic outlaw, and makes illegitimate forms of alternative economic life into a critique of conventional economic life. A cartoon from the 'One Penny Weekly' *Town Talk* in 1858 captures this well. On one half of the panel, a highwayman robs a woman on a coach, on the other a fat banker holds a pen and deposit book over a woman in an office. The first is titled 'Entire Liability 17 –', the second 'Limited Liability 18 –'.[1] *Punch* cartoons comparing railway entrepreneurs to highwaymen (Taylor 2005: 140), or satires of management such as David Brent, are in that sense the mirror image of the celebration of 'bandits' like Robin Hood, Pancho Villa or Dillinger. So when Hobsbawm (1965, 1972a) cautiously praised the social bandit as a 'proto-revolutionary' force, he was opening up some of the ways in which the robber becomes celebrated by the people, and my argument builds on his insights whilst expanding their implications. 'Where the bonds of government and lordship were loose, Robin Hood was a recognised community leader' (Hobsbawm 1972a: 49).

It may well be that social bandits have a particular appeal in specific contexts where the state is weak, or power is exercised at the point of a sword, but the broader category of the economic outlaw seems to have been of interest to many people for a very long time indeed. No society is likely to be free from crises of legitimation, and this sort of celebration of crime as resistance questions the boundaries between what is deemed right and what is deemed wrong, between the morality of the sheriff or the policeman and that of the bank robber. And all too often, the former are corrupted and venal, whilst the outlaw is brave and authentic. As Bob Dylan tells us in his 1966 song 'Absolutely Sweet Marie', 'To live outside the law you must be honest.'

This questioning of the boundary between probity and vice is one with many other twentieth-century parallels. When Edward Alsworth Ross wrote his *Sin and Society* over 100 years ago he was railing against the ways that the robber barons were corrupting US politics and commerce, and his metaphors are familiar ones:

> The shedder of blood, the oppressor of the widow and the fatherless, long ago became odious, but latter-day treacheries fly no skull and crossbones flag at the masthead. ... The modern high-power dealer of woe wears immaculate linen, carries a silk hat and a lighted cigar, sins with calm countenance and a serene soul, leagues or months from the evil.
>
> *(1907: 7, 10)*

Ross's 'criminaloid' mutates into Edwin Sutherland's 'white collar criminal', the respectable and amoral businessman whose crimes merely lack social recognition (1983, Minkes and Minkes 2008). Symmetrically, the debate on 'social crime' which developed from Hobsbawm's social bandit seeks to take the supposedly odious and make them comprehensible, or even heroic. As the literary critic William Empson suggests, the poor and excluded criminal 'can be a critic of society; so far as he is forced by this into crime he is the judge of the society that judges him' (in Pearson 1975: 11). Contemporary cultural criminology takes both of these moves as axiomatic, attempting to understand the inequalities and institutions that produce something called 'crime', as well as the creative agency of those individuals and groups who engage in it (Ferrell *et al.* 2008).

However, it seems to me that this is far from the only thing that the economic outlaw does, because they make and blur some other categories, too. Most evidently, this is a phenomenon in which the 'fact' and the 'fiction' have been intertwined for at least 700 years, and in which cultural representations of many different kinds come to constitute the object itself. Take Bob Dylan's 1967 song 'John Wesley Harding'.[2] The lyrics say little about the fact that he seems to have liked killing black people, but instead reiterates a version of the nomadic Robin Hood.

> John Wesley Harding
> Was a friend to the poor
> He trav'led with a gun in ev'ry hand
> All along this countryside
> He opened many a door
> But he was never known
> To hurt an honest man.

Or, Walter Schiavone, a Comorra boss in Naples, who has a villa just like that of Tony Montana from *Scarface*. That's because he gave his architect a copy of the film, having seen it many times and deciding he wanted a place like that (Saviano 2008: 245). As we saw in chapter six, the linkages between the US Mafia and the US entertainment industry are endless, with low life imitating art, and art taking its material from Senate hearings and wiretaps (Gambetta 2009: 258, *passim*). Seal's outlaw 'script' is now firmly constituted as a way of understanding character, context and action. It is a template with deep roots, all the way back to Robin Hood in north-western Europe at least, but these themselves are misty entanglements of ballads and histories, films and documentaries, songs and newspaper stories. The 'truth' of the outlaw is not either history or fantasy, but both, with the actions and accounts of bandits themselves often being constituted by their understandings of what it means to be a noble robber, and the fascinations of historians and journalists being shaped by the sedimentation of myth and the interests of their times. The predilection for particular sorts of hats, or a certain use of language and manner, is shaped and amplified by media representations. As Seal insists, if we treat the outlaw as 'folklore' it can be both truth and fiction at the same time, thus exorcizing the ghost of whether historical truth can be told, at the same time as encouraging us to take folk and popular culture seriously (1996: 182).

This is a very concrete example of a site where economy and culture are interwoven, too. The representations of outlaws have been sold by a huge range of cultural intermediaries and, since at least Martin Parker's entering of his 'True Tale of Robin Hood' in the London Stationers' Register in 1632, they have been an important part of the product sold by the cultural industries. The dizzying variety of ways in which these representations have been traded spans the collecting bowl of a travelling troubadour and the marketing strategy of a global entertainment corporation, but they all share this sense that these are characters and stories that people will pay money for. To decide whether the latest Robin Hood film, the Playmobil duo 5878 'Bandit and Policeman' bubblepack, or *The Little Book of Management Bollocks*, is economy *or* culture requires a determination of relative interests which is simply impossible to disentangle. We might point out that the 2010 *Robin Hood* had made $311 million within the first few months after its release, or that it is the latest manifestation of a cultural archetype that we first find documented in *Piers Plowman* over 700 years ago. Both accounts are correct, and to reduce either one to the other is to miss the richness and complexity of the ways in which selling ideas or an image does not necessarily sell out the outlaw.

This brings me to my final blurring, that of critique and co-optation. Outlaws can occupy both positions, and it is not possible to decide, once and for all, whether their politics is progressive or conservative. For example, as we saw in chapter seven, Ned Kelly has been used in many different ways over the past century. Indeed, the mutability of his figure is such that he can even be co-opted to sell banking:

> In April 1994, the Western Australian-based Challenge Bank began an expensive print and television advertising campaign featuring Ned Kelly. Although Ned's legend has only limited appeal in Western Australia, the bank's advertising agency still managed to sell this rather odd sales pitch. Perhaps the myth has come full circle. Australia's most famous bank-robber has become an appropriate icon for promoting respectable banking. From folk hero to national hero, from outlaw to advertising gimmick, from bank-robber to bank-seller: there seems to be no end to the convenience of Ned Kelly in Australian culture.
>
> *(Seal 1996: 179)*

Just as Jack Sparrow DVDs can bear anti-piracy notices, and ex-Mafiosi write cookery books, so we could treat the appropriation of the outlaw and the gang as just another example of the voracious appetites of the contemporary culture industries. The counter culture can very easily just become a resource for selling Che Guevara rebellion on a T-shirt. It doesn't matter what the text is, if it can be trivialized, reproduced and commodified it will be, as many critics of mass culture have insisted for a century or so (Horkheimer and Adorno 2002). This is happening, but at the same time it is worth pausing and considering just what all these characters seem to be saying. The context may well be global capitalist entertainment corporations, but the content very often brings us back to the sort of critique that Saint Augustine articulates. In other words, like the 'Fuck Work' sticker which we met in chapter eight, it seems quite possible that a cultural representation could be both co-opted and critical at the same time. We can never really know what the trickster, or the masked bandit, really 'means' because it means what its audience think it means, despite what cultural critics might like to claim. It might be comforting for some people to put Jack Sparrow and David Brent in a box, but they will keep escaping.

So in all of these four dimensions – legitimate/illegitimate, fact/fiction, economy/culture and co-optation/critique – the economic outlaw and alternative business present us with a masked, liminal and troubling object. According to my reading of things, this is an interesting phenomenon which doesn't sit easily within the sort of categories that we might like to put it in. As soon as we think we have it pinned down as one sort of thing, explained away as this or that, then it shifts shape and becomes something else. Correspondingly, and like the counter culture of work and organization more generally, it doesn't present itself as an easy object to be analysed by the sort of academic disciplines that might approach it – history, cultural studies, literature, film, criminology or even the business school. The outlaw, like the counter culture more generally, always evades us.

Justified objections

> Commodified fantasy takes no risks: it invents nothing, but imitates and trivialises. It proceeds by depriving the old stories of their intellectual and ethical complexity, turning their action to violence, their actors to dolls, and their truth telling to sentimental platitude. Heroes brandish their swords, lasers, wands, as mechanically as combine harvesters, reaping profits. Profoundly disturbing moral choices are sanitized, made cute, made safe. The passionately conceived ideas of the great story-tellers are copied, stereotyped, reduced to toys, molded in bright coloured plastic, advertised, sold, broken, junked, replaceable, interchangeable.
>
> *(Le Guin 2003: xiv)*

Before moving towards a sort of conclusion within which I say what *I* think all this stuff 'means' (which is also what it *can* mean, or what I would *like* it to mean), I want to deal with some of the more or less obvious objections to the arguments I have made so far. As I indicated in the first chapter, they can all be summarized as a charge of fantasy, whether that is of a gendered, classed or more general kind. As a middle-aged white man from England, I seem to have ended up writing about some figures from my childhood, and then claiming a sort of romantic importance for them as if it were uncomplicated for a law-abiding employee like me to be fascinated by crime, or for a man to be celebrating violent forms of homo-sociality, or a professor at Warwick Business School to claim he understands what it is like to be poor. Or, for that matter, for me to be suggesting that Robin Hood means the same to everyone, and means the same the world over – but I delivered my apologies and explanations about that aspect of my method in chapter one. The question of what things 'mean' is inseparable from the person who makes the meaning, and so it is with readers, many of whom will doubtless have doubted the meanings I have made here. Let's begin with the question of violent crime.

Gillian Spraggs is clear enough in her judgement concerning the forms of good fellowship that Robin Hood and his ilk promise – 'It's an attractive ideology, communistic, egalitarian. ... There is just one really major problem with it. It is an ideology of robbers and parasites' (2001: 85). Whilst I don't think that 'robbers' or 'parasites' are objective terms here, I take Spraggs to be saying that the 'ideology' that justifies the noble robber is pretty much the same one that justifies a gang kicking someone to death because they had a row in a nightclub. In practical terms, most of the people I have written about here are the same sort of people who I would probably cross the road to avoid and hate to have moving in next door. As someone said to me after a talk I did on this a few years ago, 'never mind Robin Hood, what about the robbing bastards?' The fantasy of the outlaw is very little like the facts of criminal violence. The explosive bloodshed which can be found in a wide range of images of crime and law enforcement often trades on the idea that to be a masculine hero means being justified in revenge (Sparks 1996), but the moral economy of aggression is rarely this simple. In Clint Eastwood's 1992 Western *Unforgiven*, a dime novelist, W. W. Beauchamp, is lectured on how violence really happens. There is nothing glamorous about it, being a matter of terror, pissed pants and pain. As Sante (1998: 289) points out, much of our interest in low-lifes is hence no more than rubbernecking, a vicarious thrill that is merely given academic legitimation in a book like this one which can only sell its tawdry glamour and cheap thrills because it has never really experienced them.

The debate that followed Hobsbawm's original 'social bandits' argument revolved around these sorts of questions. Anton Blok contrasts the myth of the bandit with the reality of what bandits often actually did, in Sicily for example, which of course included working for the rich and powerful, extorting from the poor, and intimidating and killing those who attempted to work for change (Blok 1972, Hobsbawm 1972b, Slatta 2007). Even the most romantic commentators on the radical meanings of piracy have to acknowledge that real Captain Jack Sparrows were involved in appalling torture, violence, rape, slavery and so on (Kuhn 2010: 157). There is nothing intrinsically good about being an outsider, and many outlaws who we should probably be very suspicious about. To take a more contemporary example, the Fascist Feme, Free Corps or freebooters were outlaw figures, too – self-proclaimed outcasts who assassinated communists, Jews, liberals and any other 'enemies' of Germany in the 15 years before the institutionalization of National Socialism in the 1930s. Captain Ehrhardt, a dispenser of 'Volkish' justice, was 'a glamorous figure – part Tarzan, part Robin Hood, part James Bond – and thousands of adolescents sought to imitate his style' (Cantor 1970: 132). It is easy enough to ignore the inconvenient and brutal facts in order to concentrate on selling the misty legends.

As I have indicated all the way through the book, these are often just boys' legends, too. Spraggs is clear on this in her condemnation of Turpin *et al.*, noting that goodfellowship excludes women, except as objects of sexual recreation (2001: 85). Hobsbawm's two-and-a-half page appendix to *Bandits* – 'Women and Banditry' – mentions a few exceptions (1972a: 135), but women are largely absent from the stories I have told here, being more often props and placeholders for home, food, children and sexual services. In the original Old English sense, they couldn't even become outlaws, since they were not full legal subjects in the first place. There are exceptions – Grace O'Malley, Phoolan Devi and Calamity Jane – but in the most extreme cases the society of men sequesters itself away from women and children, and the camaraderie thus engendered is of wildness, speed, movement and competitive banter. The conditions of possibility for the reproduction of this outlaw utopia are denied in its practices. If women are admitted into the stories, they tend to be possessed of extraordinary abilities. Perhaps they are disguised as men, or are capable of magical deception. They might be superb shots with a pistol, or are particularly ruthless fighters or leaders. In order to gain admittance to the myth, they have to become witches or supermen. Of course, more recent versions of these representations have tended to admit a woman or two into the gang – strong female pirates, or Maid Marians who can fight and shoot a bow – but the core members are almost always male. As for the brooding romantic individual, following the inspiration of Byron's 'Corsair' they are all male, stroking their stubbled chins and staring into the distance with beautiful eyes.[3] It seems that women rarely have the internal depth to be tortured by thoughts of history, freedom and revenge. Only in the characteristics of chivalry and nobility do we find a fairly constant relation between the male outlaw and the woman. Like the poor, elderly and children, they are treated well and spared violence. Ironically, it is in the very act of categorizing women as other to the violent world of men that such men then become noble, exclusion of one kind being sanctified by an exclusion of another.

Finally, we might well raise our eyebrows at the political economy of this set up. Brecht, in his notes for the *Threepenny Opera*, suggests that his version of Macheath, Messer, should be played as a bourgeois character. He explains:

> The bourgeoise's fascination with bandits rests on a misconception: that the bandit is not a bourgeois. This misconception is the child of another misconception: that a bourgeois is not a bandit. Does this mean that they are identical? No: occasionally a bandit is not a coward.
>
> *(in Ruggerio 2003: 51)*

The bourgeois conceit is that in sympathizing with the bandit, they are showing sympathy to the poor and dispossessed. In fact the real bandits are the bourgeois themselves, except that they are too cowardly to realize it and then do something about changing the world that allows them to be the people that they are. At its heart, these are Hobsbawm's reservations, too. It is all very well identifying with the noises that social bandits make, but how will that get turned into political change? 'Bandit-heroes are not expected to make a world of equality. They can only right wrongs and prove that oppression can be turned upside down' (Hobsbawm 1965: 24). That is to say, outlaws might be exemplars, but they are not useful models of organization, strategy or outcome. They have no theory of change, and often no theory of capitalism, let alone patriarchy or imperialism. And when we get to the more collective forms of organized crime, Hobsbawm sees little reason to even classify these as examples of social banditry at all because 'gangsters have a vested interest in private property, as pirates have a vested interest in legitimate commerce, being parasitic upon it' (Hobsbawm 1965: 53).

Roberto Saviano's diagnosis of the contemporary Comorra is pretty much the same: 'The logic of criminal business, of the bosses, coincides with the most aggressive neo-liberalism. The rules, dictated or imposed, are those of business, profit and victory over all the competition. Anything else is worthless. Anything else doesn't exist' (2008: 113). The diagnosis could be one which suggests that there is nothing very radical or interesting here that can't be explained by economic interests, so if you want to change the world, why begin with Jack Sparrow? Sometimes the business model involves stealing from the rich, because they do have more money than the poor, but it could just as well involve working for the rich and stealing from the poor. Dispose of the rhetoric and the romanticism, which is no more than ideology, and you see these alternatives as mainstream opportunism. Perhaps even something which could be used to teach people in business schools how to understand the principles of management strategy, or the Economics of Self Interest 101.

> ... a pirate ship more closely resembled a Fortune 500 company than the society of savage schoolchildren depicted in William Golding's *Lord of the Flies*. Peglegs and parrots aside, in the end, piracy was a business. It was a criminal business, but a business nonetheless, and deserves to be examined in this light.
>
> *(Leeson 2009: 6)*

Or when, in Levitt and Dubner's best-selling *Freakonomics* they write about the economics of drug dealing, they do so not to comment on the social context that produces the corners we might see on *The Wire* but to illustrate the relationship between labour-market supply and reward (2006: 79, *passim*). In sum, and to take the title of this book quite literally, these are just alternative businesses, and like most businesses they do it in order to get profits. Whether a leftist analysis of class politics and the economic base, or a Chicago school analysis of supply and demand, the message is the same. Never mind stealing from the poor to give to the rich, Robin Hood *et al.* steal from anyone in order to get rich.

These are all good and justified objections, and as I was writing this book I was often enough convinced by them. My imagination, shaped by a lifetime of saturation in Hollywood's dream factory, fails to understand the realities of violence and poverty, mistakes a narrow sexist homosociality for utopianism, and ends up being seduced by ideology rather than understanding economic determination. I have no doubt that this is true, and that other sorts of explanations would work well with the material I have collected here. My only escape route, and it is the same one for all three objections, is to ask whether these sorts of accounts tell us *everything* about the outlaw, because my sense is that they actually end up leaving out a great deal. They explain a lot, but they don't explain things *away*. If I'm right, and the characters in this book can be understood to simultaneously create and blur boundaries – between economics and culture, reality and fantasy, law and morality, and critique and co-optation – then there is more to be explored here. This is not to say that we should be uncritical of an 'outlaw politics', if such a phrase makes any sense, more to insist that there is a politics to these enduring images that should not airily be dismissed as a patriarchal, bourgeois fantasy.

Myth today

> A myth is, of course, not a fairy story. It is the presentation of facts belonging to one category in the idioms appropriate to another. To explode a myth is accordingly not to deny the facts but to re-allocate them.
>
> *(Gilbert Ryle, in Pearson 1983: 205)*

If you broadly accept that I have identified a species of figures from popular culture who share a certain family resemblance, then a possible question might simply be to ask: why have these characters been stock elements for so long? What are the attractions of Seal's (1996, 2009) 'outlaw hero cycle'? It is difficult not to ask this as a broadly functionalist question, in the strict sociological definition of the term, simply because we are then asking what role these representations play in our social and psychic lives. Why are they there? In one preliminary sense, since these representations are part of the standard products of the entertainment industries, we can conclude that they are repeated because they sell. Roland Barthes claimed that 'mass culture is a machine for manufacturing desire', and this could be understood as suggesting that the desire was not there in the first place until some marketing men created it in a meeting. Perhaps this works sometimes for a new flavour of crisp, but marketing clearly cannot sell everything, and anyway Martin Parker's ballad of Robin Hood predates mass culture by most definitions. So why do things sell? Is it true that if they did not sell, they would not be repeated? But that tells us very little, other than that capitalism produces more of the things that generate profits, and less of the things that do not. So, why do these particular characters have such endurance? There seem to be (at least) two ways in which we might answer that question.

One would take inspiration from a simplified version of Durkheim's sociology and suggest that showing deviance is itself functional. It is, he says 'a factor in public health, an integrative element in any healthy society' (1895/1982: 98). The law breaker marks the boundary between accepted and unacceptable, and when we see what happens to the scapegoat, we can be reminded of the importance of staying on the straight and narrow. Rather like the skeleton of the highwayman in the gibbet on the crossroads, we are encouraged to internalize the lessons of discipline and punishment, and to share the offence which the action provokes to our 'collective feelings'. In that sense, we could say that we are being warned by these characters, and they should be seen as an example of the socialization of the citizen, an injunction to avoid the sort of deviance that will end with your neck being stretched (Pearson 1975: 103). We could get to pretty much the same point through a simplified version of Marxism, too, though with more of an emphasis on the economic lessons, and the ways in which ideology resigns people to a life of servitude and wage slavery. The problem with such accounts of Jack Sparrow *et al.* is that very often (though not always) they do get away. Even when they die in a hail of bullets, like *Butch Cassidy and the Sundance Kid* (1969), they die young and pretty, and are celebrated after their deaths. If we were really being marched to watch the executions, *pour encourager les autres*, then we would not expect the victims to look quite so sexy, the perfectly aimed arrow to cut the hangman's rope quite so often, or even to argue with Judge Barry before their execution. As James Scott noted:

> If the courts are filled with truculent and defiant criminals … their behaviour amounts to a sign that domination is nothing more than tyranny – nothing more than successful exercise of power against subordinates too weak to overthrow it but proud enough to defy it symbolically.
>
> *(1990: 58)*

So if the content of the myth of the noble robber doesn't fit with the sort of morality play which we might expect from ideological functionalism, let's try a sort of half-way house explanation. The historian Robert Darnton describes tricksterism as a 'holding operation': 'It permits the underdog to grasp some marginal advantage by playing on the vanity and stupidity of his superiors. But the trickster works within the system, turning its weak points to his advantage and therefore ultimately confirming it' (1984: 59). So perhaps the pleasure that we get from watching deviance of various forms provides what Albert Cohen famously called a 'safety valve' (1966). Like the carnival, the world can be turned upside down for the day, only to be put firmly back on its feet in the morning (Scott 1990: 168). This is still a broadly functionalist explanation, in the sense that it suggests that representations of economic outlaws contribute to reinforcing a dominant economic order, but it is an explanation that begins to summon the idea that people might be projecting all sorts of desires onto these images of deviance. The interesting thing about the safety-valve explanation, whether aimed at sport, sado-masochism or watching horror movies, is that it is based on an economy of repressed pleasures and possibilities. Civilization bottles up discontents, and these need to be bubbled away in case the vessel itself explodes. This is to posit that these desires are monsters from the Id, anti-social impulses which are gratified by Robin Hood and David Brent, the primitive spasms of the lizard brain that need to be controlled and commanded by the social Superego (Duncan 1996: 117). This sort of explanation hence assumes the need for repression, and justifies the status quo precisely in terms of this sort of function. The fact that it functions imperfectly is yet further proof that it needs to be there, because the small leaks imply that there is a massive explosion waiting for the society that lets the genie out of the bottle.

This form of explanation is purely speculative, despite its ubiquity, but follows an ancient lineage of argument from Plato, Hobbes and Freud to contemporary market economics. If we don't give them bread and circuses, we end up with the war of all against all. But what if we invert the moral of the story, and make society the source of the discontent? Phil Cohen, in an early paper that prefigured some key ideas from the Birmingham Centre for Contemporary Cultural Studies, suggested that youth subcultures offered magical resolutions to the contradictions of the everyday. Well, let's quote him more precisely: 'It seems to me that the latent function of subculture is this: to express and resolve, albeit "magically", the contradictions that remain hidden in the parent culture' (1997: 94). Cohen suggests that the procession of subcultures represented structural transformations of 'the basic problematic or contradiction which is inserted in the subculture by the parent culture' (op. cit.). Rather than seeing subcultures as pathological eruptions of monkey madness, they become articulated as imaginative responses to structural tensions and contradictions in the social. This is a development of the anthropologist Claude Levi-Strauss's definition of myth in pre-industrial societies, as a form of thought which 'progresses from the awareness of oppositions towards their resolution' (1963: 224). It can't actually solve these oppositions, of course, but mediates them, and is latent, in the sense that the participants in such imaginings do not *necessarily* connect their fantasies with the social conditions that generated them. But then, almost by definition, fantasy cannot be a manifest function. If its cause and aim were clear to all, it would no longer be fantastic, but part of a mission statement or set of sensible policy proposals. So Cohen's point was something to do with a certain sort of fantasy, but not a fantasy in terms of its common sense of ungrounded escapism, a castle in the air. Rather than running away, this was a fantasy that took everyday materials and re-worked them into some sort of account that helped resolve them. Not solve them, because that would require social structural change, but to re-imagine hidden injuries, to construct an account of underdogs as heroes, and the powerful as the bumbling Keystone Cops and stupid managers.

This is important, because it allows us to connect back to Durkheim in a different way. One of the usual textbook criticisms of what people understand as functionalism nowadays is that it can't deal with social change. If something exists, it must be functional. If it is functional, it must continue to exist. *Quod erat demonstrandum.* But this wasn't actually what Durkheim said. Using the example of crime, he points out that all societies will have crime, even what he calls a 'community of saints', but that the nature of that crime will certainly vary:

> Nothing is good indefinitely and without limits. The authority which the moral consciousness enjoys must not be excessive, for otherwise no one would dare attack it and it would petrify too easily into an immutable form. For it to evolve, individual originality must be allowed to manifest itself. But so that the originality of the idealist who dreams of transcending his era may display itself, that of the criminal, which falls short of the age, must also be possible.
>
> *(1982: 101)*

This is an extraordinarily important point, because it normatively loosens social structure in order to claim that to have saints we must have sinners. But he doesn't stop there, because he's perfectly happy to acknowledge that one person's saint is another's sinner:

> Nor is this all. Beyond this indirect utility, crime itself may play an useful part in this evolution. Not only does it imply that the way to necessary change remains open, but in certain cases it also directly prepares for these changes. ... Indeed, how often is it an anticipation of the morality to come, a progression towards what will be! According to Athenian law, Socrates was a criminal and his condemnation was entirely just. However, his crime – his independence of thought – was useful not only for humanity but for his country.
>
> *(op. cit., 102)*

This is a point at which Durkheim begins to sound like the Karl Mannheim of *Ideology and Utopia* (1936). Utopians are those who have fantasies that are in tension with the prevailing order, and the distinctions between satire, crime and visionary social change are ones that have no trans-historical purchase. Your bandit is my freedom fighter, your criminal is my utopian. That is the whole point of a sociology of knowledge – to insist that knowledge is social, and that judgement can only happen in context. Now Durkheim's instincts certainly wouldn't have taken him this far. He mentions Socrates, and the persecution of heretics in the middle ages, but seems reluctant to mention anything more contemporary. Given his attitude to Marxism, this should not surprise us.[4] Mannheim certainly goes further, because he is willing to suggest that utopian ideas are found in a variety of settings, including religious sects and socialist organizations. But if we put these two ideas together, then it becomes possible to suggest that Captain Jack Sparrow is an example of Durkheim's 'independence of thought', and Mannheim's description of 'the utopian mentality': 'A state of mind is utopian when it is incongruous with the state of reality in which it occurs' (1960: 173). As we saw in the previous chapter, we don't watch films in which deserving people get promotions after long years of service, or happily chat at water-coolers about the charismatic character of their boss and their deserved pay raise. We watch comedies about stupid bosses and buy 'Fuck Work' stickers. Or, we watch stylish bank robbers and sharp-suited Mafiosi. We watch Robin Hood and his friends as they evade the cruel and stupid Sheriff.

When James Scott was documenting the arts of resistance, he largely concentrated on societies in which power was centralized and visible. The 'hidden transcript' which documents 'infapolitical' resistance to the kings, slave owners and tax collectors is precisely that – hidden from the official accounts (1990). So if Scott's analysis works to understand many of the ways in which domination is contested by a fart and a story, or in the pub, market or carnival, perhaps Jack Sparrow allows us to see how the this sort of analysis might work within the global culture of late capitalism. In complex societies, where power is multiple and often disguised as the freedom to do something and be someone, the fictionalization of resistance is a good way to hide dissent. The quite explicit criticisms that Robin Hood and his band make are disguised in plain sight, and even made profitable, by turning them into a blockbuster which can then be explained away as 'merely' fantasy. The trickster would do that, in order to survive within a culture in which everything becomes product. In terms of the critics, the logic is now reversed, and we begin to be able to explain just why so many people might be persuaded to dismiss the outlaws, rather than attending more carefully to what they say. Old stories that were whispered and sung have now become action figures marketed by global entertainment corporations, but they are still stories about resistance, accounts of the corruptions and stupidities of the powerful, and swaggering heroes that we can admire.

Fantasy economics and social change

Given any vaguely Marxist account of contemporary wage labour and capital, it should hardly surprise us that economics might actually be central to large parts of fantasy. The day-to-day reality of work for most people is one of repetition and humiliation. The making and selling of widgets, combined with the fact that other people in suits speak to you like someone with learning difficulties, is not an experience of labour and exchange that allows all desires to be satisfied. As we saw in the previous chapter, this is a knowledge which is embedded in popular cultural accounts of time, work, of the boss, of corporations. It seems necessarily an experience of limits, of dependence, perhaps of a certain fear and self-loathing, and as other authors have suggested, escape from, and reflection upon, these conditions is manifested in popular culture in various ways (Dyer 1993,

Newitz 2006). So too when we see the bandit, the buccaneer, the bank robber, perhaps we imagine a different relation to labour, to our co-workers, and perhaps even ourselves. When Hobsbawm labels the social bandits as primitive rebels, he seems to be implying that more sophisticated forms of rebellion would be rather better. He may well be right in practical terms, but we also could understand primitive to mean more elemental, more part of the fabric of everyday life. This is what James Scott does in his anthropology and theory of 'the arts of resistance' in colonial societies (1985, 1990), and it is what I am claiming for this aspect of popular culture in capitalist societies. It's a background noise, a resistance below the line, a permanent suspicion, an embedded sense of injustice which makes it likely that we cheer for Robin and laugh when the Sheriff is made to look like a fool.

We know that Jack Sparrow would not have worried too much if he was threatened with DVD piracy. And when we hear Tony Soprano's rationalizations for illegitimate economic activity, we recognize them as condemnations of our own organizations and economies. The rich deserve to be stolen from, and the poor deserve to eat better. The powerful are greasy and silver tongued and keep their states and organizations going through lies and threats. This book demonstrates that these fictions can be read as thought experiments about the nature of economy and belonging. They provide speculations about the pains and pleasures of labour, of what it means to be a subject of power or to be free, of where the legitimate economy begins or ends. Of course, texts can be read in many different ways, and not everyone who watches *Pirates of the Caribbean* will be participating in the radical imagination.[5] They might be – enjoying the relation between masculinity and violence (Sparks 1996: 353); doing research on discovering new ways to commit crimes; a little in love with Jack Sparrow; being dazzled by the special effects; or just taking the kids to see anything at the cinema to keep them quiet. All these individual reader responses are quite possible, yet the very ubiquity and similarity of these figures suggests that they are doing something interesting at a general level, that they are not merely coincidences, but social facts that require explanation.

Now any structuralist worth their salt would at least have us asking why so many of these figures have thematic features which appear to be concerned with various sorts of borders. At the historical, spatial and imaginative edges of the economy and state we find outlaws of various kinds. On the borders of and between states there are pirates and smugglers. Finally, within the city and the state, between the legitimate and illegitimate economies we find the Mafia and organized crime. This question of boundaries can be understood quite literally, in terms of the possibilities of escape from state control into the wild mountains and seas, or it could refer to the lonely roads that pass through forests between the walled towns. These are James Scott's 'nonstate' spaces, sites where the trickster can hide from the gaze of power (1998). The highwayman and bank robber can use these roads, with the former escaping to the anonymity of the city tavern after holding up the coach, and the latter driving to the hideout after the bank robbery.

FIGURE 1 A structure for holding outlaws

	Individual	Group
Outside	Outlaw	Outlaw gangs, banditti & pirates
Between	Highwayman and bank robber	Smugglers
Inside	Gentleman burglar	Urban gangs and organized crime

With the coming of urbanization, the border has just as often become an involution within the city, separating the underworld from the straight world. The city has become a place for hiding in full view, because the nameless crowds might as well be the densest forest.

Over the 700 years since early versions of Robin, in the myths of the global north, what we have tended to see is the development of more collective and more urban versions of the economic outlaw. Whilst it is easy enough to find exceptions, there have been fewer outlaws and more gangsters created in the last century, though the myths of the individual and the outside are still just as common in the parade of representations as action figures, cartoon characters and remakes of films. The idea of 'organized crime' represents a sort of echo of the contemporary culture of organizing — one in which the outlaws have learnt from the global merchants and the city has become a new jungle.

Structuralist separations apart, I think what these figures share is an embedded criticism of conventional political economy. That is to say, they reflect and encourage a questioning of what it means to work for your living, or to do what you are told. They also hold out the possibility of living free from interference, of a material plenty without labour, and an authentic relation to self and others which is not based on lying and smiling through your teeth. Representations of economic outlaws are fantasies, but this isn't meant as a dismissal. In the simplest sense, a fantasy is a desired state, possibly even a utopian one, so there are some good reasons to investigate fantasy, particularly if it is one that seems so collective and enduring. This sort of assertion does beg the question of what happens when someone reads a Robin Hood comic, or watches Jack Sparrow in the cinema, and I am not simply suggesting that they end as revolutionaries because of some hidden messages in the text. The question is a bigger one than that, because it involves explaining why 700 years of popular culture has displayed such fascination with a set of heroes who set their faces against the 9 to 5, and insist that you should not believe what you are told. This is what Carl Rhodes has called the 'critique *in* culture' (Rhodes 2007), which is to suggest that documenting this sort of popular cultural dissent which is right in front of us is also to encourage speculation concerning the limits of, and alternatives to, market managerialism (Parker 2002, Rhodes and Parker 2008). In his response to Hobsbawm, which suggests that the 'social bandit' is a largely romantic myth (or 'construct', even), Anton Blok goes on to say:

> Though such constructs may not correspond to actual conditions, they are psychologically real, since they represent fundamental aspirations of people … The myth of the bandit (Hobsbawm's social bandit) represents a craving for a different society, a more human world in which people are justly dealt with and in which there is no suffering. These myths require our attention.
>
> *(1972: 500, 502)*

This is not to rule out the possibility that such myths might also be fantasies that reflect lots of other things, too, and aficionados of psychoanalytic and psychodynamic explanations will be likely to think that I have avoided some hard questions here (Duncan 1996). So too will those with an interest in how readers and viewers respond to the messages in the mass media. But I am happy enough with the very broad generalizations I have made about my cultural texts here and, like Durkheim, don't want to make too many detailed claims about what goes on inside your skull.

Stand and deliver

> … consolation from imaginary things is not an imaginary consolation. On the contrary, it is the only real consolation that modern people have.
>
> *(Scruton 2005: 10)*

This book has explored these images of economic outlaws and alternative business in order to make a general argument about their subversive pleasures. That, I think, is why these archetypes have been so enduring. Whether we understand this in terms of utopian fantasy, the magical resolution of contradictions or a hidden transcript probably doesn't matter that much. All explanations are social, and all assume that imagination (the possibility that things could be otherwise than they are) is both a cause and a consequence of social change. However, more generally this is also an argument about the frontiers of the economic and the organized, and about the ways that certain 'impossible objects' – whether 'Fuck Work' stickers or outlaws – both make and blur the boundaries between insides and outsides. We often refer to a thing called 'the market', or 'work', as if these were uncomplicated things, and the figure of the economic outlaw allows us to see how conceptions of markets and labour have been imagined, legitimated and policed. There are a variety of proper histories which show us how ideas of the market have been naturalized over the past 400 years or so (Griswold 1983, Agnew 1986, Zimmerman 2006, Poovey 2008), but this rather more improper history attempts to show one of the ways in which this naturalization is also contested, or denaturalized. The convergence between these views is the insistence that economics is necessarily entangled with politics and culture, and the organization of work is never a mere matter of efficient necessity. The boundary between the organized economy and criminal activity is always a political issue, one inscribed with all sorts of assumptions about what can be bought, sold, owned or taken and who should benefit.

This dissolving of boundaries must apply to this book, too, and to this author, working in a business school, trading on the outlaws and trying to sell some product.[6] So the materials of the counter culture of organization could also become vehicles for teaching organizational behaviour in business schools, and all this sparkling violence and dissent might simply become a resource to be strip-mined for market managerialism. To some extent, it already has been. At the time of writing, Walt Disney Pictures and Jerry Bruckheimer films are planning the global roll-out of the latest mega-blockbuster – *Pirates of the Caribbean: On Stranger Tides*. The accountants will be laughing all the way to the advertising agency, and the Harvard Business School case study on global marketing won't be far behind. The use of Dilbert cartoons in management teaching is emblematic of this problem, but so are the presentations of pirates as case-study material for business strategy (Leeson 2009), or a book like *Tony Soprano on Management: Leadership Lessons Inspired by America's Favourite Mobster* (Schneider 2004). Many entrepreneurs and management gurus would probably rather like to think about themselves as swashbuckling types, or outlaw characters daring to be different. Richard Branson, Donald Trump and Tom Peters have all 'dared to be different', and 'lived on the edge', too. So perhaps there is something rather suspicious going on here, when global pop stars are claiming outlaw chic, internet entrepreneurs claim to be bandits on the digital frontier, and business school people claim to be on the side of Robin Hood?

In the UK, the business school academic generally lacks cultural capital, largely because the economic utilitarianism of business has always sat uneasily with the pretensions to cultural reproduction which are held in other parts of the university (Lawson 1998). Knowledge about business might claim to be really useful knowledge, but it is unlikely to help the Professor of Management have tea with the Professor of History. But this is not a stable state of affairs. As the business school becomes a central part of the university, and the university becomes more like the business school, it becomes possible to absorb disciplines that seem to have nothing to do with management. It is hence quite possible that a wider sense of culture and history might become the next fashionable turn that would begin to provide the cultural capital that is widely lacking within the business school. Just as corporations gain some reflected status by sponsoring The Rolling Stones, Mick Jagger plays Ned Kelly, and Keith Richards becomes Jack Sparrow's dad in the third *Pirates of the Caribbean* film, so could management academics sponsor themselves by claiming to understand cultural resistance. The business school has managed to ingest everything else that it has been faced with so far, and there seems to be no good reason why the economic outlaws and their alternative businesses might not become both a topic and a resource, too, inlawed whether they like it or not. This turn would itself be part of the culture of organization, a further demonstration that there is nothing that can not be made useful (and profitable) for someone in an organized world. Of course there is also the possibility that *The Little Book of Management Bollocks*, Jack Sparrow's raised eyebrow and the Playmobil duo 5878 'Bandit and Policeman' bubblepack might encourage further experiments in imagination, too. I suppose the central issue, then, is whether you believe that imagination is merely a childish distraction or the beginning of something new, something that doesn't exist but could.

The economy or market is very often naturalized as a space with laws of its own. I hope this book has begun to show that this is a social space that is surrounded by badlands which are inhabited by characters who tangle fiction and fact, and have made profits for many by deciding to be free. I don't think that there are any spaces that are simply economic, or simply cultural, but instead a series of myths and fantasies that began as songs and have now become blockbuster films with cross-marketing opportunities and McDonald's Happy Meal toys. Yet the same roots can produce a story with a very different shape, in the names of Oleksa Dovbush, Angelo Duca, Schinderhannes, Diego Corrientes, Phoolan Devi, Che Guevara or the masked Subcomandante Marcos. What we can (and, I think, do) learn from Robin Hood, Jack Sparrow and John Dillinger is that there might be honourable and authentic alternatives. Not worked-through theories, but other ways of being, other ways of making a living without losing your soul. Sometimes these are collectives – a family, or a gang, or crew of free people. Sometimes these are individuals with integrity and a lucky streak. But whichever fantasy you might prefer, the contradictions remain. When you walk out of the cinema, or raise your head from the book, you remember that work waits in the morning, but that work has paid for a glimpse of something else.

NOTES

1 Knowing the outlaw

1 Indeed, in this 1959 book Hobsbawm seemed unaware of the post-Second World War internationalization of the Mafia, referring to its 'decline' (1965: 44).
2 Though this is less true now than it was, as economic relevance and impact become increasingly more ubiquitous criteria.
3 Playmobil also sell pack 3161 Bank Robbers, 3814 Bandit and 7458 Bandit with Horse.
4 Another area in which is when organizations are themselves treated as cultures, and ideas about 'corporate culture' and the like are used to think through questions of motivation, management techniques and so on. I'll say a little more about this in the next chapter, and see Parker 2000.
5 If you want to know a bit more about other people's methods of reading different forms of culture for evidence about work, organization and economy, have a look at Czarniawska and Guillet de Monthoux (1994); Hassard and Holliday (1998); Smith *et al.* (2001); De Cock and Land (2006); Bell (2008), particularly chapter one; Rhodes and Westwood (2008); or the papers that follow Rhodes and Parker (2008).

2 The many myths of Robin Hood

1 Women could not be outlawed, since they had no legal status. They could only be abandoned, or 'waived' (Rees 2001: 55).
2 A category only repealed in civil proceedings in English law in 1879, and in criminal in 1938.
3 The earliest appearance is actually in French, but only as Robin, in the *Jeu de Robin et Marion* of *c.* 1280. Robin des Bois may in fact be the inspiration for Robin Hood. See also Holt 1960: 103.
4 It continued to be popular, with at least three films and seven TV shows being made during the twentieth century.
5 A development echoed by the 'dime novels' of the USA, with cowboys and outlaws as their heroes. See chapter five.
6 Sullivan also later turned *Ivanhoe* into an opera, performed in 1891.
7 Oddly, one of the best known of Martin Parker's ballads was *When the King Enjoys His Own Again*, presumably known to Tennyson.

8 Who was actually the outlaw Thomas Jones (1530–1609) but who was written about first in 1763 in a volume entitled *The Joker, or Merry Companion* (Rees 2001: 220, 284).
9 See http://robinhoodtax.org.uk/ (accessed 5th March 2010).
10 An excellent source on Robin Hood and twentieth-century popular culture is Allen Wright's www.boldoutlaw.com.
11 In one of which, *Son of Robin Hood* (1958), the son turns out to be a daughter.

3 Pirate utopianism

1 For more on metaphors of piracy in the context of intellectual property, see Land 2007.
2 For example, another famous Captain Jack was the warrior Kintfuash of the Californian Modoc tribe, who was hung in 1873 for rebellion against the expropriation of his land by the whites. His body was embalmed and displayed in Eastern cities as a carnival attraction, price of admission ten cents (Brown 1991: 240).
3 Though there is no agreement over the etymology of this 'Jolly Roger'. It could relate to a colloquialism for the devil, 'Old Roger'. It could be a corruption of Ali Raja, a Tamil pirate captain. Most likely it comes from *Jolie Rouge*, the bloody flag of combat (Cordingly 1999: 142).
4 Just as Eustace Folville, the outlaw I mentioned in chapter two, was pardoned after fighting for the crown in the 1330s. See Tilly 1985.
5 For contemporary versions of this unequal division of profits between financiers and pirates in Somalia, see Kemp 2009: 89, 231.
6 See also Griswold 1983 and Agnew 1986.
7 For a fuller account of the Defoe authorship controversy, see Cordingly's introduction to Johnson 1998, or Burl 2006: 265–70. On Defoe's fascination with the boundaries between crime, morality and the market, see Backscheider 1989: 476, *passim*; Ruggerio 2000b.
8 In a strange piece of intertextuality, Exquemelin also makes reference to an 'Island of Pines' (2000: 128). This was the previous name for an island off the south-west coast of Cuba, now called the 'Isla de la Juventud' (Isle of Youth). It has also been known as the Isle of Parrots, and 'Isla de Tesoros' (Treasure Island). The distinction between utopian writing, travel writing, the diary and fiction is unclear in many of these early texts. Similarly, there is often confusion over authorship. No one knows who Exquemelin was, and Louis Le Golif's *Memoirs of a Buccaneer*, discovered in France at the end of the Second World War, and though supposedly written in the 1690s, may even be a forgery (Lewis 2006: 38). This book is cited by Do or Die (1999) as a source for homosexuality on Tortuga.
9 James Surowiecki (2007) has proposed that contemporary management could learn from the link between forms of democracy which solve the problem of CEO self-interest and that of employee motivation. He suggests, half joking, 'The Management Lessons of Captain Kidd'. Clearly Surowiecki knows little about Kidd's ignominious career, and seemingly nothing at all about the many attempts at worker self-management (Parker *et al.* 2007).
10 Which became Libertatia in the 1952 film *Against All Flags*, and was destroyed by Errol Flynn, an ex-Robin Hood, in order to keep the ships of the East India Company safe.
11 Kuhn (2010: 126) makes a similar argument, noting that Hobsbawm's definitions of what counts as politics and political consequences could be contested.

4 Robbers and romantics

1 Which then connects romanticism with existentialism, and provides a powerful myth in which authenticity and externality are related. See Wilson 1963 for a mostly uncritical review of this idea.

2 As with Robin Hood, pirates, robbers and smugglers, most of the characters are male, though Spraggs does dedicate an appendix to some rare examples of the female highway robber in fact and fiction (2001: 264, *passim*).
3 A pocket-sized, short and cheap book.
4 Though Ainsworth borrows many elements from Edward Bulwer-Lytton's novel *Paul Clifford*, a story of a romantic highwayman published four years previously.
5 In *The Beggar's Opera* he is thinly disguised as the character Peachum, who is opposed to Macheath, a fairly decent highwayman who claims to be robbing from the rich.
6 There are other readings here, too. Two of Macheath's gang are called Robin (Hood?) and Wat (Tyler?).

5 Outlaws and the frontier

1 Though whether the Western really is a genre might be a questionable point. A film like *Fort Apache* (1948) actually contains a whole series of different genres – comedy of manners, slapstick, musical, romance and Western.
2 As Cole Younger is made to say in *The Long Riders* (1980), 'When all this is over, I'm going to write me a book. Make myself even more famous than I already am.'
3 See also John Gast's 1872 painting 'American Progress', in which the westward moving settlers are accompanied by an angel gazing at the horizon (Durham and Hill 2005: 149).
4 And later made into a film of the same title with John Wayne in 1935.
5 This interest in Western slang seems to echo the interest in the cant of London villains I mentioned in the previous chapter.
6 A historical episode given a rather different spin in John Wayne's *Chisum* (1970), which pits Billy the Kid against W. G. Murphy, a cruel local businessman intent on buying all the land in the valley.
7 Though there were many circuses and travelling shows across the world which continued to use variants of the name.
8 Who also appeared in one of the first US highwaymen films, *Dick Turpin*, from 1925.
9 To which might be added, anyone who concentrates power, such as a family patriarch, trading-post owner, politician or judge.
10 A masked nobleman created in 1919 by Johnston McCulley and the subject of many pulp stories and films. Zorro means 'fox' in Spanish, and he rights wrongs in California during the Spanish colonial era.
11 Parodied in *Butch Cassidy and the Sundance Kid* (1969), in which a member of the gang nicknamed 'News' reads accounts of their exploits from clippings.
12 Made into a film with Alan Ladd in 1953.
13 Wister's book is also deeply homoerotic, as if the Western man is a real man – 'at this deeply feminine remark, the Virginian looked at her with such a smile, that, had I been a woman, it would have made me his to do with what he pleased on the spot' (1998: 167).
14 Though he also suggests variations on this theme, in terms of 'vengeance' and 'professionalism'. His interpretation of the latter theme does not fit with the analysis I am suggesting here, simply because he suggests that the team of professional gunslingers' plot necessarily equates to an ideological accommodation with the employment requirements of large organizations.
15 A suggestion made by other thinkers, too. See, for example, Derrida (1992) and Tilly (1985).
16 Just how violent these towns actually were is open to question. See Horan and Sann (1954), Nolan (2003), Ames (2004).
17 Bearing in mind that the Western film became a globalized phenomenon, popular outside the ordinary range of English-speaking or European countries, with film production taking place in India, Japan, Russia and many other countries (Simpson 2006: 241, *passim*).

18 See, for an early example, *Apache* (1954). In *Dances with Wolves* (1990), a white man discovers harmony by joining the natives. 'I knew for the first time who I really was', he says. This plot is essentially revived for the 3D science-fiction film *Avatar* (2009).

19 Though the appropriation of the hyper-masculine cowboy by some gay men does suggest something about the tractability of cultural representations which is broadly helpful for my argument here.

20 Or, in *Ride the High Country* (1962), 'The day of the forty-niner is over. The day of the steady business man has arrived.'

21 William H. Whyte's *The Organization Man*, a scathing critique of obedience and collectivism, was first published in 1956, the same year as the release of *The Searchers*.

22 I am grateful to Ruud Kaulingfreks for his observation that there were plenty of cowboys in South America, too, but that the figure of the cowboy never became a focus for resistance there. This seems to underline the North American particularity of the early myth, and suggests no necessary link between anti-modernism and this particular group of workers.

6 The Mafia

1 For exceptions, see Arlacchi 1988, Enderwick 2009, Gond, Palazzo and Basu 2009.

2 For detail on this rather condensed assertion, see chapter seven in Parker 2002. Note also that this chapter is primarily concerned with the USA and Sicily. There are many other illegal business organizations now referred to as 'Mafias' – in Italy the Comorra, 'Ndrangheta and Sacra Corona Unita, and elsewhere the Russian Mafiya and organized criminals in South Africa, Bulgaria, India, Chechnya and so on. There are many similarities and differences between their organizational structures and business practices (Southwell 2006, Glenny 2009, and see chapter seven).

3 The 'Racketeer Influenced and Corrupt Organizations' act of 1970, designed to attack organized crime. There are suggestions that the name is a pun on Edward G. Robinson's character 'Rico', a version of Capone, in the film *Little Caesar* (1931).

4 In this sub-genre, see also *The Mafia Manager: A Guide to the Corporate Machiavelli* by the mysterious V.

5 This estimate comes from SOS Impresa in 2010, an Italian retail lobby group, and is based on government figures.

6 (1) From old French *maufer*, god of evil; (2) from Arabic *mihfal*, assembly of many people; (3) from Arabic *mafia*, place of refuge; (4) from 'Mazzini Autorizza Furti, Incendi, Avvelenamenti', 'Mazzini (a leader of the Risorgimento) Authorises Robberies, Arson and Poisoning'; (5) from *maha*, the Arabic word for the tufa stone caves that Garibaldi and his men hid in during the Risorgimento; (6) from Arabic *mascias*, being self-confident (Lewis 1984: 25; Sterling 1991: 54; Dickie 2004: 144).

7 Though Nick Gentile, the boss of Pittsburgh from 1915 onwards, claimed that a 'council' arrangement existed before Luciano, as did the five families. He complained that the council was a place where eloquence was the key issue in resolving disputes, and not logic (Dickie 2004: 219, 227). For organizational structures in Sicily, see Gambetta (1993: 100, *passim*), though see Arlacchi (1988: 44) for a more decentralized view.

8 For an edited collection of papers that connect the Mafia, trust and economics, see Gambetta 2000.

9 It was only really after the invention of durable recording technologies, combined with the legally generous provisions of the Racketeer Influenced and Corrupt Organizations Act, that evidence about the Mafia could become mobile, and effective in a judicial context.

10 The Mafia is a violent organization, responsible for many deaths. The Sicilian village of Corleone, which had a population of 18,000, had 153 murders between 1944 and 1948 (Lewis 1984: 95) Forty years later, in the first six months of 1989, 428 people were

murdered in Sicily. These are big numbers, but consider some others. In Bhopal, India on 13th December 1984, about 15,000 people were killed, and ten times as many injured by a release of chemicals from the Union Carbide plant. In the USA, in 2008, 4,340 people were killed in industrial accidents, 85,000 from alcohol-related deaths, and 435,000 from tobacco-related deaths. These are bigger numbers. See Gond *et al.* 2009.

11 See Gambetta (1993: 262, *passim*) for more accounts of this ritual. Like the pirate 'articles', contemporary accounts of highwaymen suggested an initiation ritual, too, in which all prior loyalties were set aside in favour of a bond that would exceed all others (Spraggs 2001: 151).

12 On the Mafia and the peasant, see Burrell 1997: 64, *passim*.

13 But not always male. See Sarah Vowell's essay, 'Take the Cannoli' (2002).

14 See also the marvellous description of Don Fabrizio in di Lampedusa's *The Leopard*.

15 The opening shot of *The Godfather* has the undertaker Amerigo Bonasera pleading with Don Corleone for a favour. He begins 'I believe in America … '.

7 Modern bandits

1 A fear found in the USA as well (Burrough 2005: 17).

2 The individualization of some of these terms is predicated on the existence of the group – as in gangster and mobster.

3 Keg Steakhouse and Bar's 'Billy Miner Pie'.

4 For accounts of Irish highwaymen who resisted the British and probably informed bushwacker mythology, see Seal 1996: 69, *passim*.

5 To add historical accuracy, or irony, one of the gang's suits of armour was used in the film. See Seal (1996: 168) for a copy of the film poster.

6 McCarty (2004: 126) called Ness 'a Wyatt Earp for the twentieth century'.

7 Again, one of the few women, a matter to which I will return in the final chapter.

8 On the confused etymology of 'hooligan', see Pearson 1983: 255.

9 In May 2010, 70 people were killed in the Tivoli Gardens suburb of Kingston as a result of organized resistance to Coke's extradition to the USA. Coke was widely seen as a local benefactor and force for stability, with suggestions that this was tolerated by local politicians in return for votes.

8 The counter culture and organization

1 See Wray-Bliss (2003) for amplifications of this kind of argument.

2 Though several people have pointed me to Batman's 'Wayne Enterprises' and Iron Man's 'Stark Industries' as exceptions here.

3 And the 'probably' here is very interesting, in terms of the different 'freedoms' that different workplaces might offer their employees.

4 Boren is President and Founder of INATAPROBU, the International Association of Professional Politicians and Bureaucrats which recognizes excellence in 'dynamic inaction, orbital dialoguing, communicative fuzzification and creative non-responsivity' (jimboren.com/inataprobu.html). He has also written books called *The Bureaucratic Zoo* and *When in Doubt Mumble*.

5 Most of the websites cited in this chapter were accessed some time in 2004.

6 Apologies for the ethnocentricity of the following examples. Popular culture of the TV variety is rarely genuinely global.

7 At the time of writing, the series is being remade, but with the anti-work satire just as pointed.

8 Less ribald, but just as powerfully, Matanle *et al.* have also shown how Japanese salary-man manga comics can represent popular challenges to management authority (2008).

9 It is also worth noting that the industrial sociology tradition tended to focus on (and perhaps romanticize) male factory work. The representations I have presented are primarily about life in offices, and hence about women's work, too. This (in part) reflects changes in the location of work and the segmentation of labour markets.

10 An absorption of anthropology that was prefigured by some of the ironic accounts of the 'management tribe' that I mentioned in the previous section.

11 Thanks to Paul Grivell for the first example, Sam Warren for the second, Wendy Brown for the third, Jude Courtney for the fourth and *The Idler* (2005) for the fifth.

9 Popular political economy

1 Thanks to James Taylor for this example.

2 The spelling should, as the attentive reader will have noticed, be Hardin.

3 The only exception I have come across outside fanzine and slash fiction is Tennyson Jesse's Captain Lovel in her *Moonraker* (1927).

4 See 'Marxism and Sociology' in Durkheim 1982.

5 No apologies to Stevphen Shukaitis for borrowing his phrase.

6 Which will perhaps make some small contribution to the profits of the business, management and accounting list in the social sciences profit centre of the Routledge imprint now owned by Taylor & Francis, which itself forms part of the publishing arm of the global information corporation Informa PLC.

BIBLIOGRAPHY

Ackroyd, S. and Thompson, P. (1999) *Organisational Misbehaviour*. London: Sage.

Adler, T. (2007) *Hollywood and the Mob*. London: Bloomsbury.

Agnew, J.-C. (1986) *Worlds Apart: The Market and the Theater in Anglo-American Thought*. Cambridge: Cambridge University Press.

Alvesson, M., Bridgman, T. and Willmott, H. (eds) (2009) *The Oxford Handbook of Critical Management Studies*. Oxford: Oxford University Press.

Ames, J. (2004) *The Real Deadwood*. New York: Chamberlain Bros.

Amin, A. and Thrift, N. (2004) *The Cultural Economy Reader*. Oxford: Blackwell.

Anand, N. (2006) 'Cartoon Displays as Autoproduction of Organizational Culture.' In: Rafaeli, A. and Pratt, M. (eds), *Artifacts and Organizations*, 85–100. Mahwah, NJ: Lawrence Erlbaum Associates.

Arlacchi, P. (1988) *Mafia Business: The Mafia Ethic and the Spirit of Capitalism*. Oxford: Oxford University Press.

Armstrong, S. (2008) *War Plc: The Rise of the New Corporate Mercenary*. London: Faber & Faber.

Asbury, H. (1927/2002) *The Gangs of New York*. London: Arrow Books.

Backscheider, P. (1989) *Daniel Defoe*. Baltimore: Johns Hopkins University Press.

Balmain, J. (2001) *The Office Kama Sutra*. San Francisco: Chronicle Books.

Balsamo, W. and Carpozi, G. (1997) *The Mafia: The First 100 Years*. London: Virgin Books.

Barry, D. (2000) *The Chivalry of Crime*. London: Jonathan Cape.

Barthes, R. (1977) 'Rhetoric of the Image.' In: Heath, S. (ed. and trans.), *Image Music Text*, 32–51. London: Fontana.

Beaton, A. (2001) *The Little Book of Management Bollocks*. London: Pocket Books.

Bell, E. (2008) *Reading Management and Organization in Film*. London: Palgrave.

Billington, R. and Ridge, M. (2001) *Westward Expansion*. Albuquerque, NM: University of New Mexico Press.

Blok, A. (1972) 'The Peasant and the Brigand: Social Banditry Reconsidered.' *Comparative Studies in Society and History* 14/4: 494–503.

Boozer, J. (2003) *Career Movies: American Business and the Success Mystique*. Austin, TX: University of Texas Press.

Boren, J. (2003) *How to be a Sincere Phoney: A Handbook for Politicians and Bureaucrats*. Whitsboro, TX: Birdcage Publications.

Bowden, M. (2001) *Killing Pablo*. London: Atlantic Books.

Brown, D. (1991) *Bury My Heart at Wounded Knee*. London: Vintage.

Bruce, S. (1999) 'Introduction.' In: Bruce, S. (ed.), *Three Early Modern Utopias*, ix–xlii. Oxford: Oxford University Press.

Burg, B. (1985) *Sodomy and the Pirate Tradition*. New York: New York University Press.

Burl, A. (2006) *Black Barty: Bartholomew Roberts and His Pirate Crew 1718–1723*. Stroud, UK: Sutton Publishing.

Burnett, J. (2003) *Dangerous Waters*. New York: Plume.

Burrell, G. (1997) *Pandemonium: Towards a Retro-Organization Theory*. London: Sage.

Burrough, B. (2005) *Public Enemies*. London: Penguin.

Burroughs, W. (1999) *Word Virus: The William Burroughs Reader*. Ed. J. Grauerholz and I. Silverberg. London: Flamingo.

Callon, M. (ed.) (1998) *The Laws of the Markets*. Oxford: Blackwell.

Callon, M., Millo, Y. and Muniesa, F. (eds) (2007) *Market Devices*. Oxford: Blackwell.

Cantor, N. (1970) *The Age of Protest*. London: George Allen and Unwin.

Carey, P. (2001) *True History of the Kelly Gang*. London: Faber and Faber.

Carlson, P. (2006) 'Myth and the Modern Cowboy.' In: Carlson, P. (ed.), *The Cowboy Way*, 13–21. Stroud, UK: Tempus Publishing.

Chwastiak, M. (2007) 'War Incorporated.' Paper presented at Critical Management Studies 5 conference, University of Manchester.

Cleverley, G. (1971) *Managers and Magic*. London: Longman.

Cohen, A. (1966) *Deviance and Control*. Englewood Cliffs, NJ: Prentice Hall.

Cohen, L. and Tyler, M. (2004) '*The Office* (27 November 2003 – 18 January 2004), The Photographers' Gallery, London: A Review.' *Work, Employment and Society* 18/3: 621–9.

Cohen, P. (1997) 'Subcultural Conflict and Working Class Community.' In: Gelder, K. and Thornton, S. (eds), *The Subcultures Reader*, 90–9. London: Routledge.

Cook, J. (ed.) (2005) *The Colossal P. T. Barnum Reader*. Urbana, IL: University of Illinois Press.

Cooper, R. (1990) 'Organisation/Disorganisation.' In: Hassard, J. and Pym, D. (eds), *The Theory and Philosophy of Organisations*, 167–97. London: Routledge.

Cordingly, D. (1999) *Life among the Pirates*. London: Abacus.

Courtis, J. (2000) *The Bluffer's Guide to Management*. London: Oval Books.

Cox, J. (1998) 'Robin Hood: Earl, Outlaw or Rebel.' *International Socialism*, March (Spring). http://pubs.socialistreviewindex.org.uk/isj78/cox.htm.

darkmatter (2009) Special Issue on 'Pirates and Piracy', 5. www.darkmatter101.org, accessed 25th January 2010.

Czarniawska, B. and Guillet de Monthoux, P. (1994) *Good Novels, Better Management*. Chur, Switzerland: Harwood Academic.

Darnton, R. (1984) *The Great Cat Massacre*. New York: Basic Books.

Davenport-Hines, R. (1997) *Gothic: Four Hundred Years of Excess, Horror, Evil and Ruin*. New York: North Point Press.

Davis, J. (2002) *The Circus Age*. Chapel Hill, NC: University of North Carolina Press.

De Cock, C. and Land, C. (2006) 'Organization/Literature: Exploring the Seam.' *Organization Studies* 27/4: 517–35.

DeMeo, A. (with Mary Jane Ross) (2003) *For the Sins of My Father*. London: Aurum Press.

Derrida, J. (1992) 'The Force of Law.' In: Cornell, D., Rosenfeld, M. and Carlson, D. (eds), *Deconstruction and the Possibility of Justice*, 2–67. New York: Routledge.

Dickens, P. and Ormrod, J. (2007) *Cosmic Sociology*. London: Routledge.

Dickie, J. (2004) *Cosa Nostra: A History of the Sicilian Mafia*. London: Hodder and Stoughton.

Dickson, P. (1996) *The Official Rules at Work*. London: Robson Books.

Dixon-Kennedy, M. (2006) *The Robin Hood Handbook*. Stroud, UK: Sutton Publishing.

Do or Die (1999) 'Pirate Utopias.' *Do or Die* 8: 63–78. www.eco-action.org/dod/no8/pirate.html.

Doel, M. and Clarke, D. (2002) 'An Invention without a Future, a Solution without a Problem.' In: Kitchin, R. and Kneale, J. (eds), *Lost in Space*, 136–55. London: Continuum.

du Gay, P. and Pryke, M. (eds) (2002) *Cultural Economy*. London: Sage.

Duncan, M. (1996) *Romantic Outlaws, Beloved Prisons*. New York: New York University Press.

Duncombe, S. (1997) *Notes from Underground*. Bloomington, IN: Microcosm Publishing.

Durden Smith, J. (2003) *The Mafia*. London: Arcturus.

Durham, J. and Hill, R. W. (eds) (2005) *The American West*. Warwickshire: Compton Verney.

Durkheim, E. (1982) *The Rules of Sociological Method*. Basingtoke: Macmillan.

Dyer, R. (1993) 'Entertainment and Utopia.' In: During, S. (ed.), *Cultural Studies Reader*, 272–83. London: Routledge.

Earle, P. (2004) *The Pirate Wars*. London: Methuen.

Ellis, N. (2008) '"What the Hell is *That*?"' *Organization* 15/5: 705–23.

Ellms, C. (2006) 'Voyage to Execution Dock.' In: Lewis, J. (ed.), *The Mammoth Book of Pirates*, 134–47. London: Robinson.

Enderwick, P. (2009) 'Applying the Eclectic Framework.' *Critical Perspectives on International Business* 5/3: 170–86.

Exquemelin, A. (2000) *The Buccaneers of America*. Mineola, NY: Dover Publications.

Ferrell, J., Hayward, K. and Young, J. (2008) *Cultural Criminology*. London: Sage.

Fishall, R. (1981) *Bureaucrats: How to Annoy Them*. London: Sidgwick and Jackson.

Gabbard, G. (2002) *The Psychology of the Sopranos*. New York: Basic Books.

Gambetta, D. (1993) *The Sicilian Mafia: The Business of Private Protection*. Cambridge, MA: Harvard University Press.

——— , D. (2009) *Codes of the Underworld*. Princeton, NJ: Princeton University Press.

Gambetta, D. (ed.) (2000) *Trust: Making and Breaking Cooperative Relations*. Electronic edition, Department of Sociology, University of Oxford. www.sociology.ox.ac.uk/papers/trustbook.html (first published by Blackwell, 1988).

Gelfer, J. (2002) *The Little Book of Office Bollocks*. Chichester: Summersdale.

Glenny, M. (2009) *McMafia*. London: Vintage.

Godelier, M. (1985) 'The Object and Method of Economic Anthropology.' In: Lackner, H. and Seddon, D. (eds), *Relations of Production: Marxist Approaches to Economic Anthropology*, 49–126. London: Routledge.

Gond, J.-P., Palazzo, G. and Basu, K. (2009) 'Reconsidering Corporate Social Responsibility through the Mafia Metaphor.' *Business Ethics Quarterly* 19/1: 57–85.

Griswold, W. (1983) 'The Devil's Technique: Cultural Legitimation and Social Change.' *American Sociological Review* 48: 668–80.

Groening, M. (2004) *Work is Hell*. London: HarperCollins.

Halford, S. (2004) 'Towards a Sociology of Organisational Space.' *Sociological Research Online* 9/1. www.socresonline.org.uk/9/1/halford.html.

Hall, S. and Jefferson, T. (eds) (1976) *Resistance through Rituals*. London: Hutchinson.

Hancock, P. (2008) 'Fear and (Self) Loathing in Coleridge Close.' *Organization* 15/5: 685–703.

Hassard, J. and Holliday, R. (eds) (1998) *Organisation-Representation*. London: Sage.

Hassrick, R. (1974) *Cowboys: The Real Story of Cowboys and Cattlemen*. London: Octopus Books.

Hay, D., Linebaugh, P., Rule, J., Thompson, E. and Winslow, C. (eds) (1977) *Albion's Fatal Tree*. Harmondsworth: Peregrine.

Heath, J. and Potter, A. (2004) *Rebel Sell*. Chichester: Capstone Publishing.

Hesmondhalgh, D. (2007) *The Cultural Industries*. London: Sage.

Hill, C. (1969) *Reformation to Industrial Revolution*. Harmondsworth: Pelican.

—— (1978) *The World Turn'd Upside Down*. London: Penguin.

Hill, H. (with Gus Russo) (2004) *Gangsters and Goodfellas*. Edinburgh: Mainstream Publishing.

Hobbs, D. (1997) 'Professional Crime: Change, Continuity and the Enduring Myth of the Underworld.' *Sociology* 31/1: 57–72.

—— (2001) 'Organizational Logic and Criminal Culture on a Shifting Terrain.' *British Journal of Criminology* 41: 549–60.

Hobsbawm, E. (1965) *Primitive Rebels*. New York: W.W. Norton & Co.

—— (1972a) *Bandits*. Harmondsworth: Pelican.

—— (1972b) 'Social Bandits: Reply.' *Comparative Studies in History and Society* 14/4: 503–5.

Hobsbawm, E., Samuel, R., May, M., Thompson, E., Linebaugh, P., Hay, D., Hirst, P. and Rock, P. (1972) 'Distinctions between Socio-Political and Other Forms of Crime.' *Bulletin – Society for the Study of Labour History*, Autumn, 25: 5–21.

Holt, J. (1960) 'The Origins and Audience of the Ballads of Robin Hood.' *Past and Present* 18/1: 89–110.

Horan, J. and Sann, P. (1954) *Pictorial History of the Old West*. London: Spring Books.

Horkheimer, M. and Adorno, T. (2002) 'The Culture Industry.' In idem, *Dialectic of Enlightenment*, 94–136. Stanford, CA: Stanford University Press.

Hornung, E. W. (1898) 'The Ides of March.' http://www.worlds-best-detective-crime-and-murder-mystery-books.com/idesofmarch.html.

Hyde, L. (2008) *Trickster Makes This World*. Edinburgh: Canongate.

Hympendahl, K. (2003) *Pirates Aboard*. Dobbs Ferry, NY: Sheridan House.

ICC International Maritime Bureau (2011) *Piracy and Armed Robbery against Ships. Annual Report*. London: International Chamber of Commerce.

Jack, G. (2002) 'After Cultural Economy.' *Ephemera* 2/3: 263–76. www.ephemeraweb.org.

James, L. (ed.) (1978) *Print and the People 1819–1851*. Harmondsworth: Peregrine.

Johnson, C. (1998) *A General History of the Robberies and Murders of the Most Notorious Pirates*. London: Conway Maritime Press.

Kaulingfreks, R., Lightfoot, G. and Letiche, H. (2009) 'The Man in the Black Hat.' *Culture and Organization* 15/2: 151–65.

Kemp, R. (2009) *Pirates*. London: Michael Joseph.

Knight, S. and Ohlgren, T. (eds) (1997) *Robin Hood and Other Outlaw Tales*. Kalamazoo, MI: Medieval Institute Publications. http://www.lib.rochester.edu/camelot/teams/robhgenint.htm.

Kontorovich, E. (2004) 'The Piracy Analogy.' *Harvard International Law Journal* 45/1: 183–237.

Kuhn, G. (2010) *Life under the Jolly Roger*. Oakland, CA: PM Press.

Lamborne Wilson, P. (1995) *Pirate Utopias*. Brooklyn, NY: Autonomedia.

Land, C. (2007) 'Flying the Black Flag.' *Management and Organizational History* 2/2: 169–92.

Langewiesche, W. (2006) *The Outlaw Sea*. London: Granta.

Lapouge, G. (2004) *Pirates and Buccaneers*. London: Hachette Illustrated.

Lash, S. and Urry, J. (1994) *Economies of Signs and Space*. London: Sage.

Lawson, A. (1998) 'Culture and Utility: Phrases in Dispute.' In: Jary, D. and Parker, M. (eds), *The New Higher Education: Issues and Directions for the Post-Dearing University*, 273–87. Stoke-on-Trent: Staffordshire University Press.

Le Guin, U. (2003) 'Foreword.' In idem, *Tales from Earthsea*. London: Orion Books.

Lea, J. (1999) 'Social Crime Revisited.' *Theoretical Criminology* 3/3: 307–25.

Leeson, P. (2009) *The Invisible Hook: The Hidden Economics of Pirates*. Princeton, NJ: Princeton University Press.

Levi-Strauss, C. (1963) *Structural Anthropology*. London: Penguin.

Levitt, S. and Dubner, S. (2006) *Freakonomics*. London: Penguin.

Lewis, J. (ed.) (2006) *The Mammoth Book of Pirates*. London: Robinson.

Lewis, N. (1984) *The Honoured Society: The Sicilian Mafia Observed*. London: Eland.

Linebaugh, P. and Rediker, M. (2000) *The Many-Headed Hydra*. Boston: Beacon Press.

Longrigg, C. (2005) *No Questions Asked: The Secret Life of Women in the Mob*. New York: Miramax.

Longrigg, C. and McMahon, B. (2006) 'Fresh Cheese and Sweet Nothings.' *The Guardian*, 15th April.

Lupton, D. and Noble, G. (2002). 'Mine/Not Mine: Appropriating Personal Computers in the Academic Workplace.' *Journal of Sociology* 38/1: 5–19.

Mannheim, K. (1960) *Ideology and Utopia*. London: Routledge and Kegan Paul.

Martin, D. and Shephard, C. (1998) *The American West 1840–1895*. London: John Murray.

Mason, M. (2008) *The Pirate's Dilemma*. London: Allen Lane.

Matanle, P., McCann, L. and Ashmore, D. (2008) 'Men Under Pressure.' *Organization* 15/5: 639–64.

Matthews, J. (2006) *Pirates*. London: Carlton Books.

Matza, D. (1964) *Delinquency and Drift*. New York: John Wiley.

McCarty, J. (2004) *Bullets over Hollywood: The American Gangster Picture*. Cambridge, MA: Da Capo Press.

McDonald, B. (2010) *Gangs of London*. Preston: Milo Books.

McIntosh, M. (1971) 'Changes in the Organization of Thieving.' In: Cohen, S. (ed.), *Images of Deviance*, 98–133. Harmondsworth: Penguin.

Mennell, S., Murcott, A. and van Otterloo, A. (1992) *The Sociology of Food*. London: Sage/ International Sociological Association.

Minkes, J. and Minkes, L. (eds) (2008) *Corporate and White Collar Crime*. London: Sage.

Mitchell, D. (2006) 'A Short History of New England Privateering.' In: Lewis, J. (ed.), *The Mammoth Book of Pirates*, 318–22. London: Robinson.

Moore, L. (1997) *The Thieves Opera*. London: Viking.

Morley, G. (1990) *Smuggling in Hampshire and Dorset 1700–1850*. Newbury: Countryside Books.

Newitz, A. (2006) *Pretend We're Dead: Capitalist Monsters in American Pop Culture*. London: Duke University Press.

Nolan, F. (2003) *The Wild West*. London: Arcturus Publishing.

Orwell, G. (1968) 'Mark Twain – The Licensed Jester.' In idem, *The Collected Essays, Journals and Letters of George Orwell, Volume II*, 325–8. London: Secker and Warburg (orig. pub. 1943).

—— (1965) 'Raffles and Miss Blandish.' In idem, *Decline of the English Murder and Other Essays*, 15–20. Harmondsworth: Penguin (orig. pub. 1944).

Osborne, L. (1998) 'A Pirate's Progress.' *Linguafranca* March, 8/2 http://linguafranca. mirror.theinfo.org/9803/Osborne.html.

Padgett, J. and Ansell, C. (1993) 'Robust Action and the Rise of the Medici.' *American Journal of Sociology* 98/6: 1259–1319.

Page, M. (1972) *The Company Savage*. London: Cassell & Company.

Parish, J. (1995) *Pirates and Seafaring Swashbucklers on the Hollywood Screen*. Jefferson, NC: McFarland & Co.

Parish, J. and Parker, M. (eds) (2001) *The Age of Anxiety: Conspiracy Theory and the Human Sciences*. Oxford: Blackwell.

Parker, M. (2000) *Organisational Culture and Identity*. London: Sage.

—— (2002) *Against Management*. Oxford: Polity.

—— (2005) 'Organisational Gothic.' *Culture and Organization* 11/3: 153–66.

—— (2009) 'Capitalists in Space.' In: Bell, D. and Parker, M. (eds), *Space Travel and Culture: From Apollo to Space Tourism*, 83–97. Oxford: Blackwell.

Parker, M., Fournier, V. and Reedy P. (2007) *The Dictionary of Alternatives: Utopianism and Organization*. London: Zed.

Parkinson, C. (1958) *Parkinson's Law, or the Pursuit of Progress*. London: John Murray.

Partridge, B. (1958) *A History of Orgies*. London: Anthony Blond.

Pearson, G. (1975) *The Deviant Imagination*. Basingstoke: Macmillan.

—— (1983) *Hooligan: A History of Respectable Fears*. Basingstoke: Macmillan.

Pearson, J. (1995) *The Profession of Violence: The Rise and Fall of the Kray Twins*. London: HarperCollins.

Philips, E. (2002) *The Tiny Book of Boss Jokes*. London: HarperCollins.

Pileggi, N. (1985) *Wiseguy*. New York: Simon and Schuster.

Pistone, J. (with Richard Woodley) (1987) *Donnie Brasco: My Undercover Life in the Mafia*. New York: New American Library.

Polyani, K. (2001) *The Great Transformation: The Political and Economic Origins of our Time*. Boston, MA: Beacon Press (orig. pub. 1944).

Poovey, M. (2008) *Genres of the Credit Economy*. Chicago: University of Chicago Press.

Punch, M. (1996) *Dirty Business: Exploring Corporate Misconduct*. London: Sage.

Puzo, M. (1969) *The Godfather*. London: William Heinemann.

Quinn, T. (1999) *Smugglers' Tales*. Newton Abbot: David & Charles.

Rainger, J. G. (2006) 'French Cowboys.' In: Carlson, P. (ed.), *The Cowboy Way*, 181–92. Stroud, UK: Tempus Publishing.

Rawlinson, P. (1998) 'Mafia, Media and Myth.' *The Howard Journal of Criminal Justice* 37/4: 346–58.

—— (2002) 'Capitalists, Criminals and Oligarchs – Sutherland and the New "Robber Barons".' *Crime, Law and Social Change* 37: 293–307.

Ray, L. and Sayer, A. (1999) *Culture and Economy after the Cultural Turn*. London: Sage.

Rediker, M. (1987) *Between the Devil and the Deep Blue Sea*. Cambridge: Cambridge University Press.

—— (2004) *Villains of All Nations*. London: Verso.

Rees, D. (2004) *My New Filing Technique Is Unstoppable*. New York: Berkeley Publishing Group.

Rees, E. (2001) *Welsh Outlaws and Bandits: Political Rebellion and Lawlessness in Wales, 1400–1603*. Birmingham: Caterwen Press.

Rehn, A. (2004) *The Serious Unreal*. Helsinki: Dvalin.

—— (2008) 'Pop (Culture) Goes the Organization.' *Organization* 15/5: 765–83.

Reiner, R. (2002) 'Media Made Criminality.' In: Maguire, M., Morgan, R. and Reiner, R. (eds), *The Oxford Handbook of Criminology*, 346–416. Oxford: Oxford University Press.

Rhodes, C. (2001) 'D'Oh: The Simpsons, Popular Culture and the Organizational Carnival.' *Journal of Management Inquiry* 10/4: 374–83.

—— (2007) 'Outside the Gates of Eden: Utopia and Work in Rock Music.' *Group and Organization Management* 32/1: 22–49.

Rhodes, C. and Parker, M. (2008) 'Images of Organizing in Popular Culture.' *Organization* 15/5: 627–37.

Rhodes, C. and Westwood, R. (2008) *Critical Representations of Work and Organization in Popular Culture*. London: Routledge.

Richards, J. (1977) *Swordsmen of the Screen*. London: Routledge and Kegan Paul.

Robb, P. (1998) *Midnight in Sicily*. London: Harvill Press.

Rogozinski, J. (1997) *Dictionary of Pirates*. Ware, UK: Wordsworth Editions.

Ross, E. A. (1907) *Sin and Society*. Boston: Houghton Mifflin Company.

Ruggerio, V. (2000a) *Crime and Markets*. Oxford: Oxford University Press.

—— (2000b) 'Daniel Defoe and Business Crime.' In idem, *Crime and Markets: Essays in Anti-Criminology*, 157–77. Oxford: Oxford University Press.

—— (2003) *Crime in Literature*. London: Verso.

Rule, J. (1977) 'Wrecking and Coastal Plunder.' In: Hay, D., Linebaugh, P., Rule, J., Thompson, E. and Winslow, C. (eds), *Albion's Fatal Tree*, 167–88. Harmondsworth: Peregrine.

Rutherford-Moore, R. (1998) *The Legend of Robin Hood*. Chieveley: Capall Bann Publishing.

Saga, J. (1995) *Confessions of a Yakuza*. Tokyo: Kadansha International.

Sante, L. (1998) *Low Life: Lures and Snares of Old New York*. London: Granta.

Saviano, R. (2008) *Gomorrah: Italy's Other Mafia*. London: Pan.

Schaefer, J. (2003) *Shane*. New York: Laurel-Leaf (orig. pub. 1949).

Schneider, A. (2004) *Tony Soprano on Management: Leadership Lessons Inspired by America's Favourite Mobster*. New York: Berkley Books.

Scott, J. (1985) *Weapons of the Weak: Everyday Forms of Peasant Resistance*. New Haven, CT: Yale University Press.

—— (1990) *Domination and the Arts of Resistance*. New Haven, CT: Yale University Press.

—— (1998) *Seeing Like a State*. New Haven, CT: Yale University Press.

Scott, W. (1996) *Ivanhoe*. Oxford: Oxford University Press (orig. pub. 1819).

Scruton, R. (2005) *News from Somewhere*. London: Continuum.

Seal, G. (1996) *The Outlaw Legend: A Cultural Tradition in Britain, America and Australia*. Cambridge: Cambridge University Press.

—— (2009) 'The Robin Hood Principle: Folklore, History and the Social Bandit.' *Journal of Folklore Research* 46/1: 67–89.

Sharpe, J. (2005) *Dick Turpin: The Myth of the English Highwayman*. London: Profile Books.

Siebert, R. (1996) *Secrets of Life and Death: Women and the Mafia*. London: Verso.

Simpson, P. (2006) *The Rough Guide to Westerns*. London: Rough Guides Ltd.

Slatta, R. (2007) 'Eric J. Hobsbawms's Social Bandit: A Critique and Revision.' *A Contra Corriente* 4/3: 22–30.

Slotkin, R. (1992) *Gunfighter Nation*. New York: HarperCollins.

Smircich, L. (1983) 'Concepts of Culture and Organisational Analysis.' *Administrative Science Quarterly* 28: 339–58.

Smith, W., Higgins, M., Parker, M. and Lightfoot, G. (eds) (2001) *Science Fiction and Organisation*. London: Routledge.

Snelders, S. (2005) *The Devil's Anarchy*. Brooklyn, NY: Autonomedia.

Southwell, D. (2006) *The History of Organized Crime*. London: SevenOaks.

Sparks, R. (1996) 'Masculinity and Heroism in the Hollywood Blockbuster.' *British Journal of Criminology* 36/3: 348–60.

Spraggs, G. (2001) *Outlaws and Highwaymen*. London: Pimlico.

Stanley, J. (ed.) (1996) *Bold in her Breeches*. London: Pandora/HarperCollins.

Sterling, C. (1991) *The Mafia*. London: Grafton.

Surowiecki, J. (2007) 'The Pirates' Code.' *New Yorker Online*, 9 July. www.newyorker.com/online/2007/07/09/070709on_onlineonly_surowiecki, accessed 14th July 2007.

Sutherland, E. (1983) *White Collar Crime: The Uncut Version*. Yale University Press.

Taylor, J. (2005) 'Business in Pictures: Representations of Railway Enterprise in Britain 1845–70.' *Past and Present* 189: 111–45.

Tennyson, A. (1881) 'The Foresters, or Robin Hood and Maid Marian.' http://www.lib.rochester.edu/camelot/rh/forest.htm.

Tennyson Jesse, F. (1981) *Moonraker*. London: Virago (orig. pub. 1927).

Thier, D. (2010) 'Somali Pirates Say They'll Play Robin Hood in Haiti.' http://www.aolnews.com/2010/02/01/somali-pirates-say-theyll-play-robin-hood-in-haiti, accessed 16th March 2010.

Tilly, C. (1985) 'War Making and State Making as Organized Crime.' In: Evans, P., Rueschmeyer, D. and Skcocpol, T. (eds), *Bringing the State Back In*, 169–87. Cambridge: Cambridge University Press.

Townsend, R. (1970) *Up the Organisation*. London: Michael Joseph.

Trolinger, J. B. (2006) 'Rodeo Cowboy.' In: Carlson, P. (ed.), *The Cowboy Way*, 170–80. Stroud, UK: Tempus Publishing.

Turner, C. (2004) *Planet Simpson*. London: Random House.

Twain, M. (1985) *Roughing It*. New York: Penguin Classics.

ul Haq, M., Kaul, I. and Grunberg, I. (eds) (1996) *The Tobin Tax*. New York: Oxford University Press.

V. (1997) *The Mafia Manager*. New York: St Martin's Press.

Vowell, S. (2002) *Take the Cannoli: Stories from the New World*. London: Hamish Hamilton.

Wagner, J. (2006) 'Cowboy: Origin and Early Use of the Term.' In: Carlson, P. (ed.), *The Cowboy Way*, 22–31. Stroud, UK: Tempus Publishing.

Warren, S. (2006) 'Hot Nesting: A Visual Exploration of Personalised Workspaces in a Hot-Desk Office Environment.' In: Case, P., Lilley, S. and Owens, T. (eds), *The Speed of Organization*, 119–46. Copenhagen: Copenhagen Business School Press.

Weber, M. (1978) *Economy and Society: Volume 1*. Berkeley: University of California Press.

Weiner, R. (2006) 'Cowboy Songs and Nature in the Late Nineteenth Century.' In: Carlson, P. (ed.), *The Cowboy Way*, 155–69. Stroud, UK: Tempus Publishing.

Williams, R. (1976) *Keywords*. London: Fontana.

Willis, P. (1977) *Learning to Labour*. Farnborough: Saxon House.

Willmott, H. (1993) 'Strength Is Ignorance; Slavery Is Freedom: Managing Culture in Modern Organisations.' *Journal of Management Studies* 30/4: 515–52.

Wilson, C. (1963) *The Outsider*. London: Pan.

Winslow, C. (1977) 'Sussex Smugglers.' In: Hay, D., Linebaugh, P., Rule, J., Thompson, E. and Winslow, C. (eds), *Albion's Fatal Tree*, 119–66. Harmondsworth: Peregrine.

Winter, S. (2006) 'Hollywood out to Make a Killing from Mafia Police.' *Sunday Express*, 9th April.

Wister, O. (1998) *The Virginian*. Oxford: Oxford University Press (orig. pub. 1902).

Woodard, C. (2007) *The Republic of Pirates*. New York: Harcourt Brace Jovanovich.

Wray-Bliss, E. (2003) 'Research Subjects/Research Subjections: The Politics and Ethics of Critical Research.' *Organization* 10/2: 307–25.

Wright, W. (1975) *Sixguns and Society*. Berkeley: University of California Press.
—— (2001) *The Wild West*. London: Sage.
Zeigler, R. (2006) 'The Cowboy Strike of 1883.' In: Carlson, P. (ed.), *The Cowboy Way*, 86–103. Stroud, UK: Tempus Publishing.
Zimmerman, D. (2006) *Panic! Markets, Crises and Crowds in American Fiction*. Chapel Hill, NC: University of North Carolina Press.

INDEX

Note: 'n' after a page number indicates a note; 'f' indicates a figure.

'Absolutely Sweet Marie' (Dylan) 143
Ackroyd, S. 137, 139
Adams, James 'Grizzly Bear' 78
Adams, Scott 134
The Adventures of Robin Hood
    (1938 film) 29
The Adventures of Robin Hood
    (TV show) 29
The Adventures of Robin Hood and His
    Merrie Men (1952 film) 29
'afterlife' of heroes 27
Ainsworth, William Harrison 64, 66
The Alamo (1960 film) 85
Aldine Publishing Company 112
alternative business: crime as 149–150;
    and legitimacy of outlaws 142–3;
    modern bandits' justifications for 127;
    and outlaws 7–8; and pirates 47
Alton Towers 136
American Fur Company 76
American Indians 73, 86
The American Sea-Rovers (Exquemelin) 38
Ames, J. 83
An Account of the History, Manners, and
    Customs, of the Indian National . . .
    (Heckewelder) 73
Anand, N. 139
anarchism 50
Andreotti, Gulio 103
Anecdotes, Bon Mots, Traits, Stratagems
    and Biographical Sketches of the most
    remarkable Highway-men . . . (anon.) 67

Arlacchi, Pino 96, 108
Asbury, Herbert 92, 123
The Asphalt Jungle (1950 film) 101
As You Like It (Shakespeare) 20
Atkey, Philip 114
Atkins, John 47–8
'Attack by Bandits' (Rosa) 54
Augustine 142
An Authentic Life of Billy the Kid the
    noted Desperado of the South (Garrett) 71
authorities: Hobsbawm on bandits'
    resistance to 4–7; as incompetent
    83; outlaws' justified opposition to
    116–17; Robin Hood and resistance
    to 16. *See also* social protest/resistance;
    the state
Avery, Henry 37

Bailey, David 121
ballads: about highwaymen 62–4; about
    pirates 37; about Robin Hood –, 12;
    about smugglers 59; about the West 83;
    and capitalism 150; and opposition to
    authority 116
Balsamo, W. 93, 95–6, 98, 104
bandits. *See* social bandits
Bandits (Hobsbawm) 4, 6, 24
banditti 53–6
barbed wire 74
Barker, Ma 119
Barnum, Phineas T. 78
Barrie, J. M. 39

Barrow, Clyde 11–0
Barry, Redmond 117
Barthes, Roland 106, 150
Bass, Sam 83
Beaton, Alistair 129–30
Beeching, Jack 51
The Beggar's Opera (Gay) 66
Belmondo, Jean Paul 53
Bergin, Patrick 10
Berlusconi, Silvio 104
Berry, Charlotte de 44
biker gangs 126
Billy the Kid 71
Black Bart. *See* Roberts, Black Bart
Blackbeard; or, the Captive Princess (Cross) 39
Black Hand gangs (*Mano nera*) 50, 92
Blackmore, R. D. 60
Blok, Anton 6–7, 147, 157
Boetticher, Budd 87
Bokkenrijders 26
Bollywood 126
Bonnet, Stede 48
Bonney, Anne 44
Bonnie and Clyde (1967 film) 120
'Boone and Crockett Club' 74
Bourguignon, Louis Dominique
  ('Cartouche') 53
Boyle, Jimmy 122
Brasco, Donnie. *See* Pistone, Joe
Brecht, Bertolt 148
Brent, David (fictional character) 3
Brown, Dee 77
Browne, Joe 92–3
'Buffalo' Bill 78–9
Buntline, Ned 78
Burl, A. 35–6, 46, 47
Burrough, B. 120
Burroughs, William 44
business. *See* alternative business
business schools 7, 158
Byron, George Gordon 39, 56

Caitlin, George 73
Caleb Williams (Godwin) 55
Cannery, Martha Jane ('Calamity Jane') 77
capitalism: and organized crime 94; and
  pirates 50; and smuggling 58;
  urbanization of 53; and the Western
  70–1, 89. *See also* economy
Capone, Al 101
Capone, Frank 105
Cardinale, Claudia 53
Carey, Peter 115
Carpozi, G. 93, 95–6, 98, 104
cartoons 29, 134–5

Casino (1995 film) 96–7
Cassidy, Butch 83
Castellano, Paul 108
Catchpole, Bessie 60
A Challenge for Robin Hood (1967 film) 29
Charles I 2
Chettle, Henry 20
Ching Yih Saou 48
Chopper (2000 film) 122
Chopper: From the Inside (Read) 122
Chronicle at Large (Grafton) 20
Clarke, D. 111
class system 61, 113–15
Cobham, Maria 44
Cody, 'Buffalo' Bill 78–9, 89
Cofresi, Roberto 48
Cohen, Albert 151
Cohen, Phil 152
Colombo, Joe 93
comics 29, 164n8(ch8)
Complete History of the Highwayman
  (Smith) 63
conservatism: Hobsbawm on bandits
  and 26–7, 149; of Robin Hood 29–30
Coolidge, Calvin 104
Cooper, Courtney Ryley 120
Cooper, James Fenimore 72–3
copyright, Parker and 1, 12
Cordingly, D. 45
Cornwallis, C. W. 67
The Corsair (Byron) 39, 56
Costello, Frank 104
Costner, Kevin 10, 29
counter culture. *See* work, counter
  culture of
cowboys: definitions of 80; as figure
  of resistance 163n22; as Western
  outlaw-hero 81–5. *See also* the West
Cowboys and Indians 85
Cox, Judy 28
crime: definitions of 6–; as resistance 143
Cross, James 39
Crow, Walter 77
Crowe, Russell 2, 29
cultural products: and highwaymen 68;
  simultaneously co-opted and critical
  145–6. *See also* films; novels; television
  shows; toys
cultural studies 137
culture: and economics of the West
  76–80; and economy 8–9, 11–12,
  129–30, 133, 145

dacoit 27
Dacus, Joseph 71

Dalton Gang 82
Dampier, William 38–9
Dances with Wolves (1990 film) 163n18
Darnton, Robert 151
Defoe, Daniel 37–8, 65–6
Dellacroce, Aniello 108
DeMeo, Albert 108
DeMeo, Roy 108
De Palma, Brian 104
deregulation and the Mafia 101
Dickens, Charles 67
Dickie, J. 50, 102
Dilbert cartoons 134
Dillinger, John 119–20
dime novels 76–9, 82–4, 160n5(ch2)
Dimsdale, Thomas J. 82
Disney, Walt 29
dissent, disguised 154
Dodge, Richard 73
Doel, M. 111
Donald, Angus 29
Donnie Brasco (1997 film) 93
*The Downfall/Death of Robert, Earl of
    Huntingdon* (Munday and Chettle) 20
Dubner, S. 149
du Maurier, Daphne 61
Duncombe, Stephen 135
Durkheim, E. 151, 153–4
Du Vall, Claude 64
Dyer, R. 3
Dylan, Bob 143–4

Earle, P. 33, 36
Earp, Wyatt 79
Eastwood, Clint 147
economy: and business ethics 99–101;
    and culture 8–9, 11–12, 76–80, 129–30,
    133, 145; and the Mafia 94–9; outlaws
    as critique of conventional political
    156–7; popular culture as hostile to 2–3;
    and smuggling 57–8
Edison, Thomas 78
Egan, Pierce 23, 123
Ellms, Charles 42
Empson, William 144
Ephron, Nora 93
Eppolito, Louis 94
Escobar, Pablo 126
ethics 99–101
Eustace the Black Monk 26
excise men 59
Exquemelin, Alexander 38, 161n8(ch3)

Fairbanks, Douglas, Sr. 28–9
Falkner, J. Meade 60

Fielding, Henry 65–6
films: about highwaymen 68; about
    modern criminals 122; about 1930s
    gangs 120–1; about noble bandits 114–
    15, 117; about pirates 40–1; about
    Robin Hood 28–9; about smugglers 61;
    about the Mafia 92–4; about the West
    78–9, 81, 83–4; about Yakuza 126;
    early 20th-century 111. *See also* popular
    culture
Floyd, Charles Arthur 'Pretty Boy' 118–19
Flynn, Errol 29
Folville, Eustace 16, 19, 161n4(ch3)
food, and Mafia 106–7
Forbes, Athol 59
*The Foresters, or Robin Hood and Maid
    Marian* (Tennyson) 23–4
Forest Laws 16
Franchetti, Leopoldo 102
Freakonomics (Levitt and Dubner) 149
'Free Traders' 58
the frontier. *See* the West; the Western
'Fuck Work' sticker 133, 138–40

Gabbard, G. 107
Gallo, 'Crazy Joe' 93
Gambetta, D. 93, 107
gangs: Black Hand gangs (*Mano nera*) 50,
    92; Chinese Triads (Tong) 123, 126;
    names of 124; of 1930s 118–20; in
    the 19th century 123–4; outlaws as
    113, 118–27; transition to organized
    crime 125–7; Yakuza 125–6
The Gangs of New York (Asbury) 92, 123
gangsters. *See* Mafia
Garrett, Pat 71
Gay, John 65–6, 123
*A General History of the Robberies
    and Murders of the Most Notorious
    Highway-Men . . .* (Smith) 62
*General History of the Robberies and Murders
    of the Most Notorious Pyrates . . .*
    (Johnson) 33, 39, 43–4
genre 162n1(ch5)
Getting Gotti (Hill and Polici) 93
Giuliano, Salvatore 25
Glidden, Joseph 74
G-Men (1934 film) 120
Godelier, Maurice 8
The Godfather (1972 film) 105–6
The Godfather (Puzo) 93, 99–101
The Godfather Part II (1974 film) 102
Godwin, William 55
Golden Age of pirates 34, 48
Goodfellas (1990 film) 94

'goodfellows' 107
gothic sublime 54
Gotti, John 93
Gough, Richard 21
Grafton, Richard 20
Gravano, Sammy 'The Bull' 93
Great Chain of Being 36
The Great Train Robbery (1903 film) 78
Greene, Richard 29
Grey, Zane 79
The Grey Fox (1983 film) 115
Griffith, D. W. 92
Groening, Matt 134
Grotius, Hugo 32–3
Gulliver, Isaac 58, 60
Guthrie, Woody 118

Halford, S. 139
Hardin, John Wesley 71, 144
Hart, William S. 79
Hassrick, R. 72
Hayward, Louis 68
Heckewelder, John 73
Hedgepeth, Marion 83
Hickok, James Butler ('Wild Bill') 77–8
highwaymen 61–5, 162n2(ch4)
Hill, Christopher 57, 69
Hill, Henry 93, 96, 98, 108
Hind, James 63
Hitchcock, Alfred 61
Hobbs, D. 125
Hobsbawm, Eric: on commonalities
    of 'noble bandit' myths 24–6; debate
    about theories of 147; on the Mafia
    109–10; on political change 149; on
    political conservatism of bandits 26–7;
    on social bandit as leader 143; on
    social banditry 4–7
Hodd (Thorpe) 29
Hollywood, influence on the Mafia
    92–5, 144
homosexuality 161n8(ch3), 163n19
Hoover, J. Edgar 120
Hornung, E. W. 113
How to Steal a Million (1966 film) 115
Hudson's Bay Company 76
Hunt, Leigh 23
Hunting Grounds of the Great West
    (Dodge) 73
Huston, John 101

Ibrahim, Dawood 126
Ideology and Utopia (Mannheim) 153
'The Ides of March' (Hornung) 113
Inagawa-Kai clan 126

individualism: vs. the market 85; and
    outlaws 112–18; and the West 71,
    75, 80–1
intellectual piracy. *See* piracy
International Maritime Bureau 49
internet 135–6
The Invisible Hook (Leeson) 50
Isle of Pines (Neville) 38
Italian-Americans Civil Rights League 93
Italian Job (1969, 2003 films) 120
Itami, Juzo 126
Ivanhoe (Scott) 22–3, 55

Jack Sheppard (Ainsworth) 66
Jack Sparrow. *See* Sparrow, Jack, Capt.
    (fictional character)
Jamaica Inn (du Maurier) 61
James, Frank 88
James, Jesse 71, 83
Janosik 26
Jefferson, Thomas 48
Jennings, Al 79
Jesse, Fryniwyd Tennyson 44
Johnson, Charles 39, 62
Johnson, Charles, Capt. 33, 46–7
Johnston, Tom 58–9
'John Wesley Harding' (Dylan) 144
Jolly Roger 50, 161n3(ch3)
Joseph, Chief 86

Kaulingfreks, Ruud 163n22
Keats, John 21–2
Kelly, 'Machine Gun' 119
Kelly, Ned 115–17
Kemp, R. 33, 49, 109
Kennedy, Joseph 104
Killigrew, Elizabeth 44
Kingsley, Charles 73
Kipling, Rudyard 61
Kirtland, Caroline 73
Kontorovich, E. 49
Kray, Ronald and Reginald 121–2
The Krays (1990 film) 122

La Buse, Olivier 48
Lafitte, Jean 48
Lafitte, Pierre 48
Lai Choi San 48
L' Amour, Louis 79
Land, C. 37, 41, 50–1
Langland, William 18–19
Lansky, Meyer 97
Lapouge, Giles 33–4, 37
Las Vegas 97
'Law of the Privateers' 41–2

Leblanc, Maurice 114
Leeson, P. 50, 149
Le Guin, U. 146
'Letter of Marque and Reprisal' 35
Leutze, Emanuel 73
Levi-Strauss, Claude 152
Levitt, S. 149
Lewis, J. 42, 103, 105
Libertalia 43–4
Life, Times and Treacherous Death of Jesse James (Triplett) 71
The Life and Adventures of Frank and Jesse James and the Younger Brothers (Dacus) 71
Life in London (Egan) 123
The Life of Jonathan Wild the Great (Fielding) 65–6
Life of Robin Hood (Ritson) 21
Little Big Horn Association 74
The Little Book of Management Bollocks (Beaton) 129–130, 132, 139–140
Lodge, Thomas 20
London, as jungle 65
Lonely Tyrant 135
Longrigg, C. 98
Lorna Doone (Blackmore) 60–1
Luciano, 'Lucky' 93, 96–7
Luny, Thomas 60
Lupin, Arsène (fictional character) 114–15
Lupton, D. 139
Lytell Geste of Robyn Hode 19

Maclaine, James 64
Madagascar 43–4
Mafia: business ethics of 99–101; compared to legitimate business 91–2, 94–6, 100–1, 109; etymology of 96, 163n6; familial bonds of 104–7; fantasy vs. reality of 108–9; films about 92–3; and food 106–7; and Hollywood 92–3, 144; and Las Vegas 97; and moral code 25; and 'nonstate' space 98; organizational structure of 96–7, 163n7; profitability of 95; reasons for success of 97–9; Sicilian 97, 102–3; skull and crossbones 50; as social bandits 5; and the state 101–4; and women 106–7
magical powers 26, 60
The Magnificent Seven (1960 film) 84–5
Maid Marian (Peacock) 23
Manchu, Fu, Dr (fictional character) 126
manifest destiny 73–4
Manners, Customers and Condition of the North American Indians (Caitlin) 73
Mannheim, Karl 153–4
Mare Liberum (Grotius) 32–3

Martin, Steve 93
Mason, Matt 50
mass-media technologies 71
Masterson, Bat 79
Matador Land and Cattle Company 76
Matsell, George W. 123
McCanles, David 77
McCarty, John 92, 97
McIntosh, Mary 125
McMahon, B. 98
McVicar, John 122
Medak, Peter 121
Melbourne-Cooper, Arthur 111
merchants 36
The Merry Adventures of Robin Hood (Pyle) 23
Millie, Bessie 60
Mills, Ann 44
Miner, Bill 115
minorities: as pirates 45; and the West 76, 86
Mission, James, Capt. 43–4
Mitchum, Robert 84
Mob Cop (Eppolito) 94
The Mohocks (Gay) 123
Moonfleet (Falkner) 60
Moonraker (Jesse) 44
Moore, Lucy 68
moral code 25
Motor Pirates (1906 film) 111
mountain men 72–3, 78
Munday, Anthony 20
Murder Incorporated 97
Murrieta, Joaquin 82–3
Muskogee Daily Phoenix 118
My Blue Heaven (1990 film) 93
My New Filing Technique Is Unstoppable (Rees) 135

Napoleon 59
Native Americans. *See* American Indians
Nelson, 'Baby Face' 119
Neville, Henry 38
Nevison, William 62
'Newgate novels' 66
A New Home – Who'll Follow? (Kirtland) 73
New Voyage Round the World (Dampier) 38–9
Nichols, George Ward 77
Noble, G. 139
'noble bandit' 24–8, 113–15
noble savage 38, 54, 72, 73–4
Nolan, N. 77

'nonstate' space: city as 65, 91, 98;
countryside as 52; of outlaws 155–6;
the West as 70
North Carolina Maritime Museum 49
North West Company 76
novels: about Robin Hood 29; about
the Mafia 93–4; educational purposes
of 67; the Western 79. *See also* dime
novels; penny dreadfuls

Oakley, Annie 78
Oceans 11 (1960, 2001 films) 120
The Office (TV show) 3
Office Monkey (TV show) 134
Office Profanity Kit 133–4
Office Voodoo Kit 133
Oliver Twist (Dickens) 67
O'Malley, Grace 44
*On the Treatment of the Dangerous
and Perishing Classes of Society*
(Cornwallis) 67
The Oregon Trail (Parkman) 73
Organizatsiya 126
organized crime. *See* Mafia
Orwell, George 80, 114
Osborne, L. 49, 51
O'Sullivan, John 73
O'Toole, Peter 115
Outlaw (Donald) 29
'outlaw hero cycle': defined 9, 27;
as established archetype 112; and
Mafia 103; and pirates 30, 52;
popularity of 150
outlaws: and alternative social
organization 7–8; commodification
of 145–6; as critique of conventional
political economy 156–7; function
of representations of 150–3; as gangs
113, 118–127; highwaymen 61–5;
history of, shaped by representations
of 12–13; as individuals 112–18;
myth vs. reality of 147–8; nobility
of 113–18; in old English law 16–17;
robbers/banditti 53–6; smugglers
57–61; structures for holding 156f;
as symbol of dissent 3–4; and trickster
figures 17–19; as Western hero 81–5;
and women 148, 160n1(ch2); and
work 154–5. *See also* pirates; Robin
Hood; specific outlaws; urban outlaws;
the Western
outsiders 53, 56, 68. *See also* outlaws

Parish, J. 40
Parker, Bonnie 119

Parker, Henry 60
Parker, Martin 1–2, 12, 15, 18
Parkman, Francis 73
Peacock, Thomas Love 23
Pearson, Geoffrey 123
Pearson, John 121–2
penny dreadfuls 23, 64–5, 112, 123–4
Penny Satirist 66–7
Perowne, Barry 114
Peter Pan (Barrie) 39
Pileggi, Nicholas 93
Pinkerton, Allen 83
The Pioneers (Cooper) 73
piracy: and anarchism 50; as business
149; and economics 50; Golden
Age of 34, 48; intellectual 32, 50;
privateering as state-licensed 35;
and 21st-century mercenaries/
private armies 49; and violence
41–2, 46
Piracy Reporting Centre, International
Maritime Bureau 49
pirates: and authority by consent 42;
city-states of 43–4; commodification
of 33, 49–50; exclusion from
merchant/state alliance 36;
female 37, 44–5, 48–9; films about
40–1, 44–5; historical overview
of 34–7; as maritime Robin Hoods 37;
moral code of 41–2; racial
heterogeneity of 45; representations
of 37–41, 51; and sexuality 45;
support of commoners for 36–7;
21st-century 49
The Pirate's Dilemma (Mason) 50
Pirates of the Caribbean (film) 3, 32, 158
The Pirate Wars (Earle) 33
Pistone, Joe 93, 98, 105
Playmobil 10, 145, 160n3(ch1)
Plummer, Henry 82
Polici, Sal 93
*Political and Administrative Conditions in
Sicily* (Franchetti) 102
political change 149
popular culture: cultural resistance as
'safety valve' 9; as disguised dissent 154;
dismissal of, as insignificant 3; as
economic product 10–11; fear of
negative influence of 66–7, 82–3, 111;
gangs in 123–7; and highwaymen 62–5;
as hostile to economic order 2–3;
and smugglers 59–61; and work 138.
See also ballads; films; novels; social
practices; toys
Porter, Edwin 78

President's Commission on Organized
  Crime 95
'Pretty Boy Floyd' (Guthrie) 118
Primitive Rebels (Hobsbawm) 4, 24
Princess Productions 134
private armies 49
privateering 35, 49
prohibition 103
property, and definitions of crime 61–2
Provenzano, Bernardo 'Tractor' 98
Public Enemies (2009 film) 120
Public Enemy (1931 film) 119
Punch 143
Puzo, Mario 93
Pyle, Howard 23, 43

Rabat-Salé 43
radicalism: of pirates 41–2, 47; and
  Robin Hood 20; of the West 89–90.
  See also conservatism
Raffles, Arthur J. (fictional character)
  113–14
'Raffles and Miss Blandish' (Orwell) 114
Raft, George 93, 121
Ratsey, Gamaliel 63
Rawlinson, P. 94
Read, Mark Brandon 'Chopper' 122
Read, Mary 44
Rediker, M. 36, 42–3
Rehn, Alf 9–10
resistance. *See* social protest/resistance
Rhodes, Carl 156–7
Richards, Jeffrey 28, 30, 40, 68
Ritson, John 21
robbers 53–6
Roberts, 'Black Bart' 35–6, 42, 46–8
Robin and Marian (1976 film) 29
Robin Hood: claiming the name of,
  for moral purposes 17; contradictory
  figure of 4; as cultural commodity 19,
  21, 23, 28–9; as dispossessed noble 20;
  Kelly as Australian 117; key elements
  of narrative regarding 2, 19, 24–8;
  representations of 18–23, 28–31;
  Robin des Bois as inspiration for
  160n3(ch2); and Western
  outlaw-heroes 83
Robin Hood (1922 film) 28–9
Robin Hood (1973 film) 29
Robin Hood (2010 film) 2, 29
Robin Hood (TV show) 29
Robin Hood and His Merry Men
  (1908 film) 28
Robin Hood and Little John (Egan) 23
Robin Hood and the Pirates (1960 film) 49

Robin Hood: Prince of Thieves (1991 film)
  10, 29
Robin Hood Tax 28
Robin of Sherwood (TV show) 29
Robinson Crusoe (Defoe) 37–8
Rob Roy (Scott) 55
Rocky Mountain Fur Company 76
Rogers, Will 78
Rohmer, Sax 126
The Romance of Smuggling (Forbes) 59
romanticism: influence of, on outlaw
  images 53; and Rosa's paintings 53–4
Rookwood (Ainsworth) 64
Roosevelt, Theodore 74
Rosa, Salvator 53–4
Ross, Edward Alsworth 143
Roughing It (Twain) 74, 77–8
Rule, John 61
Rutherford-Moore, R. 28
Ryle, Gilbert 150

'safety valve' of popular culture 9, 151–2
Sante, L. 124–5, 147
Saviano, Roberto 109, 149
Scarface (1983 film) 104
Schaefer, Jack 84
Schiavone, Walter 144
Schiller, Friedrich 54–5
Schinderhannes 25
Schneider, Anthony 95, 158
Sciarra, Marco 53
Scorsese, Martin 96
Scott, James 18, 52, 140, 151, 154. *See also*
  'nonstate' space
Scott, Walter 22–3, 55
Scruton, R. 157
sea, as international territory 32–3
Seal, Graham 9; on 'afterlife' of hero 27;
  on commonalities of 'noble bandit'
  myths 24; on key elements of 'noble
  bandit' narratives 26; on magical powers
  of bandits 26; on marketing Ned Kelly
  145; on origins of outlaw figures 30;
  outlaw as folklore 144–5; 'outlaw hero
  cycle' 71, 103, 112
The Searchers (1956 film) 88
Selkirk, Alexander 38–9
A Sense of Freedom (Boyle) 122
Sepulchral Monuments of Great Britain
  (Gough) 21
sexuality 45, 161n8(ch3), 163n19
Shakespeare, William 20
Shane (Schaefer) 84
Shelton, 'Stag' Lee 86
Sheppard, Jack 66

Sheriff of Nottingham 2
The Shootist (1976 film) 85
Siegal, 'Bugsy' 93, 97
'The Significance of the Frontier in
American History' (Turner) 74–5
The Simpsons (TV show) 134
Sin and Society (Ross) 143
slaves 41, 45, 86
Smircich, L. 137
Smith, Adam 58
Smith, Alexander 62–3
smugglers 57–61
The Smugglers Intrusion (Wilkie) 60
'A Smuggler's Song' (Kipling) 61
Snell, Hannah 44
social bandits: Blok on 6; Hobsbawm on
4–7; Mafia 5; myth vs. reality of 147–8
social protest/resistance: banditry as
primitive form of 4–6; disguised 154–5;
piracy as form of 50–1; popular culture
as disguised 154; and smuggling 57–8;
taking from the rich/giving to the
poor 24–5, 63–4; and trickster
figures 18; of the Western hero,
to industrialization 71, 84, 89; and
work 138–41. *See also* the state
Somali pirates 31
The Sopranos (TV show) 94–5, 100, 105,
107–8, 109
Sparrow, Jack, Capt. (fictional character) 3,
50, 51. *See also* pirates
Sparrows Can't Sing (1963 film) 121
Spraggs, Gillian 62, 68–9, 147, 162n2(ch4)
the state: as corrupt 83; Italian 103–4;
and the Mafia 1014; and violence 102
Sterling, Clare 97, 99, 108
Stevenson, Robert Louis 39
The Story of the Kelly Gang (1906 film) 117
Stukeley, William 21
subcultures 152
The Successful Pirate (Johnson) 39
Sullivan, Arthur 23
Surowiecki, James 161n9(ch3)
Sutherland, Edwin 101, 143
Swiss Family Robinson (Wyss) 38

Talbot, Mary Ann 44
The Tale of Gamelyn (Lodge) 20
tattoos 126–7
taxes 28, 57
Taylor, Buck 78
Teignmouth by Moonlight (Luny) 60
television shows: about pirates 29;
about Robin Hood 29; about
smugglers 61; and counter culture 134;

noble bandits 114; the Western 79–80.
See also popular culture
Tennyson, Alfred 23–4
theft, craft vs. project model of 125
The Robbers (Schiller) 54–5
the West 71
The Winning of the West (Roosevelt) 74
The Thomas Crowne Affair (1968, 1999
films) 115
Thompson, P. 137, 139
Thoreau, Henry 74
Thorndike, Russell 60
Thorpe, Adam 29
Threepenny Opera (Brecht) 148
Tilghman, Bill 79
Tilly, Charles 142
Todd, Richard 29
'To J. H. R. in Answer to his Robin
Hood Sonnets' (Keats) 21–2
Tong (Chinese Triads) 123, 126
*Tony Soprano on Management: Leadership
Lessons Inspired by America's Favorite
Mobster* (Schneider) 158
Tortuga 43
Town Talk 143
toys 10, 145, 160n3(ch1)
trading companies 36
train robberies 82
Treasure Island (Stevenson) 39
trickster figures: and bandits 25–6;
Darnton on 151; and Robin Hood
17–19; smugglers as 58–9; Ward as 116
Triplett, Frank 71
Trot, Nicholas 47–8
The True History of the Kelly Gang
(Carey) 115
'A True Tale of Robin Hood' (Parker)
1–2, 12, 15, 18
Turner, Frederick Jackson 74–5
Turpin, Dick 64
Twain, Mark 74, 77–8, 80
Twm Sion Catti 26

Unforgiven (1992 film) 147
urbanism 52
urban outlaws 65–7; dominance of,
after 19th century 113
utopia: pirate city-states as 43–4; vs.
prevailing order 153–4

van der Schlossen, Kobus 26
Veerappan 27
violence: and business organizations
164n10; of early New York gang
culture 124–5; and the Mafia 163–4n10;

and the Mafia's Murder Incorporated
97; of merchant/legal codes 46; and
moral code 25; of pirate life 41–2, 46;
and the state 102; toward unjust
authority 19–20, 24; and the West
76–7, 84–5, 88
The Virginian (Wister) 75
*The Vision of William concerning Piers the
Plowman* (Langland) 18–19
Vizzini, Calò 98–9, 108
Volstead Act 103
Vory tattoos 126–7

'Walking' (Thoreau) 74
Ward, Frederick 'Thunderbolt' 116
Warren, S. 139
Watch, Will 59–60
Waverley (Scott) 55
Wayne, John 79, 85, 88
Weber, M. 102
the West: commodification of 77–80,
85–6, 89; creation of myths about 72–5;
and escape 80; and individualism 71, 75,
80–1; industrialization of 76, 88–9; and
minorities 76; natural law vs.
industrialism/capitalism 88–9; as
Promised Land 75; and violence 76–7,
84–5, 88; visual representations of 73;
and women 86–7
the Western: and capitalism 71; films
78–9, 81, 83–4; and minorities 86;
novels 79; outlaw heroes of 81–2;
Robin Hood and outlaw heroes of 83;
television shows 79–80. *See also*
cowboys
Westward Ho! (Leutze) 73
'white collar crime' 101, 143
Wild, Jonathan 65
wild west shows 78
Wilkie, David 60

Williams, Raymond 52, 137
Willis, P. 137
Wilson, Lamborne: on Libertalia 44;
pirates as example of alternative social
organization 47; on pirate sexuality 45;
on Rabat-Salé 43
Winslow, C. 59
Wiseguy (1985 film) 93
Wister, Owen 75, 79, 162n13(ch5)
women: exclusion of, from bandit myths
148; exclusion of, from Mafia 106–7;
and highwaymen 162n2(ch4); and the
Mafia 106–7; and outlaws 148, 160n1
(ch2); as pirates 37, 44–5, 48–9; as
smugglers 60; and the West 86–7; and
work 165n9
work: and cultural studies 137; gothic
representations of 130–1; positive views
of 131; as repressive 136; and social
protest/resistance 138–41; and women
165n9. *See also* work, counter culture of
work, counter culture of: books about
133–4; context of 132; corporations as
evil in 132–3; meanings of 140–1; as
money-making enterprise 138–9; and
outlaws 154–5; representations of 131,
134–6; scholarly interest in 137–40;
subversion and 131; television shows
about 134
Wright, Allen 161n8(ch2)
Wright, W. 84, 87
'Writ of Outlawry' 16
Wynne, Emmanuel 34
Wyss, Johann 38

Yakuza 125–6
Yamaguchi-Gumi clan 126
Younger Gang 82

Zorro 82, 162n10(ch5)